The Southern Manifesto

D0764179

The Southern Manifesto

Massive Resistance and the Fight to Preserve Segregation

John Kyle Day

University Press of Mississippi   Jackson

www.upress.state.ms.us

The University Press of Mississippi is a member
of the Association of American University Presses.

Copyright © 2014 by University Press of Mississippi
All rights reserved
Manufactured in the United States of America

First printing 2014
∞
Library of Congress Cataloging-in-Publication Data

Day, John Kyle, author.
  The Southern Manifesto : massive resistance and the fight to preserve segregation / John Kyle
Day.
     pages cm
  Includes bibliographical references and index.
  ISBN 978-1-62846-031-5 (hardback) — ISBN 978-1-62846-032-2 (ebook) 1. Segregation
in education—Law and legislation—Southern States—History. 2. Discrimination in educa-
tion—Law and legislation—Southern States—History. 3. Civil rights movements—Southern
States—History—20th century. 4. Segregation in education—Law and legislation—United
States—History. 5. Discrimination in education—Law and legislation—United States—His-
tory. 6. Southern States—Race relations—History—20th century. 7. Topeka (Kan.). Board of
Education—Trials, litigation, etc. 8. Brown, Oliver, 1918–1961—Trials, litigation, etc. I. Title.
  KF4155.D39 2014
  344.73'07980975—dc23   2013044475

British Library Cataloging-in-Publication Data available

IN HONOR OF J. K. DAY, M.D.

Woe unto him that buildeth his house by unrighteousness, and his chambers by wrong; that useth his neighbor's service without wages, and giveth him not for his work.

—Jeremiah, 22:13 KJV

Contents

Acknowledgments

Robert Collins suggested the topic from which this book evolved. I thank my colleagues with whom I studied and under whom I served during my education at Fayetteville and Columbia, with whom I taught at Quincy and Monticello, and who read and edited various drafts, the librarians who facilitated my research, and the present and former staff of the University Press of Mississippi for taking this manuscript to completion.

This book was financially supported by the University of Missouri–Columbia, the Lyndon Baines Johnson Foundation and Dwight D. Eisenhower Foundation, the Deep South Regional Humanities Center at Tulane University, the Institute for Southern Studies at the University of South Carolina, Phi Alpha Theta National History Honor Society, and the University of Arkansas at Monticello.

The Southern Manifesto

Introduction:

The Manifesto That Made Massive Resistance

On March 13, 1956, ninety-nine members of the Eighty-Fourth United States Congress promulgated the Declaration of Constitutional Principles, popularly known as the Southern Manifesto. This southern *profert* formally stated opposition to both federally mandated public school desegregation as declared in the U.S. Supreme Court decision *Brown v. Board of Education* (1954) and the emerging Civil Rights Movement that ultimately destroyed the southern caste system known as Jim Crow. Today, the Southern Manifesto is justifiably viewed as the single worst episode of racial demagoguery in the era of postwar America (1948–1973). Yet, at the time, most members of the Southern Congressional Delegation boasted that they played a part in the statement's drafting, while many claimed that they had conceived of the project in the first place. While historians recognize the name of the Southern Manifesto and agree on these basic facts, the document remains both misunderstood by scholars and largely forgotten by the public-at-large. Historians disagree over who conceived of this statement, who wrote it, and its implications for postwar American history in general and the Civil Rights Movement in particular.[1]

The neglect to thoroughly consider the high drama inherent in the political consequences of the Civil Rights Movement obscures a full comprehension of this most important social revolution in American history. This misunderstanding partly stems from the lack of critical analysis of the United States Congress and its role in combating *Brown*'s implementation. Historians typically use the memoirs of contemporary insiders to study the Senate, while political scientists usually focus upon the U.S. House of Representatives. In contrast, this book employs the theoretical model of David R. Mayhew's *Congress: The Electoral Connection*. Mayhew's theory that the United States House of Representatives is the immediate reflection of American public opinion is widely accepted. That is, as members of the House of Representatives stand before the electorate every two years, their professional energies are primarily directed toward satisfying the concerns of the constituents who elected them so that they may be returned to Congress. The House's incumbents are thus permanent seekers of reelection. But, as United States senators are subject to election only every six years, while just approximately one-third of the Senate membership stands before their constituents every two-year election cycle, senators are generally thought to be more insulated from the electorate and, therefore, possess much more freedom of action. Applying Mayhew's theory to the Southern Congressional Delegation in general and the Senate's Southern Caucus in particular, this study uses the promulgation of the Southern Manifesto as a test case to understand how the postwar Southern Congressional Delegation successfully preserved white supremacy and thus satisfied the concerns of their enfranchised white constituents for decades after Jim Crow was dubbed illegitimate by most other Americans and became a diplomatic embarrassment to the United States before the court of world opinion.[2]

Indeed, the most immediate impact of the *Brown* decision was within the realm of national partisan politics. Assuming it would take most southern school districts at least one year to comply with the desegregation edict, *Brown*'s corollary, known as *Brown II* (1955), vaguely ordered southern school districts to desegregate "with all deliberate speed." This ambiguous timetable made the first school year of planned large-scale desegregation incidentally coincide with the 1956 national elections. In the winter of 1955–1956, seminal events in the Civil Rights Movement—such as the Emmett Till lynching in Mississippi as well as the Montgomery Bus Boycott and the Autherine Lucy riots in Alabama—brought the struggle for black freedom to national attention. In January 1956, the opening of the second session of the Eighty-Fourth Congress brought a series of civil rights and education appropriation bills out of committee for formal consideration by both the House of Representatives and the Senate.

The South's congressional incumbents thus feared that if they did not block *Brown*'s implementation, the consideration of these civil rights bills, and attempts to deny federal school funding to districts that openly defied the Supreme Court's edict, their white constituents would support opposing candidates in both the 1956 Democratic primaries and the general election. Specifically, another third-party movement threatened the Southern Congressional Delegation if the Democratic Party formally endorsed *Brown* and supported federal civil rights legislation. Potentially more potent than the 1948 Dixiecrat Revolt, another southern third party devoted to states' rights and white supremacy would divide the Democrats to the advantage of the popular Republican incumbent, President Dwight David Eisenhower. Such a scenario inevitably produced a major turnover in elected officials throughout the South. Republicans and/or intransigent segregationists could be elected throughout Dixie, defeating Democratic incumbents. The South faced the loss of control over congressional committees, the basis of its federal political power and the bulwark of the southern caste system. The Democrats, moreover, lost their congressional majorities and faced a major political realignment, whereby the New Deal coalition disintegrated and the Democracy became the nation's minority party.

The Southern Congressional Delegation counterattacked with the Southern Manifesto. This statement harnessed state level defiance of *Brown* to shield southern national officeholders from charges that they were acquiescent to desegregation, ensuring their continued dominance of congressional committees. The statement's language was framed in such a way so as to satisfy both intransigent segregationists (those who supported formal defiance of the federal judiciary) and so-called southern moderates who, though intellectually, politically, and socially committed to segregation, nevertheless believed that formal opposition to *Brown* was both futile and irresponsible.

The Southern Manifesto ultimately produced a moderate national consensus toward the Civil Rights Movement. This statement allowed the white South to dictate the interpretation of *Brown II*, setting the slothfully circumspect timetable for the implementation of public school desegregation with the consent of both national political parties. It provided the Southern Congressional Delegation with the means to effectively delay federal civil rights legislation for years to come. The Solid South remained the geographic base of the Democratic Party and the New Deal coalition was sustained. The death of Jim Crow largely came on white southern terms.

Throughout the text, the generic use of the term *segregationist* is avoided to describe those white southerners who opposed implementation of *Brown.* Because there were no white southerners active in formal partisan politics who can be considered as *integrationists* (advocating the complete desegregation of southern society), the term *segregationist* does not provide an adequate description of *Brown*'s opponents. In order to describe those white southerners who actively worked against *Brown*'s implementation, the term *intransigent segregationist* is employed. Recent scholarship portrays a significant contingent of white southerners seeking "strategic accommodation" with desegregation mandates.[3] Those white southerners who bespoke of compliance with federal desegregation decisions, however, never supported complete integration. They most often described themselves as *southern moderates*, which is used in this text. The various degrees of white southern opinion is explained herein.

1. The Upheaval: Interposition and Moderation

The southern caste system of Jim Crow collapsed after World War II because of large impersonal social forces and the actions of individuals who sought to fulfill the American promise. Economic and population growth created an urban industrial base that brought the South into the modern consumer economy. These developments provided the means for African Americans to dismantle the institutions that denied them their constitutional rights. In turn, a significant number of white southerners accepted the changes to their society brought about by the initial success of the Civil Rights Movement. By the end of the first decade after World War II, most Americans believed that Jim Crow could, should, and would be abolished.

The South exemplified America's robust demographic and economic growth after World War II. The baby boom and intracontinental migration changed the national demography, especially in the former states of the Confederacy. During the 1950s, the South's population grew as much as, while industry expanded more than, any other region. A modern consumer economy developed through the mechanization of agriculture, farm consolidation, and industrial expansion. The South was "living through an upheaval, more profound," *U.S. News & World Report* proclaimed, "than the Secession."[1]

African Americans were particularly affected by postwar growth, but remained second-class citizens. Reflecting the demographic trends of the twentieth century United States, African Americans moved from rural to urban areas en masse, particularly to northern cities. Consequently, they experienced significant gains in literacy rates, higher education enrollment, union membership, purchasing power, and average life span. Despite these positive developments, black annual income lagged well behind that of whites; most blacks were still denied access to the full range of educational opportunities offered to other Americans. "The gap between what the Negro now achieves and what he might achieve," *Time* concluded, "indicates that he is the nation's most wasted resource."[2]

The roots of the Civil Rights Movement lay in postwar economic and demographic growth, but the most important victories for black freedom came from the legal assault against Jim Crow. During the first half of the twentieth century, the National Association for the Advancement of Colored People (NAACP) worked through the federal judiciary to destroy the southern caste system's legal foundations. The NAACP's legal challenge gave black southerners access to the benefits of postwar prosperity and encouraged the social protests that came thereafter. By 1956, the NAACP made de jure racial segregation illegitimate in the American common law.[3]

The NAACP's most important legal victories came in higher education and voting rights. In successive cases, the NAACP made the federal judiciary rule that segregated law and graduate schools failed to provide equal educational opportunities for black students and were thus in violation of the Fourteenth Amendment. The NAACP successfully challenged black disenfranchisement in *Smith v. Alright* (1944), which declared Texas's Democratic white primary unconstitutional. The end of the South's lily-white primaries changed elections forever. In 1944, fewer than 200,000 black southerners were registered to vote. By 1948, there were approximately 1.3 million; in the 1956 general election, an estimated 3 million black southerners voted.[4]

The NAACP's legal victories over Jim Crow culminated with *Brown v. Board of Education of Topeka, Kansas* (1954). A combination of five cases that each addressed the validity of segregated schools, *Brown* applied desegregation to primary and secondary education and conclusively abolished the "separate but equal" doctrine established in *Plessy v. Ferguson* (1896). *Brown's* corollary, known as *Brown II* (1955), ordered American school districts to desegregate their educational facilities "with all deliberate speed," and gave federal and state courts general guidelines for enforcement of the ruling.[5]

Desegregation of American public education thereafter enjoyed substantial, albeit strictly limited, success. Within one year of *Brown*, approximately 10 percent of southern black schoolchildren attended desegregated schools. With the exception of Washington, D.C., and Texas (which underwent large-scale desegregation of public schools and accommodations), *Brown's* implementation was confined to school districts in the border states and Upper South. No school districts in Alabama, Florida, Georgia, Louisiana, Mississippi, North and South Carolina, and Virginia moved toward compliance.[6]

The NAACP thereafter continued to sue school districts in federal court that resisted *Brown*, and forced municipalities to desegregate other areas of public life. Consequently, the 1956–57 school year marked the first widespread federally mandated desegregation of school districts and communities throughout the South. *Brown* was, according to the black-oriented *New York Amsterdam News*, "the greatest victory for the Negro people since the Emancipation Proclamation."[7]

The NAACP undermined Jim Crow's legal foundations, but the procurement of full citizenship for African Americans was more precarious, for the vestiges of the caste system remained embedded in southern culture. Only by direct challenge was Jim Crow ultimately overthrown. After *Brown*, black southerners were no longer "afraid of bombs and burning crosses," *Ebony* professed, or "intimidated by economic reprisals and floods of hate that flow alike from the mouths of white sharecroppers and Southern Congressmen."[8]

The tocsins for the modern Civil Rights Movement came the year after *Brown* with Emmett Louis Till's lynching in Mississippi and the Montgomery Bus Boycott in Alabama. These two events drew northern journalists to the South in droves and thus notified the American people of the coming revolution. The mass media, furthermore, laid bare the blatant injustice of the southern caste system before the world. "There are as many Yankee reporters dropping off planes and trains," complained the Charleston, S.C., *News and Courier*'s Thomas R. Waring, "as there were carpetbaggers in the 1860's." After Till's corpse was recovered from the bottom of the Tallahatchie River, his mother held an open casket funeral in their hometown of Chicago, Illinois, then toured the country to tell her story. An estimated seventy-five reporters from throughout the nation attended the murder trial of the two accused attackers, who were declared innocent by an all-white male jury. The murderers quickly sold an exclusive interview to nationally syndicated *Look*, in which they boasted of killing Till. Likewise, the Montgomery Bus Boycott drew widespread media attention during the winter and spring of 1955–1956, while its leader, the Rev. Dr. Martin Luther King, Jr., became an international celebrity. In this milieu of favorable media coverage, King optimistically predicted to "get rid of segregation in most areas of American life by 1963," the centennial of the Emancipation Proclamation.[9]

1.1 Emmett Louis Till. Courtesy of AP Images.

In this early stage of the black freedom struggle, King's prophecy seemed a fair assessment. A significant part of the white South recognized that, at the very least, America's newfound postwar prosperity and world leadership were inextricably tied to the end of pro forma white supremacy. The strong socioeconomic forces and federal court decisions that brought the South more in step with the rest of the United States increasingly made Jim Crow incompatible with the cultural ethos of postwar America. Most notably, almost every Christian denomination of the white South formally endorsed desegregation, as did most ecumenical organizations. Desegregation enjoyed substantial support, moreover, among southern college students. "We have attempted to make clear the ethical, social, and religious mandate against segregation," the editor of the University of North Carolina's *Daily Tar Heel* proclaimed, "and have advocated desegregation with all possible speed."[10]

The possibility of peaceful desegregation, with fundamental social change thereafter, was realistic. Population and economic growth, educational accessibility, legal reform, and religious leadership made possible the beloved community sought by civil rights workers. Yet, while some white southerners initially embraced the prospect of reorganizing into a freely democratic society, events quickly showed that when pressed, most actively opposed changes that threatened the superior status they enjoyed within the narrow confines of Jim Crow. Intransigent segregationists fought bitterly and successfully to blunt the integrationist thrust that promised, or in their view threatened, to transform the South.

Brown's desegregation timetable incidentally coincided with the 1956 national election cycle. This coincidence made desegregation the preeminent concern of every elected official in the South. Despite its acceptance by certain sectors of the white South, a groundswell of antipathy to black equality soon emerged. The South's sociopolitical structure designed to maintain white supremacy soon became manifest, as political and economic elites quickly formed a concerted opposition to desegregation.

The Citizens' Councils were the foremost expression of formal opposition to the Civil Rights Movement. Initially created some two months after *Brown* in Indianola, Mississippi, councils quickly organized throughout the entire South. By December 1955, there were 253 chapters and 65,000 dues-paying members, located in Alabama, Arkansas, the Carolinas, Mississippi, Tennessee, and Texas. At their greatest strength in the late 1950s, the councils claimed nearly 250,000 members across the United States.[11]

The Citizens' Councils' first statewide meeting was held December 1, 1955, in the city auditorium of Jackson, Mississippi. An observer noted that the thousands gathered were composed of "well-dressed people of the sort found at Rotary meetings or dancing at the country club." Dignitaries included Democratic Governor Hugh White, Democratic United States Representative John Bell Williams, and over forty Democratic state legislators. Among the most vocal critics of desegregation in the Congress, Williams infamously dubbed *Brown* as "Black Monday," and alleged that "the Supreme

Court drove a knife into the heart of the U.S. Constitution." In the meeting's keynote address, U.S. Senator James Oliver Eastland of Mississippi called for the formation of a regional commission in the South, supported by state taxes, whose sole purpose would be to subvert *Brown*.[12]

The Citizens' Councils believed the Civil Rights Movement was designed to promote miscegenation, curtail states' rights, destroy federalism, and defeat the United States in the Cold War. A Texas councils' pamphlet rhetorically asked, "Do you want your children or grandchildren to go to school with Negroes? Do you want them to fraternize with Negroes, date them, dance with them?" The Texas Citizens' Councils professed to be a law-abiding institution, "organized to prevent the integration of Negroes into white schools." They vowed "to do so by any means at our command which falls within the law." Underscoring their devotion to peaceful means of resistance, they explained, "We do not advocate violence or any form of illegal activity." They opposed desegregation because "every individual has the right to choose his own associates." On February 10, 1956, the Lone Star State's first executive meeting was held in Waco to pass resolutions condemning *Brown* and propose an amendment to the federal Constitution that made the Supreme Court subject (and thus subservient) to congressional oversight. Maintaining that civil rights workers were aligned with the international communist conspiracy, the Oklahoma Citizens' Council adopted as its official motto, "Our White Christian Civilization is the only barrier between Soviet Dictators and World Conquest."[13]

Public reaction toward the Citizens' Councils was mixed. According to Frederick Sullens of the *Jackson News*, councilors were "thoughtful, law abiding citizens, men who stand tall in all walks of life," and were "actuated by what they sincerely believe to be the highest motives." Fellow Mississippian Hodding Carter of Greenville's *Delta Democrat-Times* disagreed, describing them as "blood brothers of the Capone mob." Among the era's foremost southern writers, Robert Penn Warren noted the anxieties of many white southerners who left the countryside for urban life. This native Kentuckian described the typical member as "a hill man, come to town from one of the counties where there aren't too many Negroes, but he is now out to preserve, he says, 'what you might name the old Southern way, what we was raised up to.'" Warren believed that a member was "not out for money, but something else. He is clearly a man of force, force that somehow has never found its way, and a man of language and leadership among his kind, the angry and ambitious and disoriented and dispossessed. It is a language that intoxicates him now."[14]

Truly, most Citizens' Councils were composed of reputable middle-class professionals who emphasized the preservation of law and order. The public officials who either formally affiliated with the Citizens' Councils or support-ed their goals condemned the use of violence as a means to preserve the caste system, and distanced themselves from those who condoned such methods. The councils, nevertheless, were organized specifically to preserve segrega-tion and white supremacy, which permitted, even relied on, state-condoned violence to sustain Jim Crow. In most instances, southern states refused to prosecute violence toward civil rights workers and, therefore, gave de facto approval to the racially motivated guerilla terrorism indicative of the south-ern polity after the Civil War.[15]

While formally denouncing mob violence, the Citizens' Councils used blatant intimidation to preserve white supremacy. After fifty-three black Mississippians signed a petition requesting the Yazoo City School Board to admit their children into the white schools, the local Citizens' Council chapter published their names in a full-page newspaper advertisement "as a public service." Thereafter, signers were denied patronage at local white businesses, so they were forced to either remove their names from the peti-tion or leave town. Financial lending houses owned by councilors, moreover, reportedly canceled $1.5 million in 1955 crop loans to black farmers in the area, while two black men were forced to remove their names from the vot-ing registrars of Isola, Mississippi, in order to get their cotton ginned. From 1954 to 1955, the number of blacks paying poll taxes in Humphreys County, Mississippi, reportedly dropped from 400 to 94.[16]

After *Brown*, Citizens' Councils drove southern politics. Southern state and local officials (many of them members) subverted the federal desegre-gation orders by resurrecting anachronistic states' rights political theories of the early Republic. They enacted numerous state laws to prevent *Brown*'s implementation. During the civil rights era, southern legislatures ultimately passed over 450 statutes designed to obstruct desegregation and hinder the activities of civil rights workers.[17]

The doctrine of interposition became the means to oppose *Brown*. Inter-position alleged that a state government possessed the right to "interpose" between its populace and the federal government when that state determined that its citizens' rights as guaranteed by the United States Constitution were infringed, until the dispute in question was resolved. The doctrine's fore-most promoter was James Jackson Kilpatrick, editor of the *Richmond News Leader*. A born and bred Okie and graduate of the University of Missouri's prestigious school of journalism, Kilpatrick was the protégé of the legend-ary newspaperman and Pulitzer Prize–winning biographer Douglas Southall Freeman. Upon Freeman's death in 1953, Kilpatrick made the *News Leader*'s

1.2 James Kilpatrick of the *Richmond News Leader.* Courtesy of AP Images.

editorial page the leading forum for critics of the Civil Rights Movement in general and *Brown* in particular. For Kilpatrick, states could simply refuse to implement a federal law when a majority of their white citizens disagreed with it. "Every State has a right to interpose its sovereignty, under certain circumstances," he explained, "as a challenge and check against encroachment by the Federal Government upon reserved powers of the States."[18]

Kilpatrick's adopted Virginia was the first state of the former Confederacy to enact interposition. In January 1956, the Old Dominion's voters approved a constitutional amendment granting the state authority to use public funds to pay students to attend private secular segregated school systems. Rather than admit black students, approximately 20 percent of Virginia's public schools had already closed since *Brown.* Set to begin that fall semester, the plan cost approximately $1 million for every 1 percent of the state's school population that chose to attend private schools. Many influential Virginians (including dean of the University of Virginia Law School Frederick D. Ribble) warned that the amendment was unconstitutional, but voters nonetheless passed it by a margin of approximately two to one. The percentages in favor were greatest in the counties with the largest black population. "Well," boasted Democratic state Senator Peck Gray, chair of the commission proposing the plan, "I guess we won the Civil War."[19]

After Virginia enacted privatization, Governor Thomas B. Stanley invited southern governors to parley in Richmond. On January 24, 1956, in the capitol's gubernatorial conference room, Stanley, Democratic governors George Bell Timmerman, Jr., of South Carolina, Marvin Griffin of Georgia, and governor-elect James P. Coleman of Mississippi issued a formal endorsement of interposition as a legal means of resistance to "encroachment of the central government." They called upon their legislatures "to protect" the South, "its sovereignty and the rights of its people."[20]

Democratic Governor Luther Hodges of North Carolina attended the conference but, as his legislature was then not in session, did not endorse the proclamation. His vacillation reflected the Tar Heel State's prevailing political winds. Upon Hodges's Special Advisory Committee on Education's recommendations, in 1955 the North Carolina Legislature passed a series of acts that made local school boards responsible for pupil admission within their respective districts, and thereby absolved the state of responsibility for *Brown*'s implementation. Hodges earlier called for "voluntary segregation," an ambiguous concept with no legal merit. North Carolina thus surrendered its law enforcement powers and allowed local school boards to simply ignore *Brown*.[21]

Either explicitly or implicitly, the southern governors who did not attend the conference nevertheless endorsed the proclamation. Democratic Governor Orval E. Faubus of Arkansas sent a delegation to study the Gray Plan so that he could make appropriate recommendations to his legislature. In his successful 1954 race for governor, the Man from Greasy Creek proclaimed that "desegregation should be solved at the local community level." After his delegation returned from the conference, however, Faubus formally endorsed interposition and privatization, and called upon Arkansas lawmakers to pass enabling legislation. Similarly, Democratic Governor Earl Long of Louisiana was elected to a third gubernatorial term at the same time that Virginia adopted interposition; he ran on a platform that included a pledge to close the state public school system rather than comply with *Brown*.[22]

The Virginia General Assembly quickly acted on Stanley's recommendations. Led by Democratic state Senator Harry Carter Stuart (the great-nephew of Confederate General J. E. B. Stuart), Virginia passed an interposition resolution for the 1956–57 school year. By a vote of thirty-six to two in the state senate and ninety to five in the House of Delegates, the Old Dominion asserted that it was "interposing the sovereignty of Virginia against the encroachment upon the reserved powers of this State, and appealing to sister States to resolve a question of contested power." Believing that such an amendment would not be passed by three-fourths of the states, Virginia

1.3 Democratic Governor Thomas Stanley of Virginia. Courtesy of Library of Virginia.

called upon other states in the Union to initiate a constitutional amendment specifically granting the U.S. Supreme Court jurisdiction in public education. According to Mississippi native Mark Ethridge of Kentucky's *Louisville Courier-Journal*, Virginians "have ridden off like headless horsemen into the woods of nullification—even though they call it interposition—and in pursuit of every evasion that slick, if not smart, lawyers may devise."[23]

The Deep South quickly followed. Alabama legislators passed constitutional amendments abolishing the public school system if the federal judiciary implemented desegregation. *Brown* was "null, void, and of no effect; and," the Heart of Dixie resolved that "as a matter of right, this State is not bound to abide thereby." Before a joint session of the General Assembly broadcast over statewide television and radio, Griffin called upon Georgia's legislators to adopt interposition. He declared that desegregation was "the most vital issue to confront this body since its creation." Accordingly, on February 9, the Peach State declared *Brown* "null, void and of no force or effect." The next week, Timmerman signed the unanimous joint legislative resolution that "condemns and protests against the illegal encroachment by the central government" on South Carolina's sovereignty, "and against the grave threat to the constitutional government implicit in the decisions of the Supreme Court of the United States." The Magnolia State's resolution, adopted February 29, declared *Brown* "unconstitutional and of no lawful effect within the territorial limits of the state of Mississippi." The resolution urged the Southern Congressional Delegation to "protect the rights of the states from the unwarranted encroachment upon their reserved powers to govern the internal and domestic affairs of the states," and to "protect the states when their constitutional rights and privileges are endangered." Federal desegregation orders were designed to "reduce these sovereign states to mere satellites, and subject us to the tyranny of centralized government, so much abhorred by the founders and for the prevention of which they exercised their finest genius." Five southern states thereafter stood in formal defiance of the federal judiciary.[24]

Georgia exemplified this counterrevolution to black equality. In his address, Griffin informed Georgians that the southern governors concluded in Richmond that the federal judiciary did not possess "jurisdiction over any State of the Union except in the case of suits between States respecting boundary disputes and the like; and suits between the States and the United States in cases of that character." The federal Constitution prevented "any State from being sued by individuals in the Supreme Court or in any Federal Court without the State's consent. For this reason, these decisions do not and cannot bind the state of Georgia." Griffin's legerdemain cited the Compact Theory and the Tenth Amendment while simultaneously employing the doctrine of implied powers. He admitted that the "right of interposition" was "not expressly referred to in the Constitution," but maintained that it nonetheless came "out of the nature and character of that instrument and the government established by it, and exists of necessity." Placing interposition within historical states' rights doctrine, he believed that "as the Supreme Court may declare laws unconstitutional when such is necessary to exercise of the authority committed to it to try cases in law in equity, so the States may declare null and void any unlawful action of the Supreme Court which interferes with the exercise of their reserved rights." In a thinly veiled warning about impending miscegenation, Griffin proclaimed "the rights possessed by every man to have a home and rear a family, to choose his own associates, to rear his children according to his belief, to stand erect in the dignity of his personality and to maintain the pride of his inheritance."[25]

Interposition advocates maintained that states had never relinquished their authority to maintain racially separate schools. The "Congress that submitted the Fourteenth Amendment for ratification established separate schools in the District of Columbia," the Georgia resolution noted, "the same State Legislatures that ratified the Fourteenth Amendment also provided for systems of racially separate public schools." Not to "assert its clear rights would be construed as acquiescence in the surrender thereof; and that such submissive acquiescence to the seizure of one right would in the end lead to the surrender of all rights," and thus "inevitably to the consolidation of the States into one sovereignty, contrary to the sacred compact by which this Union of States was created." Segregation was not of a "judicial character," but could be determined only by "the people themselves speaking through their legislative bodies." A constitutional amendment was the only means by which desegregation could be legally implemented. The resolution endorsed school privatization and threatened to "take all appropriate measures honorably and constitutionally available to the State, to avoid this illegal encroachment upon the rights of her people."[26]

As interposition gained momentum, southern states also passed laws designed to destroy the NAACP, abolish freedoms of speech and assembly, and punish recalcitrant citizens. Georgia, for instance, made it a felony to advocate desegregation within the state. Teachers who instructed integrated classes would automatically lose their state licenses. City charters of municipalities that desegregated public parks and other recreational areas would be revoked. Atlanta's two newspapers, both critical of Griffin's policies, were targeted by making it easier for county prosecutors to sue them for libel. Similarly, Mississippi made it illegal and punishable by a one-thousand-dollar fine and six months incarceration "to solicit, advocate, urge or encourage disobedience to any laws" and "nonconformance with the state of Mississippi." Public school employees were required to declare publically all organizations to which they belonged or paid dues during the past five years, and it was illegal for them "to foment or agitate litigation, or to solicit or contribute funds to finance litigation." Alabama passed legislation authorizing county school boards to "fire school teachers who belonged to any organization which advocated racial integration," and initiated an investigation into the NACCP's supposed ties to the international communist conspiracy. In June, the Heart of Dixie's attorney general, James M. Patterson, secured an injunction prohibiting the NAACP from conducting business in the state. Likewise, South Carolina officially declared the NAACP a subversive organization, which placed it under state investigation and barred members from government employment. The NAACP was "so insidious in its propaganda and the fostering of those ideas designed to produce a constant state of turmoil between the races," the Palmetto State asserted, "that membership in such an organization is wholly incompatible with the peace, tranquility and progress that all citizens have a right to enjoy."[27]

Mississippi enforced white supremacy with unmatched fervor. In November 1954, state voters approved a constitutional amendment authorizing public funds for private schools. Before the vote, some legislators reportedly murmured that "a few killings" prior to the legislative session would be the best way to ensure passage of the measure, and that the Citizens' Councils "want to persuade first but are determined to use force if necessary." In early 1956, the Magnolia State abolished common law marriages and called upon Congress to propose a constitutional amendment "granting to the States the right to regulate health, morals, education, marriage, peace and good order." The infamous State Sovereignty Commission to enforce segregation laws was created, as well as a $5,000 library fund in order to purchase books that argued for white supremacy. The campaign produced immediate affects: from 1952 to 1955, the number of registered black Mississippi voters—which had risen from a paltry 2,500 in 1946—dropped from approximately 23,000 to 8,000.[28]

Southern officials even hindered federal agents from operating within their borders. In Florida, Georgia, and South Carolina, the Federal Bureau of Investigation was not allowed to interview prisoners who alleged civil rights violations unless a state official was present. FBI agents were also forced to secure Timmerman's written authorization for civil rights investigations within his state. Alabama Circuit Judge George Wallace declared that he would arrest any FBI agent investigating jury tampering within his jurisdiction. "Invariably, when atrocious acts of violence break out we run into an iron curtain of silence," FBI Director J. Edgar Hoover informed President Dwight David Eisenhower. "The difficulties which our Agents face at times are almost indescribable," Hoover said, "the Negroes are afraid to talk and in case after case we have to wait until nightfall to go see them if we hoped to secure any information."[29]

The interpositionists spread their message across the United States and thus provided the intellectual propaganda necessary for subverting *Brown.* They predicted that regions with black majorities would inevitably experience violent resistance, as well as the degradation, if not abandonment, of their public school systems. According to Kilpatrick, progress made "toward equalization of public facilities in an area in which the vast bulk of taxes are paid by white persons and personal incomes are distressingly low, has been astonishingly good." The South would "either abandon their schools or breach the immutable law by which the South's character has been preserved. And the law is this: That white and black cannot come together, as equals, in any relationship that is *intimate, personal, and prolonged.*" Desegregation also meant that most black teachers lost their jobs and public education discontinued. Presciently, Waring predicted that "even if the schools are not abandoned it seems unlikely that the white people will submit to heavy taxation to operate schools that many of them refuse to patronize. If they are not throttled outright, the public school systems in some areas may be starved to death."[30]

Intransigent segregationists held the neo-Confederate view that the Fourteenth Amendment was illegally ratified during Reconstruction when radical Republicans denied congressional representation to former Confederate states. For Kilpatrick, "nothing could be clearer than the line of reasoning which holds that if the amendment were void at the outset, it remains void to this day, whether one thousand or ten thousand cases have been decided pursuant to its terms." The Tenth Amendment, conversely, allowed segregated public school systems because it did not explicitly prohibit segregation. While the Fourteenth was illegally procured, it was nonetheless ratified by northern states that also maintained segregated schools.[31]

To intransigents, segregation prevented violence between whites and blacks. Citing statistics that showed more crime in black communities, Waring alleged that "interracial homicide is relatively rare." With the exception of Emmett Till's murder, which Waring believed was unfairly covered by the northern press, "no lynching," he said, "has occurred in years." This Low Country newspaperman warned: "If there is riotous bloodshed it will be for the most part Negroes' blood. The thin tolerance of the ruffian and lower elements of the white people could erupt into animosity and brutality if race pressure becomes unbearable." Accordingly, "schools would be a focal point for such disturbance, first among the pupils themselves and later by enraged parents."[32]

For these intransigent segregationists, the disparity between black and white student achievement test scores proved that desegregation would prove ineffective for the former and detrimental to the latter. Failing to directly address the NAACP's argument that the lack of adequate facilities, teacher training, and other educational resources were the primary reasons that black southerners produced poorer test scores, Kilpatrick argued that "to aim at the median white child would be plainly unfair to the colored children; to lower the teaching level to a point acceptable to the colored children would be unfair to the white." Waring agreed. "Can you honestly say that you are eager to send your own child to a classroom where the majority of other pupils will be considerably more backward in their studies," he rhetorically asked, "and extremely different in social background and cultural attainment? Which would you *really* put first: your theory of racial justice, or justice to your own child?" "White parents, aware of the disparate racial mores," Kilpatrick concurred, "ought not to be denounced as bigoted fascists if they exhibit what seems to them a well-founded concern for the well-being of their children."[33]

Intransigents, moreover, consciously riled white fears of miscegenation. Kilpatrick asserted that higher rates of illegitimacy, syphilis, and gonorrhea among black southerners proved "that among large groups of the Negro population in the South, the sexual act is viewed as casually as a goodnight kiss. Further, the ugly truth is that this tendency toward promiscuity is accompanied by a dismaying tendency to violence and crimes of passion." African Americans were also supposedly less hygienic than whites, while black children came from less stable home environments. Black marital relations were "casual—even more so, in fact, than among the often-divorced personalities of Northern café society. Many Negro couples," Waring observed, "do not bother with divorce because there was no actual marriage in the first place." For Kilpatrick, to "recite certain facts of public health and jail commitments is no more to damn a whole race than it is for the automobile insurance companies, in fixing a higher rate for drivers under 25, to damn all teenagers." *Brown* meant "a social experience," he explained, "compounded of class plays and cadet hops, senior proms and home room picnics; it involves an intimate boy-girl relationship in the formative years of adolescence." Desegregation could eventually be accomplished in public accommodations but, for the white South, such a prospect could never be allowed in public schools. "In the formative years of adolescence," Kilpatrick believed, "the element of sex arises in its most dangerous and experimental form." For this adopted Virginian, "to integrate the schools of the Southern States thus is to demand a relationship forbidden by the mores of the people; and it is to risk, twenty or thirty years hence, a widespread racial amalgamation and a debasement of the society as a whole." Likewise, Waring believed that some blacks had since "progressed beyond the cultural level of the vast bulk of their own people, but are not accepted by the whites, who fear to let down any dikes lest they be engulfed in a black flood." Indeed, the "mixture of races which white Southerners have observed in Latin American countries gives them a dim view of legalizing cohabitation with Negroes." If blacks continued to move north, however, "the racial proportions may grow more nearly equal. Then the North may come more tolerant of the Southerners' view of race problems, and the South better able to handle its dwindling Negro problem. Southerners will gladly share the load." While admitting that the "views and philosophies may change through the ages," Waring believed "some basic truths stand out like the Ten Commandments. Southerners are not yet ready to accept an eleventh, 'Thou shalt not protect the purity of thy race.'"[34]

Despite this intense pressure, some southern officials did not openly defy the federal judiciary. They came to be identified as southern moderates who condemned legislative defiance as futile and misguided and pleaded for nonviolence as well as open communication among all groups concerned. To achieve real social change, moderates advocated the gradual implementation of *Brown* and advised the NAACP and other civil rights groups to practice patience and discretion in the enforcement of federal orders.[35]

The most recognized southern moderate after *Brown* was Democratic Governor Frank G. Clement of Tennessee. Clement served as an FBI agent, then an army officer in World War II, before establishing a successful Nashville law practice. Elected governor in 1952 with the largest popular vote in state history, and reelected to a four-year term

1.4 Thomas Waring of the *Charleston News and Courier*. Courtesy of the Strom Thurmond Institute.

in 1954 by fending off two intransigent challengers, Clement was then the youngest chief executive in the United States. On Sunday mornings, Clement (a friend of the renowned Baptist preacher Billy Graham) also served as a lay minister in local protestant churches.[36]

On January 23, 1956, an organized rally of some three hundred people ascended the Tennessee capitol to demand that Clement convene the general assembly to enact interposition. The motorcade displayed signs that read "Save Our Children from the Black Plague," with the U. S. and the Confederate battle flags flying ubiquitously. Protesters marched alongside bearing placards of "God the Original Segregationist," "Down with Traitors," "Segregation or War," "A Bargain: Segregation at any Cost," and "Beware: This Is Not a Pleasure Trip." The Volunteer State's Capitol Plaza, with its Great War Union and memorials to the "Boy Hero of the Confederacy," Sam Davis, and Sgt. Alvin York, is an ideal locale for evoking past southern glory. The marchers climbed the steps past the graves of President James K. Polk and President Andrew Johnson to Clarke Mills's *General Jackson on Horseback*, and passed Carmack's "Pledge to the South" into the capitol.

Clement granted the parade of intransigents an interview for over an hour, but saying the controversy was not one for the state but exclusively for federal and local authorities, he refused to endorse interposition. There to help him welcome the intransigents were a Catholic priest, a Jewish rabbi, two protestant ministers, and numerous reporters. Clement urged the group to proclaim for nonviolence, and told them that their actions only assisted the

NAACP in bringing about immediate integration. Maintaining that desegregation policies would be left to the discretion of local communities, Clement told the intransigent crowd that "pressure tactics" would not intimidate him, and that a "governor who submits to pressure, rather than following reason, would not be worthy of the office." During the rally, some threatened to attack a reporter for the black-oriented Memphis *Tri-State Defender*, to which a white security guard responded, "If you hit this man I'll lock you up. This building belongs to all the people. That reporter has as much right here as you do."[37]

Theatrics aside, Clement's policy was like that of Hodges. These Upper South governors sought to lend the moral voice of the governor's office to the cause of moderation. Both proclaimed that local school boards had the authority to implement desegregation in their districts. Clement and Hodges thereby absolved themselves of responsibility for their states' compliance with *Brown*. Federal orders must be followed at the local level, they reasoned, so gubernatorial direction was outside of their jurisdiction. Clement believed that his involvement led only to the threat of intransigent segregationists gaining a statewide forum, with the real possibility of violence as a consequence. "A few indiscriminate words on my part, as Governor," he explained, "could initiate conflict and bloodshed." He added that "it is my policy to allow local communities in the state to conduct" their "own community affairs."[38]

The moderate course of Clement, Hodges, and like-minded public officials was at best problematic and at worst irresponsible. They rightly tried to parry the interposition thrust that bespoke the South's flagrant defiance of *Brown*. But what Hodges labeled "voluntary segregation" bore little difference to Clement's call for local control. Because they shifted responsibility to local governments, segregationists openly defied both *Brown* and other federal decrees for years. Granted, the successful implementation in some areas of the Upper South was real. But just as many, if not more, of the local communities that Clement, Faubus, and Hodges claimed were best equipped to implement *Brown* endured rioting and violence, as well as distended community social relationships that lasted for generations. The moderates' capitulation ultimately forced the federals to take a much greater role in local law enforcement, school administration, and the protection of individual civil liberties. Claims that *Brown* was outside of gubernatorial jurisdiction were dubious, if not farcical. Political moderation abjectly failed.

Moderation nonetheless achieved a modicum of legitimacy in the public debate over *Brown*. Moderates generally sympathized with the aspirations of black southerners, but maintained that, with the notable exception of a few violent extremists, intransigent segregationists were merely resisting their

1.5 The Tennessee state capitol, Nashville. Courtesy of Mary Anne Sullivan.

communities' cultural disintegration. "Many a sincere deep-South Southerner does not know, or refuses to admit," the *Atlanta Constitution's* Ralph McGill explained, "that world forces are at work in the American race problem as they are in Asia and Africa." Warren agreed. Citizens' Councilors merely dreamt "of preserving the traditional American values of individualism and localism against the anonymity, irresponsibility, and materialism of the power state, against the philosophy of the ad-man, the morality of the Kinsey report, and the gospel of the bitch-goddess." They wanted "to be southern *again:* to recreate a habitation for the values they would preserve, to achieve in unity some clarity of spirit, to envisage some healed image of their own identity."[39]

Moderates argued that *Brown's* gradual implementation was the best means to alleviate discrimination and sustain public education. Activists on both sides of the debate were thus to blame for violent confrontations. Desegregation was inevitable, so southern states should work out *Brown's* implementation themselves, without federal interference. For McGill, "the trumpets of the nine black robed justices in the Greek temple on the Potomac blew down the already weakened walls of political feudalism in the South. There long will be fighting in the ruins, but it will be guerilla stuff and its denouement is sure." A slow and steady implementation could bring immediate progress without broaching southern mores. "Integration accom-

plished with a minimum of fuss in a few easy counties in otherwise recalcitrant Southern states," argued the *Washington Post*'s Benjamin Muse, a former Virginia state senator, "a healthy movement for compliance with the law
of the land could go on from there." Muse charged that "the indiscriminate
aggressiveness of the NAACP has contributed to the present attitude of resistance to the Supreme Court's anti-segregation decision and has registered
no gains." Desegregation should first be implemented in the border states,
but the Deep South should for a time be exempted. "What the Deep South
needs now," Muse believed, "is a cooling off period."[40]

Moderates also denounced the passivity of white southern progressives.
The Mississippi novelist William Faulkner, for instance, believed that southern moderates must speak up "because we will not sit quietly by and see our
native land, the South, wreck and ruin itself twice in less than a hundred
years over the Negro question." Muse claimed that "genuine progress will not
be made until the moderates on both sides rise up and make their influence
felt." Warren dissented, stressing the necessity of implementing wide-scale
desegregation quickly, but also called upon fellow whites to assume moral
leadership for the prevention of violence. Believing the southern moderate
"senses somehow that the great loyalties and deep friendships which the two
races have known will bring the region through," McGill offered cautious
optimism. They "will continue in this hope, even though the sound of guerilla fighting in the tumbled down walls of life and politics that was, all but
drowns out his words."[41]

Southern moderates' influence, however, was limited. The newsmagazine
Life praised moderation, for its proponents "emphasize why pioneers should
avoid scraping of Southern sensitivities and emotions." Civil rights workers
thus "have a double duty to talk softly," since the "task is to preserve an atmosphere in which reason, tolerance, and compromise can still operate." Nevertheless, moderates were criticized from all sides. Intransigents despised
moderates. "Segregation was and is," M. Wright of New Orleans, Louisiana,
explained, "preference not prejudice. Faulkner and his Negro friends have
the inalienable right to go North if not satisfied with the Southern status
quo." In turn, *Brown*'s advocates condemned southern moderation for its
shallowness. The commentator Roscoe Drummond noted that moderation
was sound only if "the moderates of the South will join in turning aside the
other extreme of total resistance and nullification." Another influential pundit, Walter Lippmann, said that while noble in principle, southern moderation did not "represent a practical and concrete program on which men of
moderate temper have agreed to unite," asking, "how slowly can we go without nullifying the Constitution?" Richard A. Long, an English professor at the

historically black Morgan State University in Baltimore, Maryland, considered southern moderation a myth that was "purely for intellectual and liberal consumption and has not been heard from the politicians. Being practical men, the politicians would be embarrassed by such a compound of subtlety and vacuity." He denounced the idea that southern moderates were silenced and excluded from the negotiation process. "If the work of the moderates has been so inconsequential that the first faint breeze will rip it to shreds," he explained, "it has been the work of dreams rather than substance." The NAACP's Albert E. Barnett also denounced pleas for patience because "in no case has 'privilege' surrendered of its own accord. Nor will it. If to 'go slow' is to relax pressures through the courts and public opinion, no social change will be effected." Barnett saw the Montgomery Bus Boycott as exemplary of successful efforts at "expectancy with calmness," and noted that civil rights workers practiced nonviolence while praying for their segregationist opponents. "Orderly militancy is of the essence of patience; it is moderation," the Georgian declared, "not immoderation." While both moderate and intransigent segregationists thought the NAACP subversive, the organization sought only orderly change through the judicial system, a strategy in stark contrast to contemporary Marxist revolutions where oppressed minorities employed guerilla warfare and "redress of grievances by torch, dagger and bomb, instruments that produce social chaos and involve loss of precious moral values." "The trend has been clear for twenty years," noted Thurgood Marshall, asking those who pleaded for deceleration, "how long must the cooling off period be?" If the NAACP slowed its campaign, the South would refuse to implement *Brown*. "We follow the Court's order," he maintained, "we move with 'deliberate speed.'"[42]

As intransigent segregationists controlled most southern state governments, moderation did not appeal to civil rights workers. This gradual strategy for social change failed to offer a viable means to implement *Brown*, extend first-class citizenship to black southerners, and prevent reactionary violence. Moderates offered eloquent appeals for the prevention of violence and open communication between interested parties. They nonetheless failed to acknowledge the established political and economic interests of the status quo and the inherent fears of white Americans regarding interracial sex. The Jim Crow establishment indubitably defended the status quo. Moderates' pleas for gradualism, or even the mild alleviation of social inequality, were subverted in almost every instance of confrontation. And the moderate argument was ultimately used to sustain Jim Crow for years. That white moderates had the best intentions and were altruistic in word and deed is certain. Their motivations did not, however, negate their status as members of the ruling class in the southern caste system. Moderates recognized the inherent problems of their society's steadfast commitment to white supremacy. But, as privileged members of their communities, it was difficult, if not impossible, for them to attain the intellectual distance needed to realize the solution, a forthright compliance with the law.

2. The Racial Politics of the 1956 Elections

In the wake of *Brown v. Board of Education* (1954), intransigent segregation or moderation dominated southern politics at every level of government. The Declaration of Constitutional Principles, popularly known as the Southern Manifesto, fused these distinct yet similar ideologies together. More than any other single statement of its era, the Southern Manifesto articulated the political doctrine of the white South towards the Civil Rights Movement. The authors achieved their objectives because they composed a statement supported by both intransigents and moderates within the Southern Congressional Delegation. In turn, the statement momentarily persuaded most Americans that the white South's opposition to *Brown* was, if not justified, at the very least not just irrational hysterics, and thus worthy of consideration. The Southern Manifesto made the white South's definition of race relations a legitimate point of debate in the national discussion over the emerging Civil Rights Movement. Meaningful desegregation and related civil rights legislation was thereafter stalled for years.

Though written to serve immediate practical ends, the Southern Manifesto was the culmination of years of political and legislative strategy designed to sustain Jim Crow. From the outset, the Southern Congressional Delegation in general, and the U.S. Senate's Southern Caucus in particular, blocked all legislation sought by civil rights advocates and led the counterrevolution against the federal judiciary's desegregation decrees. Their strategy was clear. Southern members of Congress openly questioned the integrity of the Supreme Court and the legitimacy of its decisions. They portrayed desegregation as unconstitutional, an integral part of the international communist conspiracy, and designed to destroy the white South's culture through widespread miscegenation.

The Senate's Southern Caucus sought foremost to undermine the United States Supreme Court's credibility and convince the American people that its justices were incompetent. The caucus's acknowledged leader, Democratic Senator Richard Brevard Russell, Jr., of Georgia, boasted to constituents that he would work to "get some real lawyers and judges on the Court who would recognize the time-honored judicial principle of *stare decisis* instead of undertaking to formulate policy in the nature of legislation." Democratic Senator James Oliver Eastland of Mississippi described the court as a "crowd of parasitic politicians" who were "indoctrinated and brainwashed by left-wing pressure groups." Senator J. Strom Thurmond of South Carolina fumed that the justices "were not worthy to wear the robes of their high office."[1]

The Southern Caucus declared *Brown* an illegal intrusion into the legislative field. For Democratic Senator Russell Long of Louisiana, "the Supreme Court has become a lawmaking body. It has undertaken in a number of instances to change the Constitution of the United States without the consent of the people." Similarly, Democratic Senator John Stennis of Mississippi alleged that the "real issue in the recent Supreme Court decision is not segregation alone. It is the usurpation of power by the Supreme Court. The Court must be curbed."[2]

The Southern Caucus urged constituents to resist *Brown*'s implementation. Thurmond believed that the "Court did not follow the Constitution in arriving at its decision. We are not bound by honor or the law to submit to the Court without resisting." Eastland told white southerners they "will not be violating the Constitution or the law when they defy this monstrous proposition." "Corrupt decisions of a Court do not change the law," he explained, "and the Supreme Court does not have the power to change the Constitution." Democratic Senator Allen Ellender of Louisiana believed that judicial review of Congress as established under *Marbury v. Madison* (1803) was erroneous. He would, furthermore, "enthusiastically support a movement to repeal the 14th and 15th Amendments to the Constitution, if I thought that there was any chance of doing so."[3]

For southerners in Congress, the most egregious aspect of *Brown* was Chief Justice Earl Warren's majority opinion that employed the work of the sociologist Gunnar Myrdal. Russell alleged that "any connection between legality and the Supreme Court decision, was, at most, purely incidental. When they forgot all the law and precedent and based the decision on a book written by a socialist psychological engineer, they pulled the rug out from under all lawyers." "There was and is still no law upon which they could base such a decision," Thurmond explained. The Supreme Court mistakenly "used sociology and psychology upon which to base their decision in the segregation suit."[4]

The Southern Caucus argued that the Supreme Court was duped by the international communist conspiracy. *Brown* was "shot through and through with politics," said Russell, "for the Negroes of the nation are organized and exert a powerful influence on our government here in Washington." These "extreme pressure groups who are not card-carrying Communists are as great a threat as the Communists." The Supreme Court ruled in favor of the "communist-dominated" NAACP, Thurmond believed. "Where did the idea of integration come from?" he rhetorically asked. "Read the 1928 platform of the Communist Party and there you will find this statement: 'Segregation must be abolished.'" Thurmond charged that Myrdal and other social scientists cited in *Brown*'s majority opinion were "members of communist front organizations, socialists, or wholly ignorant of the situation." In May 1955, Eastland and Democratic Senator Olin D. Johnston of South Carolina cosponsored a Senate resolution proposing a formal investigation of the supposed communist influence on *Brown.* In introducing the resolution, the Mississippian said that "the decision of the Supreme Court in the school segregation cases was based upon the writings and teachings of pro-communist agitators and other enemies of the American form of government."[5]

The Southern Caucus warned that desegregation inevitably led to miscegenation and the collapse of southern culture. For Russell, desegregation was "the most serious problem we have had to face since Appomattox. The history of every other country shows that integration eventually leads to amalgamation and that no mongrel race has ever accomplished much." Stennis concurred. "Placing the children side by side over the years, in primary grammar and high school grades, is certain to eventually destroy each race." He said that "the bloodstream—the racial integrity of each group—is worth saving." He predicted that white southerners would "regretfully and reluctantly abolish their public school systems if necessary to avoid enforced destruction of their own race." According to Eastland, "The future greatness of America depends upon racial purity and maintenance of Anglo-Saxon institutions, which still flourish in full flower in the South."[6]

According to these senators, the Civil Rights Movement was primarily designed to introduce intermarriage and anarchy into the South. Ellender denounced the "invasion of our states by a new and hungrier breed of carpetbaggers." He warned of "outside agitators" who were "hovering like greedy vultures for the time when racial antagonisms lead to chaos, the breakdown of governmental authority, and general lawlessness." In Eastland's view, "Anti-segregation decisions are dishonest decisions dictated by political pressure groups bent upon the destruction of the American system of Government and the mongrelization of the white race." Attempting to counteract the negative publicity that Mississippi received after the Emmett Till lynching, Eastland and the Citizens' Councils publicized the fact that, while enlisted in the U.S. Army during World War II, Till's father was executed upon his conviction of rape and murder of a local girl and the rape of two other women in

Italy. As the elder Till's reputation was well known in the community where his son was killed, the violent reaction by white ruffians after racial boundaries were crossed proved the need for rigid segregation.[7]

"Centralized control of education has historically been the escalator to absolute power for dictators," warned Thurmond, as he and his colleagues portrayed southerners—black and white alike—as a persecuted minority whose culture was destroyed by a powerfully oppressive central government. Stennis "found great peoples with patterns of conduct and customs of their own," in other regions of the country who "would not want to see their customs swept away by Court decree, especially without a single new law on the subject being passed by lawmakers." "Colored people have and want their own churches," he explained, and "they have and want their own social affairs and fraternal organizations. These go to make up the way of life of our colored people—a way of life which they do not want to give up. As part of this way of life, they want and need their own schools." Long agreed: "I'm strongly in favor of segregation, first because I believe in it, second because every White Southerner wants it and third because the great majority of colored people want it." Ellender maintained that "racial segregation, based on the principle of racial equality, involves no derogation of either race; if some believe that segregation connotes inferiority, then it is connotation which they, themselves, choose to place upon it, for the principle of segregation applies to white and negro alike."[8]

The Southern Caucus threatened black southerners with the dissolution of public education if they did not desist in pressing for *Brown*'s implementation. For Ellender, "Schools must continue on a segregated basis if the taxpayers are to continue to support the public schools, and if negro school teachers expect to continue to be employed." They realized, however, that segregation was doomed if southern officials failed to make black school facilities equal to those of whites. "If we fail," Stennis warned, "we will furnish our opposition with weapons to club us with in years to come; our inaction now will be effectively used against us later." Eastland favored shuttering the entire public school system, but Stennis dissuaded him, for "he was heaping down coals of fire on his own head when he advocated abolishing the public school system because in great areas of Mississippi the attitude of the people was that they were going to keep their public schools and by indirect methods they would also keep them separate." As a member of the Senate's District of Columbia Appropriations Committee, Stennis financially controlled the federal district's desegregation plan. He urged white southerners to follow a similar course in their own communities. "If the local people decline to vote the necessary revenue, the school authorities can't carry out the court's orders," he advised.[9]

No member of the Southern Caucus formally joined the Citizens' Councils, but all agreed with, while many promoted, their agenda. Thurmond called upon "men and women within the Citizens' Councils" to "have the intestinal fortitude to fight for the rights that are guaranteed them under the Constitution of the United States." Stennis recommended that Council leaders organize local chapters composed of "several leaders well spread out, men of calmness and judgment, who will not lose their heads and men who really have the public welfare at heart. This cannot be solved by demagoguery and irrational condemnation." Eastland became the Councils' titular spokesman, helping them organize throughout the South. After the Mississippi Councils' first statewide meeting, Executive Secretary Robert B. Patterson ecstatically told Eastland that his plenary address "outdrew Liberace and the Harlem Globetrotters by a clear 2,000." Eastland also spoke before a rally on February 9, 1956, in Montgomery, Alabama, during the height of the bus boycott. Before a crowd of some 15,000, his oft-repeated battle cry urged rebellion: "You are not required to obey any court which passed such a ruling. In fact, you are obligated to defy it." The chairman of the Alabama Councils, state Senator Sam Englehardt, Jr., praised Eastland for rallying troops to the cause. "Since that meeting," he informed the Mississippian, "we have picked up 1500 new members and have requests for new organizations in twelve counties." At a highly publicized rally in Columbia, South Carolina (with attendance around 3,700 and speeches by many of the Palmetto State's leading politicians), Eastland declared that the Councils would "protect and maintain white supremacy throughout eternity."[10]

The Southern Caucus also directed opposition to *Brown* on the state level. Russell encouraged state and local officials throughout the South to enact interposition, corresponded with intransigents across the country, and read widely on the NAACP, other civil rights advocacy groups, and many white supremacist organizations. Stennis helped draft Mississippi's interposition resolution in the weeks before its formal adoption by the legislature and regularly consulted state officeholders on strategies and tactics. He encouraged Mississippi Democratic Governor James P. Coleman that "some stronger language than the Virginia Resolution would be justified and should be used." Stennis also promoted the idea that state governors could use military intervention to prevent violence, even if in direct violation of federal orders. For the prevention of violence "to meet a given situation that might develop in any school district, I think that would be a proper use of police power." The former judge explained, "While acting as chief executive of a State," a southern governor "is beyond the Court's power."[11]

A few within the Southern Caucus, however, doubted interposition's viability. Democratic Senator John McClellan of Arkansas admitted to constituents that "Congress is powerless to pass an effective law preserving segregation since the same Supreme Court would hold any such law unconstitutional," and he was "confident that a majority of the members of Congress would oppose such a law." Ellender confided that there was little hope of annulling *Brown*, and that he "would not consent to actively support the interposition movement unless I can be convinced that it is legally sound and there is some chance of success." He admitted that *Brown* was the law of the land and that it could not be annulled save for an unlikely constitutional amendment. Local white and black leaders thus should meet together to "work out some kind of understanding as to how the Supreme Court's segregation ruling shall be applied." The Louisianan hoped "that moderation will be the watch word, and self-restraint on the part of our leaders the order of the day, to the end that unfavorable publicity can be avoided and a rational solution of this problem achieved." These moderate sentiments bespoke the need to follow the rule of law and prevent violence, yet left the murky and undefined question of which law and authorities to obey. According to Democratic Senator J. William Fulbright of Arkansas, "You can't pass laws to make men good to each other. If you sent troops south and put Negroes in every school by force, you still wouldn't change the fundamental problem."[12]

No member of the Southern Caucus ever called for physical violence to subvert *Brown*. They understood that violence hindered segregation's credibility before the court of American public opinion. "Hot-headed oratory and rash acts, whether by government officials or by private individuals or groups," Ellender acknowledged, "will not help but rather will hurt our cause." He warned constituents that "trouble-makers from outside the South will be looking with a fine-comb in an effort to discover isolated incidents that can be blown up all out of proportion to their significance," and used to present "a distorted picture of the status of the Southern negro under our segregation policies, and thereby provoke Federal intervention." "The fight we must wage must be a just and legal fight," Eastland asserted, "acts of violence and lawlessness have no place" in the campaign against *Brown*.[13]

The Southern Congressional Delegation was especially positioned to make *Brown* illegitimate in public opinion and prevent the passage of federal civil rights legislation. Because of the congressional seniority system, the white South possessed an inordinate amount of power in American politics after World War II. With southern officeholders' long tenure, the one-party states of the former Confederacy dominated Congress in postwar America. Administrative power in the Congress resided in the hands of senior office-holders who were largely immune from conforming to the policies and platforms of the national parties. The seniority system insulated tenured senators and representatives from political pressure and allowed one-party southern states to dominate nearly all rules, procedures, and legislation within the Senate, and to a similar (though lesser) degree in the House of Representatives.[14]

Southern seniority's impact within a Democratic majority was most evident during the Eighty-Fourth Congress, the first elected after *Brown*. Democrats held a forty-nine to forty-seven majority in the Senate after the 1954 midterm elections, and a twenty-nine-vote majority in the House. Because of seniority, southern Democrats chaired nine of the fifteen major standing committees in the Senate and fourteen major committees in the House. Eight of the nine southern-chaired Senate committees were generally acknowledged as the most powerful. Senate Majority Leader Lyndon Baines Johnson and Speaker of the House Sam J. Rayburn, furthermore, represented the former Confederate state of Texas. The consensus as to the best committees on which to serve led to a permanent shortage of choice assignments for new senators and representatives. It was, therefore, almost impossible for senators and representatives from states with competitive two-party political systems to get chairs or other important committee positions.[15]

Rule Twenty-Two, commonly known as the filibuster, ensured the Southern Caucus's hegemony in the Senate. Filibusters allowed for unlimited debate for pending business and a super majority to enact cloture (the cessation of debate), so that legislation could be brought to a vote. Groups of senators, therefore, literally talked to death proposed legislation they deemed unfavorable. The Southern Caucus began to use the rule in the 1920s to prevent civil rights legislation from consideration. In 1949, the Eightieth Congress's Democratic majority further strengthened Rule Twenty-Two. Led by Russell, the Senate raised the necessary majority to enact cloture from two-thirds of the senators present to two-thirds of the whole Senate, or sixty-four total. The change immediately prevented much of President Harry S. Truman's proposed civil rights legislation from formal consideration by the full Senate. "Rule XXII is the barrier at which all Congressional efforts to legislate the 'civil rights' program has been stopped dead. National conventions may approve by large majorities specific items," Arthur Krock of the *New York Times* observed, "but the Senate has been the graveyard of such pledges and the gravedigger has been Rule 22."[16]

Russell personified the Southern Congressional Delegation's inordinate influence on national politics. A master of consensus and parliamentary procedure, he was not among Congress's grandstanders. The Georgian was more comfortable behind the scenes than at the forefront of legislative debates, preferring personal negotiation in the Senate's storied cloakroom to dramatic speeches from the chamber's well. His leadership of the Southern Caucus, chairmanship of the Armed Services Committee, and crucial stewardship of the 1951 MacArthur hearings made him the single most powerful member of Congress after World War II, and arguably the most influential senator of the twentieth century.[17]

The era's politicos considered Russell the embodiment of the Senate at its best; many were in awe of the alleged Georgia Cicero. A congressional staffer described Russell as "a man of towering intellect," with "superb intuition," and "one of the most astute minds that has ever entered the Senate," while another believed him "one of the most attractive men I've ever known in my life. He is a great gentleman, a man of tremendous integrity, and one of the smartest men who ever served in the Senate." Russell's adversaries paid heed. As Democratic Senator Hubert Humphrey of Minnesota recalled, on Capitol Hill, "the man you had to pay your respects to was Dick Russell." Even NAACP Executive Secretary Roy Wilkins referred to him as "distinguished," though he carefully added that "except in the field of human rights he *is* distinguished." For journalist William S. White, Russell "acted for his nation with a gallantry and a generosity that the nation has in fact repaid with a petty discrimination against him and all his kind." The sycophant rhetorically asked, "How many times must northern liberals in their inner awareness of their professional inferiority to such Richard Russells as still survive, reassure themselves by seeing to it that every Richard Russell is kept firmly in his place. How long can the nation afford all this?"[18]

In every congressional debate over proposed civil rights legislation after World War II, Russell directed the entire Southern Congressional Delegation in conceiving legal theory, constructing policy, and formulating political strategy. His leadership was established after Democratic Senator Dennis Chavez of New Mexico introduced a bill in January 1946 to establish a permanent Fair Employment Practices Commission (FEPC). After the Truman Commission issued its 1947 report, "To Secure These Rights," Russell publicly assumed command of the Southern Caucus. On February 2, 1948, Truman sent a special message to Congress endorsing the recommendations of the commission. One month later on March 6, twenty-one senators from the eleven former Confederate states met in the office of Democratic Senator Harry Byrd of Virginia to plan their strategy against the pending civil rights legislation.[19] Members announced afterward at a press conference that they were placing themselves under the "generalship" of Russell for all future actions against civil rights bills. The episode marked Russell's formal recognition as head of the Southern Caucus, replacing Democratic Senator Tom Connally of Texas, a position which the Georgian subsequently held until his death in 1971. There was no formal membership in the Southern Caucus, dubbed by the press as the "Dixie Study Group," though it consisted of almost all of the senators from the former states of the Confederacy. Usually, Russell's staff called a meeting of what they described as the "Constitutional Democrats," who thereafter met in his office to plan their opposition. Some meetings included invited guests, such as select House members or a visiting southern governor. During his tenure, Russell posted a southern senator on the Senate floor at all times during congressional sessions for his "turn of guard duty," to prevent any "quickie," or "legislative trickery" by civil rights advocates that could allow their bills to be considered. He also pressured the Mutual Broadcasting System and the Federal Communications Commission to allow southern senators to give national radio addresses to air the group's views before the American public. As Senate aide George Reedy explained, "Southerners had learned that Russell was not going to get any of them in trouble, that as long as they went along with Russell and played fair and square, he would play fair and square with them."[20]

Prior to the 1948 Democratic National Convention in Chicago, Russell led southern delegates to join a host of northern regulars and publicly call for Truman to remove himself from consideration for the presidential nomination. In an effort to keep southern delegates in the convention hall, Russell allowed his name to be submitted as a formal challenge to the incumbent president. Yet, after Truman was nominated, Russell and most of his southern congressional colleagues endorsed the ticket and did not join the walkout led by the South Carolina and Mississippi delegations. Thereafter, he and the rest of the senior members of the Southern Congressional Delegation did not participate in either Truman's national campaign or the Dixiecrat Revolt. Their tepid rapprochement with the Democratic Party proved advantageous after Truman's surprise victory, for they kept their seniority and thus successfully blocked the president's civil rights proposals in the next congressional session.[21]

Indicative of his professional style, Russell worked within the Democratic Party to stifle civil rights. As with the rest of the senior Democratic congressional leadership of his generation, Russell played a major role in the party's legislative agenda through their committee leadership and long tenure; they were instrumental in the transformation of the federal government into a modern bureaucratic welfare state during the New Deal and World War

II. Evoking the mantra of his predecessor, Georgia's Civil War–era Senator Benjamin Hill, Russell always described the Democracy as "the party of our fathers." He thus sought the 1952 Democratic presidential nomination by trying to win the southern primaries and controlling their state delegations to the national convention. His candidacy stumbled, however, with little support outside the South. But, with General Dwight D. Eisenhower's immense popularity below Mason and Dixon's Line, Russell's campaign served to prevent the states of the former Confederacy from defecting, and tamped down southern Republicanism to a minimum. In stark contrast to Thurmond's quixotic 1948 Dixiecrat Revolt, the Georgian prevented another southern walkout in 1952, pruned Ike's coattails from becoming so large as to defeat the South's congressional incumbents, and retained southern control over federal congressional legislation through seniority. He subsequently helped place Senator John Sparkman of Alabama as the Democrats' vice presidential nominee. Southern Democrats were unsatisfied with the presidential nominee, Governor Adlai Stevenson of Illinois, and the party's platform that endorsed Truman's civil rights program. Both Russell and Senate President Pro Tempore Walter George of Georgia announced that they would not participate in the autumn presidential campaign. After Ike's campaign gained substantial traction in the South, however, Russell quickly returned from Venezuela to campaign for the Democratic ticket. George followed suit and raised some twenty thousand dollars for the national campaign. As a gesture of solidarity, Stevenson downplayed civil rights on the hustings. Russell and George considered Democratic congressional majorities the sine qua non for loyalty to the national party, while the 1952 Democratic campaign considered party unity more important than equality for African Americans.[22]

There were, however, deep fissures within the Southern Congressional Delegation's otherwise impregnable rampart against the Civil Rights Movement's legislative agenda. The foremost threat was Tennessee's two Democratic U.S. senators, Estes Kefauver and Albert Gore, Sr., who refused to caucus with their colleagues from the former Confederate states. Arriving to the Senate in 1949, Kefauver announced during the debate over Rule Twenty-Two that he would not support the Southern Caucus's successful expansion of cloture. In his unsuccessful campaign for the 1952 Democratic presidential nomination, Kefauver secured the endorsement of the Senate's strongest civil rights champion, Democratic Senator Paul Douglas of Illinois. Supporters of civil rights could be mildly supportive of Kefauver's voting record. He was a longtime proponent of federal abolishment of the poll tax and of creating a civil rights division within the U.S. Justice Department. He sought home rule for Washington, D.C., as well as Alaskan statehood, both considered crucial goals by civil rights advocates. Kefauver worked closely with both the NAACP and the powerful Harlem Democrat, U.S. Representative Adam Clayton Powell, Jr., of New York. His estrangement from the Southern Caucus, however, did not mean he supported immediate desegregation. Kefauver voted against Powell's successful amendment to Russell's 1946 School Lunch Act, which would have denied federal funding to meal programs that practiced discrimination. Kefauver also opposed a federal antilynching statute which he—like most southern reformers—thought counterproductive by constraining the power of local authorities who had drastically reduced such mob actions after World War II. After *Brown*, the Tennessean declared that he and fellow southerners could demonstrate "our good Americanism—our patriotism, by recognizing that we have no choice but to do our dead level best to comply with this new interpretation of our Constitution. To do otherwise in any respect, of course, would lead to chaos and anarchy." Kefauver also announced that he and his wife would keep their children enrolled in Washington, D.C.'s desegregated public schools. Later that year, he won re-election after a bitter campaign with Republican U.S. Representative Pat Sutton.[23]

Gore followed Kefauver's lead, but remained more intellectually committed to segregation. As with most southern congressman, Gore did not participate in the Dixiecrat Revolt of 1948. He later described Thurmond and his allies (inaccurately) as "nothing more or less than the old Bourbon leaders of the South who believed that they could once more control the southern states." First elected to the Senate in 1952, Gore defeated the long-time incumbent Kenneth McKellar in the Democratic primary, and then joined Kefauver in refusing to caucus with fellow southerners. Anticipating *Brown*, in December 1953 Gore first gave what became his standard reply to constituents: "I have been reared to believe that it would be better for white children to go to white schools and be taught by white teachers, and that it would be better for negro children to go to negro schools and be taught by negro teachers. I still believe this is the best." Civil rights workers "who would push too far, too fast" he warned, "may actually harm, rather than help, the cause for which they profess such devotion." He believed that significant social progress was manifest: with two black lawyers serving on the Nashville City Council, and Atlanta, Georgia, electing a black school board member, change was on the way. He was "not to be numbered among the extremists who refuse to believe that discrimination and injustice to the negro race do exist." He continued: "Neither am I to be numbered among the extremists in the other direction. I believe that all of us should approach such problems as this with Christian Good Will." After *Brown*, Gore professed a devotion to the rule of law while arguing that real social change could not be achieved through judicial edict. "I do not mean to imply that I am in agreement with the reasoning upon which the Court based its decision or on the results on which it contemplates," he informed a constituent. Yet, "the decision of the Court is, after all a decision by the highest Court of our land and cannot be completely ignored." After his retirement, Gore described himself as "a moderate who believed in the Constitution, who respected and supported duly constituted courts of the land, and who had compassion for oppressed fellow Americans." Like his southern col-

2.1 United States Senator Albert Gore, Sr., of Tennessee. Courtesy of the Senate Historical Office.

leagues, Gore maintained that "law cannot per se create higher moral standards, cannot correct deeply held prejudices, cannot engender the spirit of neighborliness," which he believed essential for progress in race relations.[24]

Tennessee's threat to the Southern Caucus's control over the legislative process was, though, only indicative of the tenuous nature of the Democrats' Senate majority. The political ramifications of *Brown*, that is, merely laid bare the precarious nature of Johnson's majority leadership, and forced him to negotiate the labyrinth of desegregation. Before passage of the 1957 Civil Rights Act, Johnson's voting record on civil rights was one of avoidance, if not outright opposition. His votes on civil rights legislation consisted strictly of procedural measures so, in effect, he never formally voted on a bill. He equivocated, taking neither side. His 1949 maiden speech in the Senate supported Russell's enhancement of Rule Twenty-Two. Johnson endeared himself to the Southern Caucus while not directly opposing civil rights legislation, which after World War II was never actually brought to the Senate floor until the passage of the 1957 Civil Rights Act. The Texan regularly attended the Southern Caucus after his 1948 election to the Senate. When Democratic Majority Leader Scott Lucas of Illinois was defeated in 1950, Russell could easily have been elected to succeed him. If he had assumed the leadership, however, Russell would have had to adopt the positions of the national Democratic Party. He would have to abandon the leadership of the Southern Caucus and become a national statesman rather than a regional leader. Russell was unwilling to make this move. As he told Stennis, "I wouldn't give up my heritage of the South to be president of the United States." Instead, the Georgian virtually handpicked the next majority leader, Senator Ernest MacFarland of Arizona, and made Johnson the whip. Thereafter, Johnson ceased attending the Southern Caucus so as to present himself as the leader of the entire Democratic delegation. Although the Democrats regained control of the Senate in 1954, MacFarland was defeated in the fall elections by the Republican Barry Goldwater. Johnson became majority leader and, during Eisenhower's presidency, the highest elected Democrat in the country.[25]

The sectional differences inherent in the Democrats' New Deal coalition became manifest after World War II, when economic growth created the Sunbelt, dissolved the common cause of nationalization and financial recovery, and laid bare the southern caste system before the court of world opinion and thus to the forefront of legislative debate. After the Republican landslide of 1952, Johnson and Rayburn sought to bury sectional differences and present a formal, united, and loyal opposition to the Eisenhower administration that could win Democratic majorities in the Congress. Sustaining the New Deal coalition required bridging the divide between the northern and southern wings of the party by transcending sectional antipathy over civil rights and organized labor, and stemming defections to Republicanism in traditionally Democratic districts, particularly in their southern geographic base. Their strategy was twofold. For international relations, Johnson and Rayburn provided unequivocal support for Eisenhower's foreign policy, which demonstrated national unanimity in the increasingly hostile Cold War and deflected criticism that Democrats were soft on communism. Domestically, Johnson and Rayburn emphasized traditional New Deal issues, such as agriculture support and federal development of infrastructure in the South and West, while defending states' control over fossil fuels.

To implement this strategy in the Senate, Johnson unified the Democratic delegation under his leadership through heavy financial contributions and plum committee assignments to influential colleagues. He also cleared committee assignments with the Democratic Steering Committee, chaired by Russell; assignments were distributed only after the Senate had voted upon Rule Twenty-Two. Supporters of civil rights charged that incoming senators were blackmailed into maintaining the insurmountable cloture rule, lest they be overlooked for key committee assignments. Johnson and Russell then developed the Senate Democratic Policy Committee (DPC) into a true com-

2.2 The Eighty-Fourth Congress's Senate Democratic leadership, all from below Mason and Dixon's Line. From left: Majority Whip Earle Clements of Kentucky, President Pro Tempore Walter George of Georgia, Majority Leader Lyndon B. Johnson of Texas, and Secretary of the Democratic Conference Thomas Hennings of Missouri. Courtesy of AP Images.

mittee for the formulation of public policy and a significant counterweight to civil rights supporters within the Democratic Party. Chaired by Johnson, the committee was almost completely composed of senators who either opposed or were indifferent to civil rights legislation. Through the Rules Committee, under the chairmanship of an intransigent segregationist, United States Representative Howard W. Smith of Virginia, Rayburn did much the same in the House. Johnson and Rayburn, therefore, gummed over sectional differences and sustained Democratic majorities in the Congress, while offsetting civil rights advocates' attempt to assert control over the party's legislative agenda. For the Democratic leadership, if civil rights legislation was allowed to be debated in Congress while there was a highly popular Republican president, a major political turnover in the South inevitably followed. Strong Republican gains, as well as the election of extremist race baiters, followed at the expense of senior southern Democrats. In this scenario, the committee chairmanships were surrendered. Federal civil rights legislation was passed. Jim Crow was dead.[26]

The Senate's procedural obstacles that blocked civil rights legislation were formidable. Bills could be initially filibustered from being pulled out of the hopper and introduced for consideration. If the bill was actually read and introduced, it would be sent to the proper committee, where southern chairmen simply refused to place it on the agenda. As chair of the Judiciary Committee's Subcommittee on Civil Rights, for instance, Eastland refused to release all such bills. "For the three years I was chairman," he bragged, "that committee didn't hold a meeting. I didn't permit them to meet." "I had to protect the interests of the people of Mississippi," so "I had special pockets put in my pants and for three years I carried those bills around in my pockets everywhere I went and everyone of them were defeated."[27] Even in the unlikely event that a chairman like Eastland was overruled and the bill was forced out of committee, the unsympathetic DPC then placed it on the Senate calendar on a date when the Southern Caucus would have the advantage, if it was even scheduled for consideration at all. Another filibuster could then be enacted to prevent it from being brought to the floor. Again, even if this filibuster was broken and the bill was actually brought to the floor for debate, then endless amendments could be submitted and debated, thus delaying actual consideration or fundamentally changing the bill at hand. If the bill actually survived floor debate, then another filibuster could be enacted to prevent a final vote. In the House, the situation was similar, but because there was no filibuster rule, majorities could force bills out of committee for a vote. Yet, bills passed by the House had to be reconciled with anything passed by the Senate, again allowing the possibility of another filibuster on the final version. Only then could the bill be sent to the president for signature. With the most powerful committees controlled by the Southern Caucus, the calendar organized by a DPC composed overwhelmingly of senators who were politically unresponsive to the notion of black equality, and the enforcement of Rule Twenty-Two, civil rights bills were impossible to pass under a Democratic majority led by Johnson. Only he had the power to pass such a bill, and only at a time of his own choosing.

Despite these obstacles, a more formidable civil rights coalition emerged after *Brown* that jeopardized the South's control of the legislative process. Numerous civil rights bills repeatedly failed in the Eighty-Third Congress, while a number of others from the Eighty-Fourth's first session remained bottled up in the southern-chaired committees. With Rule Twenty-Two, none of these bills could be released to the floor. But, with the help of an informal civil rights caucus, Democratic Senator Thomas Hennings of Missouri used his chairmanship of the Judiciary Committee's Subcommittee on Civil Rights to introduce four separate bills that collectively sought to strengthen the protection of voting rights in federal elections and primaries, create a civil rights division in the Department of Justice, extend federal pro-

2.3 Democratic United States Representative Reverend Adam Clayton Powell of New York. Courtesy of the Dwight D. Eisenhower Presidential Library.

tection to members of the armed forces against physical attack, and create a new federal antilynching statute. The bills were reported favorably out of his subcommittee on February 9, and set for consideration by the full Judiciary Committee on March 4, 1956. Incidentally, Hennings's civil rights legislative package was the first considered by the Judiciary Committee after Eastland became the chairman upon the sudden death of Democratic Senator Harvey Kilgore of West Virginia on February 26. The widespread support the Missourian received from across the country forced civil rights legislation to be considered in the Eighty-Fourth Congress and thrust the issue into the early stages of the national campaign season.[28]

Powell did the same in the House. In December 1955, the Harlem Democrat announced the formation of a "non-partisan civil rights bloc" in the Congress to support anti–poll tax and antilynching legislation. The group of approximately 150–200 members (mostly from the North and far West) led efforts to construct a civil rights legislative package in the House similar to that pushed by Hennings in the Senate. At the opening of the second session in January 1956, Powell also attached an amendment to HR 3305, commonly known as the Kelly Bill, an appropriation for the construction and restoration of America's public schools. The rider, quickly known as the Powell Amendment, prohibited federal funds from going to any and all school districts that refused to comply with *Brown* and initiate desegregation. Powell announced that he would try to amend all future federal education assistance measures to ensure that funds were not awarded to school districts that resisted desegregation. He explained how federal dollars continued to build Jim Crow schools and hospitals in the Deep South and chastised Eisenhower for not enforcing the Supreme Court edicts. To preempt critics that argued that his rider jeopardized all federal aid to education, he explained, "Negro people have waited many, many years for this hour of democracy to come and they are willing to wait a few more years rather than see a bill passed which will appropriate Federal funds to build a dual system of Jim Crow schools in defiance of the law."[29]

McClellan was the Senate's original sponsor of the Kelly Bill (S. 2779), first introduced January 24, 1954, nearly four months prior to *Brown.* In a strategic maneuver designed to subvert the Supreme Court's forthcoming edict and unite the Democratic Party under the aegis of what the historian Robert Collins has described as "Growth Liberalism," McClellan urged fellow senators to cosponsor the massive financial assistance to school construction. With an annual $100 million appropriation, the bill promised to channel federal funds to the most impoverished areas of the country. The Kelly Bill explicitly left local segregation laws in place. If Kelly passed, it would usurp *Brown* and provide southern states the financial resources needed to improve segregated facilities. The bill's language left the determination of funding up to the states, and consequently allowed the South to shore up segregated facilities, or at least gloss over the disparities in white and black education and refute claims that segregation was "inherently unequal."[30]

The South possessed many of the poorest school districts in the country and most in need of federal education aid. Southern education professionals, school boards, and Parent Teacher Associations lobbied strongly for federal aid to education. Despite the substantial loss of funding, however, white southern educators stressed that they would rather forgo funding than comply with *Brown.* A school superintendent told his Democratic U.S. representative, Wilbur Mills, that "we definitely need assistance for school construction in Arkansas. However, we do not need strings attached to it, especially if it must be without segregation." The state superintendent of Georgia public schools was blunter, admitting, "I wouldn't have the mint if they are after us to integrate."[31]

Congressional opposition to the Powell Amendment was swift. The Kelly Bill was immediately in the hands of southern Democrats; most agreed with their colleague, Democratic U.S. Representative John J. Flynt, Jr., of Georgia, who described the Powell Amendment as "a hydraheaded, five-fanged, cloven-hooved, and fork-tailed combination of polecat, dog, and rattlesnake." Indeed, most parties with a vested interest in federal education aid shared the *Nashville Tennessean*'s assessment that Powell was a "racial extremist," and urged African Americans to "reject his intemperate views in favor of more reasoned leadership and [they] could do themselves a service by acting accordingly."[32]

In the tumultuous milieu that *Brown* produced in Washington, D.C., Eisenhower's own promotion of black equality was equally ambiguous, but he took important steps toward supporting civil rights. Ike privately disagreed with *Brown* and did not publicly support it after its declaration. In the 1952 campaign, he had successfully courted leading intransigents, who led his southern campaign, dubbed Operation Dixie. His appointments to the Supreme Court, nonetheless, were the crucible for *Brown* and other desegregation rulings. The 1954 Republican Party platform, furthermore, formally endorsed federally mandated desegregation, whereas that year's Democratic platform made no mention of civil rights issues. By executive order, Ike desegregated public accommodations in Washington, D.C., and publicly supported the court ruling outlawing racial segregation on interstate travel. Through Vice President Richard Milhouse Nixon's Committee on Government Employment Policy, Ike's adminstration hired and approved civil service upgrades for thousands of black federal employees, and provided access to previously exclusive white-collar and supervisory positions.[33]

After *Brown*, Eisenhower sought compromise between what he perceived as two extreme positions: immediate federally enforced desegregation throughout the South or outright defiance by the former Confederate states. He worried that to label *Brown* a "Republican" decision, as Nixon repeatedly did, was to politicize the federal judiciary and diminish its prestige. Ike supported the swift desegregation of southern graduate schools, and privately boasted of his role in desegregating the army in 1946–47. He also frequently consulted with the renowned evangelical and fellow Republican Billy Graham, as well as other prominent Christian leaders like Democratic Governor Frank Clement of Tennessee and Democratic U.S. Representative Brooks Hays of Arkansas, both highly respected laymen within the Southern Baptist Convention, to explore peaceful solutions to desegregation. Collectively, they envisioned desegregation most easily implemented through the church; if integration of southern religious institutions could be achieved, then real social change would be attained and discrimination largely alleviated. Southern Christians—best positioned to address the problem—would lead the call for compliance with federal court orders. Ike believed this stratagem kept his administration out of the controversy and prevented desegregation from becoming a partisan football. Ike believed that to politicize civil rights inevitably led to a third-party movement, the dissolution of his southern support, and the potential for widespread violence and confrontation.[34]

The White House staff, however, was almost completely indifferent to the plight of black southerners, and counseled the president accordingly. "Whatever I did on civil rights was, to be sure, a tremendous additional burden on my time," Secretary to the Cabinet Maxwell Rabb, who directed the administration's civil rights policy, later remembered, and "outside the mainstream of my everyday activities." Ike disliked the concept of a specific position for civil rights issues because he thought it implied special treatment, so he gave Rabb the additional responsibility. Accordingly, any "particular problem that arose" Rabb should manage "quietly and unofficially." The president's point man on black equality believed the Civil Rights Movement was not a pressing issue until the 1960 election, so there were no "confrontations" or "open hostility" for them to address, only a "smoldering beneath the surface." Nonetheless, Rabb believed that there was "audacity and great progress" in civil rights during Ike's tenure.[35]

The lone voice of dissent within the White House was E. Frederic Morrow. Hired as special assistant to Chief of Staff Sherman Adams after working on the 1952 campaign, Morrow insisted that he was not specifically designated for minority affairs, that he should function as simply another assistant in the administration. But, as a former NAACP field secretary and the only African American in Ike's official entourage, Morrow was the Civil Rights Movement's only hope for direct access to the president. Moreover, Morrow felt the inevitable sting of American race relations in mid-twentieth century Washington, D.C. Although a graduate of both Bowdoin and Rutgers Law School, a decorated army officer, and the president's man, Morrow still bore the brunt of the capital's Jim Crow culture. Morrow was refused apartments in all but predominantly black neighborhoods and initially denied admittance into the better hotels, restaurants, and clubs. His daily treatment particularly bore the administration's duty to enforce the Supreme Court's orders to desegregate the District of Columbia.[36]

From what he described as "very personal talks," Morrow concluded that the president never "really conceived the dimensions of this problem." He believed that Ike "felt he shouldn't be harassed with this problem, because this was something where the hearts of men had to be changed, and that since he wasn't a magician or holy man, it would be difficult for him to change the hearts of men. Until this was done, therefore, nothing else could be done about the plight of the Negro in this country." Morrow remembered "that civil rights in the Eisenhower administration was handled like a bad dream, or like something that's not very nice, and you shield yourself from it as long as you possibly can, because it just shouldn't be." While expressing a deeply felt admiration and personal loyalty to the president, Morrow nevertheless argued that Ike "could never bring himself to take the one gigantic step of coming to grips with this very important and dangerous problem in American life," that ultimately proved detrimental to future race relations in the future.[37]

Morrow was the lone official in the White House who recognized the seminal changes occurring in the South, particularly in the wake of the Till lynching. He repeatedly pleaded with colleagues to consider the "dangerous situation that is now affecting the country." In addition to mass meetings, Sunday sermons, and daily press editorials, Morrow received angry letters from black leaders urging the president to publicly condemn Till's murder. In response, Morrow urged his superiors to call a meeting of prominent black leaders to "exchange views on this very dangerous problem," promote Ike's accomplishments in civil rights, and give African Americans prominent places

2.4 Republican President of the United States Dwight D. Eisenhower with special assistant Frederic Morrow. Courtesy of the Dwight D. Eisenhower Presidential Library.

in upcoming Republican functions, as well as more positions of authority. Morrow recognized the significant achievements in civil rights during the first term, but this did not mean that blacks would invariably vote Republican in 1956. "Any non-Negro would expect evidence of extreme gratitude," he argued, "but the average Negro feels that he has merely come into something that should have been his at the dawn of the Republic, and while he rejoices in his new status, he feels no extreme obligation to anyone for giving him what he believes to be his inalienable right."[38]

Despite Morrow's counsel, Ike avoided specificity on civil rights issues during his first term. Instead, he employed panegyrics to set the tone for his reelection campaign. His 1956 State of the Union Address asserted that problems in education "will not yield to swift or easy solutions, or to any sweeping action by the Federal Government." He assured Dixie that Jim Crow would not be dismantled by implicitly endorsing the Kelly Bill. Federal aid to education "should operate to increase rather than replace local and State support of schools; should give the greatest help to the States and localities with the least financial resources; and should in no way jeopardize the freedom of local school systems." The sole civil rights measure that he specifically mentioned was the congressional investigation into voting rights abuses. Nixon insisted this passage be kept; while under southern control, Congress would not act, which placed the onus on the Democratic majority. The only mention of civil rights was a celebratory passage of his administration's successes that reached a crescendo by calling upon Americans to "strive to have every person judged and measured by what he is, rather than by his color, race or religion."[39]

Ike did not want school construction threatened by such amendments as Powell's, though he often voiced support for *Brown*'s implementation. His staff and Republican congressional leaders decided, however, that the GOP would support the Powell Amendment in Congress. Ike worried how, despite his previous efforts toward civil rights, the Republicans did not increase their percentage of black votes in the 1954 midterm elections. He predicted that the Powell Amendment would produce a southern filibuster in the Senate, and thereby kill all federal aid to education in the near future. But, "in view of the Supreme Court decision, a vote against Powell would seem to be a vote against the Constitution." Nixon's stratagem won out. The president would not publicly support the Powell Amendment, but the Republican congressional delegation would work for its passage. The plan maintained Ike's southern support, while congressional Republicans ensured that civil rights legislation was debated during the election year. The strategy would provoke an irreparable fissure between the Democratic Party's northern and southern wings, help Republican candidates in close congressional races, and use Eisenhower's personal magnetism to make further inroads in the South.[40]

Policies toward other civil rights issues were formulated in a similar manner. During the height of the Montgomery Bus Boycott in late February 1956, Morrow argued for a more forthright stand by the Eisenhower administration and asked permission to meet personally with its leaders in Birmingham. Adams dismissed the proposal immediately, informing Morrow that the situation was too dangerous, both politically and personally, for "the Communist influence in the situation was tremendous, and he was certain that none of the responsible Negroes involved realized the extent of this." Rabb in particular thought African Americans were ungrateful for the administration's efforts. The cabinet secretary told Morrow that "most of the responsible officials in the White House had become completely disgusted" and there "was a feeling that Negroes were being too aggressive in their demands; that an ugliness and surliness in manner was beginning to show through." Rabb described civil rights workers as "intemperate," whose demands "so far exceeded what reasonable white people would grant" that they estranged most of their political allies. He ordered Morrow to thereafter remain silent on civil rights, and not to press his superiors any further about the issue. Accordingly, Ike publically maintained that civil rights issues were state and local affairs, though he believed that it was "incumbent on all the South to show some progress."[41]

The struggle for black freedom's political implications nonetheless showed in Ike's announcement to seek reelection. His decision to run again was problematic, as he had suffered a severe coronary thrombosis the previous September. He thus sought two objectives in his announcement. First, he would demonstrate to Americans that he had made a full medical recovery and could complete a successful second term. Secondly, he returned to his 1952 campaign strategy by sending a signal to white southerners that he was sympathetic to their interests pertaining to both the emergence of the Sunbelt and abatement of Jim Crow.

To achieve these ends, Ike validated his physicians' clean bill of health by embarking on a ten-day vacation at Secretary of the Treasury George Humphrey's Milestone Plantation, situated among ten thousand acres in the piney woods of southwestern Georgia, near the fashionable winter retreat of Thomasville. *Life* reported that Ike was greeted by an enormous crowd upon his arrival, and "in full view on a Georgia vacation, the President put himself to a final test of his fitness. He strenuously hunted and golfed and grappled with problems of office," and thus demonstrated his stamina for another term.[42] As Jackson learned in the Nullification Crisis and Indian Removal,

Sherman showed with his March to the Sea, and F. D. R. proved with Warm Springs, Ike knew that the Peach State was the South's linchpin.

By provoking Democrats to divide over civil rights issues, Ike left northern blacks to support him by default, or at least stay at home on election day. Either scenario meant the negation of this key Democratic constituency. His palliative measures toward civil rights—statehood for Alaska and Hawaii that increased nonsouthern votes in Congress, home rule for Washington, D.C., and the completion of desegregation in the federal government—won the election's civil rights debate. When introduced, his civil rights bill included such measures as a civil rights division in the Department of Justice and the elimination of the poll tax by federal amendment, the most he was willing to risk in an election year. Even such ostensibly uncontroversial remedies placed the burden on a Democratic Congress that could not break a southern filibuster. In the 1956 election, these measures succored black support in key northern swing states like Illinois and New York. Democrats thus appeared most responsible for the lack of action to guarantee constitutional rights for every American citizen.[43]

Ike made other overtures to the white South. He renewed his alliance with Texas's Democratic Governor Alan Shivers, the intransigent segregationist who helped him carry the Lone Star State in 1952. Ike also unsuccessfully tried to dump Nixon from his ticket, for the vice president had become especially unpopular in the South for his public support of *Brown.* As Ike undertook his winter southern tour, Nixon made a series of public speeches that praised "a unanimous Supreme Court, the great Republican Chief Justice, Earl Warren," who had "ordered an end to racial segregation in the nation's schools." At the previous year's annual convention of the NAACP in Atlantic City, New Jersey, Nixon proclaimed that under the Republican administration, the "greatest progress since 1865 has been made toward the objective to which this organization is dedicated." An honorary member of the civil rights organization, Nixon said that "the most important objective of all" was "the integration of the public school systems." He boasted that Ike "placed the full moral weight of his personal prestige and power behind a realistic program designed to realize our common objective." Democrats unanimously denounced Nixon's support of *Brown* as a base ploy that only proved that the decision was politically inspired and brought the Supreme Court into partisan politics.[44]

Ike consulted advisors about another vice presidential candidate. He really wanted a southern Democrat who would transform the American electorate into a Republican majority. They eliminated Shivers and Senator Spessard Holland of Florida from consideration because of their opposition to

Brown. The discussion, however, turned to Governor Frank Lausche of Ohio, who was immensely popular in the South for his antiunionism. Comparing the decision to Lincoln's selection of Andrew Johnson as the vice presidential candidate for the 1864 Union ticket, they believed that Lausche "would be a turning point in history" for American politics. As a Roman Catholic, furthermore, Lausche attracted broad working-class support. Ike, however, favored a southern Democrat like Shivers, Holland, or Robert B. Anderson. Republican National Committee Chairman Leonard Hall argued that replacing Nixon with a southern Democrat "would be a bold move and it would start a new era of politics in this country; to my mind the conservatives would then be voting for our party and not split up as they are now." If the segregation issue were not inevitably to arise, Ike thought the "answer would be to get a really good Southern Democrat." According to Press Secretary James Hagerty, whom Ike sent on his own southern tour to interview prominent officials and GOP leaders about who would be the best potential running mate, "not one person was for Nixon for Vice-President for a second term." The vice president was "in some way connected in Southerners' minds with the Negro difficulty," said Hagerty. Ike confided in his diary (with apparently no pun intended) that Hagerty was "startled by the intensity of the feeling in the south over the Negro question, currently at white heat."[45]

Ike's southern strategy immediately bore fruit. A Gallup Poll taken shortly after his announcement showed that 56 percent of southerners supported the president's reelection, a higher percentage than he received in the region in 1952. For *Life*, Ike's approach to civil rights "appeals to tolerant and fair-minded people of every race. It means that the Republican invasion of the South will not be very dramatic. But it also means that when there is a Southern Republican party, it will be there to stay."[46]

Indeed, Ike reflected the emerging political consensus regarding the Civil Rights Movement. As the nation's leading moderate, he offered public sympathy to black aspirations, but maintained that government was not ultimately responsible for preventing discrimination and alleviating racial prejudice. Like his moderate gubernatorial counterparts, Ike made *Brown* unenforceable, gave intransigents room to maneuver, and virtually ensured future confrontations between southern state authorities and the federal judiciary. Refusal to implement court orders by both the state and national executive branches gave violent intransigents—actually a small percentage of the southern white population—control of the public debate, and ultimately prevented meaningful desegregation. In this realm of domestic policy, Ike's first term was an abject failure.[47]

Like Ike, aspirants to the 1956 Democratic presidential nomination contended with civil rights issues in an election year when the eleven former Confederate states accounted for 128 electoral votes, while the border states of Kentucky, Maryland, Missouri, Oklahoma, and West Virginia totaled forty-eight more. The Democratic bastions of Arizona, New Mexico, and Rhode Island brought the total to 188. A combination of large swing states, such as California, Illinois, New York, Ohio, and Pennsylvania, could potentially provide the seventy-eight more electoral votes, or total of 266, needed to win. Despite Ike's assumed invincibility, a Democratic victory was thus plausible. To succeed, Democrats sought the New Deal strategy of past glory: retain the solid South and a number of border states while securing big city swing states. The plan meant sustaining the Democracy's support from southern segregationists, northern blacks, and organized labor, a virtual contradiction in terms.[48]

Combined with the 1948 Dixiecrat Revolt, the 1952 GOP sweep meant that southern state parties were essentially severed from the Democratic National al Committee. The state parties acted independently and were Democratic in name only. The Southern Congressional Delegation actually preferred it that way. With a Republican in the White House, southern Democrats' seniority, prestige, and visibility ensured that they not only blocked civil rights legislation, but also controlled the party agenda and exerted an inordinate amount of influence on both domestic and foreign policy. As seven of the fifteen Democratic senators who stood for reelection in 1956 came from the former states of the Confederacy (plus three more from the border states of Kentucky, Missouri, and Oklahoma), southerners sought to prevent both the eventual Democratic presidential candidate and party platform from endorsing *Brown* or federal civil rights legislation. If the Democratic Party supported civil rights, however, the 1948 scenario would likely repeat: the Deep South bolted the Chicago convention and formed a white supremacist third party, a move that threatened incumbents' chances for reelection as well as their control over congressional committees.[49]

The South was not unified in its preference for the presidency. Leading southern Democrats initially preferred Lausche. Russell and McClellan endorsed his candidacy as early as October 1955, well before the primary season, as did many intransigents like Shivers and James F. Byrnes of South Carolina, who, along with Byrd, led Ike's 1952 Operation Dixie campaign. Nonetheless, as in 1952, Kefauver and Stevenson were the front-runners for the Democratic nomination. At the outset of the campaign, a *U.S. News & World Report* poll found that Stevenson was the favorite presidential candidate among 49 percent of Democrats, while Kefauver was preferred by 17 percent, the remaining percentage divided among five other candidates. Despite Stevenson's large lead, the nomination was not a foregone conclusion in an era that still relied largely upon the convention system for the presidential nod.[50]

As the New Deal's standard bearer and darling of the influential Americans for Democratic Action (ADA), Stevenson was the heir apparent to FDR's legacy of uniting the northern and southern wings of the party, the one candidate who could sustain economic growth and an internationalist foreign policy while transcending the civil rights conundrum. In 1956, Stevenson was again not Dixie's ideal candidate, for he had lost the four largest southern states of Florida, Tennessee, Texas, and Virginia four years earlier. Accordingly, he sought to shore up his southern base. In 1955, Stevenson made extensive travels into the South, including the necessary public pilgrimage to the LBJ ranch on the Pedernales River in December to meet with both Johnson and Rayburn. Here, the three Democratic leaders likely reached a compromise on civil rights prior to the upcoming congressional session and primary season. Stevenson also employed old friends from his New Deal days, including Hays and U.S. Representative Hale Boggs of Louisiana, to serve as his advance men in the South. In October 1955, Boggs was sent to the pivotal primary state of Florida to set up local organizations. In a symbolic though maudlin gesture, Stevenson's 1955 Christmas card bore the "soldier's prayer" of the Confederate infantrymen. He also courted prominent southerners such as Thurmond. Stevenson said he was "grateful" to the Dixiecrat "for any advice and counsel" that he could provide. Stevenson would "be able to serve more effectively if" he could ask Thurmond "about what the problems are and about the best ways of meeting them."[51]

Again like Ike, Stevenson's southern strategy quickly bore fruit, for he picked up key endorsements from a large share of southern Democrats before the campaign season. As U.S. Senator Sam Ervin of North Carolina explained in his formal endorsement, Stevenson expressed "a desire to get along with the South and to understand our problems." An enthusiastic supporter of the former Illinois governor, Ervin told constituents that "in the field of race relations," Stevenson's "courageous stand for moderation has raised his stature to statesmanship on this problem." The Tar Heel predicted that "extremists will not accept this point of view. Stevenson will be hard pressed by some politicians to denounce moderation as evil and instead demand troops and bayonets to implement the Supreme Court decision in the South." Thus, "Stevenson prefers to be right rather than have the support of the professional politicians who seek to make capital of an unfortunate situation. We will watch with keen interest whether this pressure deprives him of nomination."[52]

2.5 Fulbright's Arkansas duck hunt. From left: Democratic United States Senator James William Fulbright of Arkansas, Democratic United States Senator John Sparkman of Alabama, Democratic Governor Orval Eugene Faubus of Arkansas, and former Democratic governor Adlai Stevenson of Illinois. Courtesy of the University of Arkansas Mullins Library, Special Collections.

In the early stages of the primary campaign, Stevenson took to the hustings in Florida, where civil rights was ubiquitous. He campaigned on the University of Florida campus in Gainesville, where the black student Virgil D. Hawkins was then suing the state for admission to the law school. When asked why Florida supported Eisenhower in 1952, Stevenson replied, "because of Yankees and ignorance." He then went to Georgia, where he stayed at the Governor's Mansion on Peachtree Street with former Democratic Governor Herman Talmadge, among the South's most notorious race baiters. For Stevenson, he and Talmadge "can agree on a great many more things than we disagree on, and we need one another."[53]

Stevenson's most important southern overture, however, was his Arkansas duck hunt. The hunt and barbeque was arranged by Fulbright, who had served as campaign director for the Stevenson-Sparkman ticket in 1952. The Arkansawyer arranged the two-day hunt for December 1955 in the heart of the Mississippi Delta on the four-thousand-acre plantation near Jerome known as Alice Sidney Farms. At this highly publicized fete, attended by scores of prominent Democratic Party leaders, newspapermen, and businessmen from across the South, Stevenson secured a wide swath of key endorsements and helped unify moderates and intransigent segregationists behind his nomination. The excursion demonstrated to the country national party unity, and the chance for Democrats to reach a compromise on civil rights before the congressional session and primary season when the issue entered the national debate.[54]

Kefauver also secured a base within the Democratic Party, but his strategy was different. Though the Tennessean never issued a policy statement on proposed civil rights legislation, he repeatedly called for immediate compliance with *Brown* by asserting that "the Supreme Court ruled that segregation is unconstitutional, and every member of the Senate as well as every other Federal official is bound by his oath of office to uphold the laws of this Country and the Constitution of the United States. Therefore, there is nothing any member of Congress can do to change the ruling." Hedging a bit, Kefauver alleged that the court was "wise" to leave "the final decision up to the various district courts who are closer to the people and therefore understand the situation better." This delay supposedly allowed "the problem to be worked out on a local level by people directly affected by the decision." Yet, *Brown* was "the highest law of the land, and therefore must be respected by those who have sworn to uphold the Constitution and the laws made in pursuance to it."[55]

While Stevenson was shooting ducks and receiving homage, Kefauver went to Virginia to speak against the Old Dominion's school privatization plan. He then accepted an invitation to join the executive committee of the Democratic National Committee's nationalities division, chaired by Michigan Governor G. Mennen "Soapy" Williams, among the party's staunchest civil rights advocates. They campaigned together as Williams outspokenly denounced Stevenson's moderation. Consequently, Kefauver secured endorsements from many Democrats in the Midwest, the Old Northwest, the Atlantic states, and New England, as well as that of U.S. Representative George S. Long of Louisiana's Long dynasty. Political analysts recognized that Kefauver was returning to Truman's successful campaign strategy of 1948, winning the North and West while abandoning the Deep South. Conversely, Stevenson soft-pedaled civil rights, which restored the North-South compromise that emphasized New Deal–type economic stimulus programs and a strong Cold War foreign policy. With the early primaries held in California, Florida, New Hampshire, Minnesota, and Wisconsin, Kefauver's initial strategy was technically sound. If he could win most of those contests, the Tennessean would gain the necessary momentum to enter the convention with an ample base of secured delegates.[56]

Kefauver gained the endorsement of important civil rights leaders, including the AFL-CIO vice president and head of the Brotherhood of Sleeping Car Porters, A. Philip Randolph, as well as Cecil Newman, publisher of the black-oriented *Minneapolis Spokesman*. Kefauver appointed the black attorney and NAACP official Frank Reeves to a highly visible position on his campaign staff. He also received high praise from the retired federal judge J. Waties Waring, who wrote the dissenting opinion in *Briggs v. Elliot* (1951), arguably the most important case collectively decided with the four other cases under *Brown*. Waring advised Kefauver that the sooner he supported civil rights the quicker he would get "the support of the decent people of the country outside the Deep South." Waring counseled him to disregard Stevenson's "'moderation' which is only a pretty word for cowardice, and if we Democrats run him it is easy to see the same result as in 1952. Stevenson may carry the Deep South, but nothing else."[57]

The other leading candidate for the Democratic presidential nomination was New York Governor Averell Harriman, whose most important support came from Truman. The former president convinced Harriman to embrace the Fair Deal and run on a strong foreign policy and civil rights program. In early February 1956, Truman formally endorsed Harriman in New York City with a series of high profile meetings. "I am of the opinion that some voters will be lost in the South," the Man from Missouri announced, "but we don't need the solid South to win. That was proven conclusively in 1948." As Harriman was a dark horse, the press fueled rumors of a deal between him and Kefauver, whereby the former would contribute funds to the latter's cash-strapped primary campaigns. In return, Kefauver would pledge his delegates to Harriman at the Chicago convention if his campaign stumbled. While undocumented, that such a deal was struck is possible. Kefauver was in New York City at the same time as Truman, and both candidates emphasized relatively strong civil rights policies. Truman's commitment to the original goals of the Fair Deal seem genuine, so it was certainly in all of their best interests to work toward the common goal of blocking Stevenson's renomination.[58]

Harriman's efforts in winning southern support were unsuccessful. Harriman embarked on a public hunting excursion of his own in Alabama with Folsom and Democratic U.S. Representative Frank Boykin. Hunting turkey and deer on Boykin's vast plantation near McIntosh, the New Yorker received endorsements from both politicians at a public barbeque. Harriman then journeyed to New Orleans in the hopes of giving a major foreign policy speech, but his address at the Roosevelt Hotel was poorly attended. "When Harriman arrived," one reporter remarked, "he had no known Louisiana supporters for President. When he left, observers could still find none." For white southerners, the most damning aspect of Harriman's candidacy were persistent reports that he supported the use of federal troops in the South to enforce *Brown*. Despite attempts by the Empire State's congressional delegation to refute the rumor, the perception compromised Harriman's efforts and put him beyond consideration for the white South.[59]

U.S. Senator Stuart Symington of Missouri also sought the Democratic presidential nomination. Although he was the candidate who possessed the most genuine professional relationship with black political leaders, Symington was a self-described moderate in 1956, so his speeches equivocated on civil rights issues. A staunch cold warrior and critic of Eisenhower's dovish foreign policy, Symington was positioned as the candidate with the most potential to satisfy all parties if Stevenson failed to break through. For Symington, to maintain party unity at the expense of estranging black Americans was especially dangerous in the Cold War political climate. "What worries me is that by far the majority of the people of the world are colored—tan, black, etc.," the Missourian professed to a colleague, "and the Communists are conquering the world—to me there is no question about it."[60]

Regardless of their political posture, all of the Democratic candidates had to confront the Civil Rights Movement after Autherine Lucy pushed the black freedom struggle into national partisan politics. In 1952, Lucy and her friend Pollie Ann Myers Hudson applied to the University of Alabama to study library science, but were denied admission because they were black. After three years of legal wrangling, Lucy was admitted but was banned from staying in the dormitories and dining halls, so she commuted fifty-eight miles from Birmingham to school in Tuscaloosa. As a divorcée, however, Hudson was still denied admission.[61]

The university campus was alive on the Friday evening of February 3, 1956, with thousands of students attending the rush week parties at the Greek houses lined along University Boulevard between the campus and downtown Tuscaloosa. The previous day, university President Oliver Cromwell Carmichael announced that Lucy would begin matriculation. She attended classes without major incident, but as word spread in the evening that Lucy was allowed on campus earlier that day, a crowd of students gathered downtown. Staggering out of the many bars along the boulevard, they amused themselves by singing "Dixie" and chanting "Keep 'Bama White!" The crowd then marched up the street to demonstrate on the front lawn of the white-columned antebellum President's Mansion. Another group burned a cross on the lawn of Dean William Adams. On Saturday night, the situation turned from bad to worse. The students were joined by a number of townies, mostly high school students, young white men of the working class, drunks, and

2.6 Downtown Tuscaloosa, Alabama, on the night of February 6, 1956. Courtesy of AP Images.

street toughs. Costermongers peddled little Confederate battle flags, eggs, and tomatoes. The emboldened rabble now harassed black motorists driving through the area and vandalized their vehicles. Guns and knives became ubiquitous, while the city and university police forces feigned controlling a mob that chanted, "Hey, hey, ho, ho, Autherine has got to go!"[62]

The worst was yet to come. On Monday morning Lucy, accompanied by a prominent black Birmingham businessman and a Baptist minister, arrived on campus. After a full weekend of rioting, approximately three hundred protesters greeted Lucy outside of her first class in Smith Hall. She made it into the building unscathed, but at the end of class Dean of Women Sarah L. Healy and one of Carmichael's assistants, Jefferson Bennett, escorted her into the car to drive to the next class through the ruffians, who pelted them with eggs and stones. Police passively stood by as rioters pummeled the Cadillac with rocks and shattered its windows. Carmichael tried to address the crowd, but white women shouting, "Kill her, kill her, kill her," and "Nigger lover, nigger lover!" drowned out his pleas. Lucy sneaked through the back door of Bibb Graves Hall for her next class in children's literature, while Bennett stood outside among rioters now attacking him with stones and eggs, amongst shouts of "Kill him! Kill him!" Bennett made it inside to a telephone and called Folsom to inform him that the mob was trying to lynch Lucy. Simultaneously, the University Board of Trustees met and suspended Lucy for her own "safety and the safety of the students and faculty members of the university." Afterward, a police escort drove her back to Birmingham. That night, a crowd again gathered on the front lawn of the President's Mansion. When Carmichael's wife went out to tell the crowd that he was not home, the mob threw eggs and rocks at her, and waved the Confederate Naval Jack while setting off firecrackers.[63]

On Tuesday morning, relative calm returned to the campus. The student government and six other campus organizations passed resolutions condemning the riotous violence and Lucy's suspension, though none endorsed immediate and complete desegregation. As the *New Republic* noted, "Not a single outstanding Alabamian has dared to urge publicly that the law as interpreted by our highest court must be effectuated—somehow, someday." Carmichael addressed some eight thousand students and faculty at two separate meetings, where he said that the "issue before the University is not segregation versus integration, but law and order versus anarchy." He declared that his administration would obey all court orders. He explained, "No great university can afford to defy the laws of the land and thus set an example of lawlessness before its students." Carmichael then blamed the riots on outside elements that "invaded" the university, and reemphasized that Lucy was suspended only for her own protection. The president of the student debating society, Dennis Holt, offered a more credible reason: "They did it because the mob forced them to," said Holt, "the mob won."[64]

When asked about the riot at a Birmingham press conference, Lucy said, "I can't hate them as individuals. Maybe they would have killed me if they had gotten me out. I don't know. All I could do was pray, and I thought, am I going to die?" She explained, "I didn't intend to cause all this violence and agitation among my fellow citizens and fellow students. I merely wanted an education," and added, "I will keep fighting until I get one." Family and friends sheltered Lucy at her brother-in-law's residence. He displayed a plethora of firearms for the reporters' inspection, and told them, "I'm not going to have her snatched from my care as they did the Till boy."[65]

On the advice of her attorney, Arthur Shores, Lucy immediately filed suit in U.S. District Court against the board of trustees for suspending her and Healy and for not admitting her to the dormitories and dining halls. Meanwhile, she attended classes at the nearby historically black Talladega College. In early March, the federal court ordered the university to readmit Lucy. In response, the trustees formally expelled Lucy the next day because her suit accused them of conspiring with the mob. The trustees also expelled four other students that rioted, including nineteen-year-old Leonard Wilson, president of the West Alabama White Citizens' Council. Lucy thereafter moved to New York for an extended convalescence away from the rioters and the media, and was cared for by two new members of her legal team, Thurgood Marshall and Constance Baker Motley.[66]

Most observers condemned the violence and concluded that if allowed, the mob would have murdered Lucy. Tuscaloosa Chief of Police William C. Tompkins admitted that Lucy and her entourage were in mortal danger on Monday morning while en route to her classes, but his force made only three arrests during the entire four days of rioting. Buford Boone, the segregationist editor of the *Tuscaloosa News*, ominously described the riot as "an eyewink away from murder." Boone warned that the rioters "would have killed this girl if they could have gotten their hands on her." He rightly charged that "there was no aggressive effort to control the mob," and chastised local officials for the "breakdown of law and order and abject surrender to what is expedient rather than a courageous stand for what is right."[67]

During that weekend, as torporific local and state authorities allowed chaos to reign at the university and almost let a young woman be lynched, Folsom went fishing. Upon his return, Folsom tried to stem the damage done to the public image of his administration and state by telling reporters that the "worldwide attention" brought by the riots "has been very much overplayed." Rather than explain why he failed to enforce the federal order, Folsom asserted that "a fundamental difference between races and tribes since the beginning of time" existed. In response, the executive secretary of the North Alabama Citizens' Council, Democratic state Senator Asa E. "Ace" Carter of Birmingham, condemned the violence but called for the resignation of Carmichael and the impeachment of Folsom, and alleged that they did not adequately defend the color line. A local journalist later surmised, "If he had been there and told the Ku Klux Klan that if they appeared he would split their heads and had the National Guard been there the history of the State and indeed the history of the entire South might have been different . . . But Folsom allowed the mob to win."[68]

Some Americans thought Lucy and the NAACP were to blame. "Integration is inevitable," Larry Custer of Emory University's *Wheel* explained, "but the NAACP is not helping their cause by attempting to speed the process up." Similarly, James Alger III, a student at Virginia Polytechnic Institute, thought Lucy "foolish to attempt fighting the system there; she will never be accepted by the students, and no court order or armed force can change that. If I were in their place I would resent her trying to change the order of things." *Life* agreed. "She, herself, helped create antagonism by being driven to school ostentatiously in a Cadillac," the newsmagazine opined, "by being registered ahead of others waiting in line and by suing for immediate admission to dormitory and mess as well as classes (although most whites as old as she board outside)." Such public demonstrations "emphasize why pioneers should avoid needless scraping of Southern sensitivities and emotions."[69]

Most Americans, however, condemned Tuscaloosa's hysterics. Alabam-

2.7 Autherine Lucy with her
attorney, Arthur Shores.
Courtesy of AP Images.

ans only demonstrated "their immaturity, indecency, inhumanity, and perhaps inferiority," said the University of West Virginia's *Daily Athenaeum*, "if
the white race were superior (and it is not) it would not have to insure its
position." Mark F. Ethridge of the *Louisville Courier-Journal* claimed that
such incidents have "brought up to the top in the South its worst character-
istics." For Edwin M. Yoder of the *Daily Tar Heel*, the consensus of opinion at
the University of North Carolina was "total disgust, even among those who
heartily favor segregation" at Chapel Hill. The *Nation* singled out Carmichael
and the board of trustees' actions for special criticism, for they "would have
the world believe that she was ousted because of the charges made in these
affidavits and not because of the color of her skin." They questioned "whether
this is the type of example that educators should set for American youth."
According to pundit Walter Lippmann, "It is impossible to accept the gradualism" of southern moderation, "if at the same time they have to acquiesce in
what happened at Alabama University."[70]

Lucy changed American politics. As Stevenson was the Democratic front-
runner, his moderation cost him. A week after the Tuscaloosa riot, he addressed approximately two hundred black Californians at the Watkins Hotel
in Los Angeles. Although enthusiastically received, Stevenson gave a speech

full of the typical evasive platitudes that marked his generally obtuse disregard of black equality. He then estranged the crowd in the subsequent question-and-answer session. When asked about the Powell Amendment and the proposed civil rights commission in the Department of Justice, he claimed that they were unnecessary measures. When asked if he would use federal troops to protect black southerners and enforce *Brown*, Stevenson answered, "That would be a great mistake. That is what exactly brought on the Civil War. It can't be done by troops or bayonets. We must proceed gradually, not upsetting habits or traditions that are older than the Republic." Stevenson then obscured his views about the emerging interposition movement, professing, "I don't know what it means. It sounds like nullification, but I am not clear." At the conclusion, the audience stood aghast, mumbling, "I think he's a phony," and "Can you imagine that?" Afterward, the West Coast journal *Frontier* concluded that "as long as small colored boys can be murdered in Mississippi without the protection of the law, Stevenson's moderate approach to reform will strike most Negroes as distressingly inadequate."[71]

Kefauver seized the opportunity. Speaking before the California Democratic Council in Fresno, the Tennessean denounced the "horrible murder" of Emmett Till the year before and called for the enactment of a federal statute against mob violence. He then traveled to Los Angeles for a private meeting with black Democrats at the Californian Hotel. Afterward, the NAACP Oakland chapter chairman, Reverend L. Sylvester Odom, announced that he had switched his support to Kefauver. California state Representative W. Byron Rumford of Berkeley likewise attested that Stevenson "lost a lot of support," and unless the Democratic front-runner became more assertive on civil rights, he would "have no alternative but to switch to Kefauver."[72]

The Democratic establishment defended Stevenson's approach to desegregation. As the theologian Reinhold Niebuhr attested, "Stevenson is right. Police power can deal with individual recalcitrance, but it is impotent against the collective recalcitrance of a whole community—indeed, it often tends to harden the heart of the rebellious community." Civil rights advocates, however, berated the front-runner. Both the AFL-CIO and the NAACP denounced his calls for "gradual" change, and demanded that candidates declare for *Brown*'s immediate implementation. For Carey McWilliams of the *Nation*, "It is not the function of a liberal journal of opinion to endorse candidates with uncritical enthusiasm simply because they are charming and intelligent, high minded and well-mannered."[73]

The Civil Rights Movement then reverberated in Florida, site of the next major primary. Russell won the 1952 Florida Democratic primary; his supporters, led by Holland and the Miami stockbroker F. X. James O'Brien, scrambled to gain control over the party before the 1956 primary and se-cure the Sunshine State's delegates for Lausche. They sought to force Flori-da's Democratic Executive Committee to vote for an unpledged slate for the Democratic National Convention and return the state to the former "pref-erential primary" of yesteryear, whereby the vote would be non-binding for delegates. This move allowed segregationists more leverage in opposing a strong civil rights plank, as well as any candidate who supported it, at the national convention. In 1952, the faction openly opposed the Stevenson nomination and helped secure Eisenhower more than a one-hundred-thou-sand-vote majority in the general election, though Russell did not partici-pate. On January 23, 1956, prior to the arrival of the presidential candidates in Florida, Russell came to the state, ostensibly for a testimonial dinner in honor of Democratic U.S. Senator George Smathers in Miami. Russell's ef-forts were truncated, however, for immediately after dinner he was rushed to the hospital, suffering a serious case of influenza. Despite the Georgian's efforts, the Executive Committee kept the pledged slate format, while many leading Florida Democrats, including Smathers and Governor Leroy Collins, planned to endorse Stevenson formally after their own primary wins. State officials postponed the ruling on the desegregation lawsuit at the University of Florida until after the presidential primary on May 29. Segregation re-mained the preeminent topic in the gubernatorial primary as all candidates formally opposed immediate compliance with *Brown*.[74]

Kefauver's Florida campaign remained supportive of *Brown*, which pro-duced some precarious situations. In the small farming community of Mi-canopy, Kefauver addressed a group of young students in the school audito-rium. As he was about to leave, thirteen-year-old Wayne Saunders jumped up and asked him: "We are in a small school but a wonderful school. We are getting along fine and we like it. Mr. Kefauver, won't you help us keep us this way—the Negro school on one side of town, ours on the other? Mr. Kefau-ver, please, won't you keep the colored people off to themselves? Please keep Florida schools white." Kefauver was clearly caught off guard and, unable to deflect the child's oration with his usual folksy banter, quickly left the audi-torium. He soon regained his composure, though, and addressed journalists covering the episode. He recognized that someone had clearly scripted the boy's speech. One of his own supporters, Louise Graham, had arranged the confrontation to show Floridians that Kefauver supported segregation.[75]

Other Kefauver supporters tried to convey this notion too. Prior to Ke-fauver's arrival, Philip Barton, one of his state organizers, issued a statement declaring that Kefauver was for continued segregation. When Kefauver and Barton appeared together in a press conference, however, the Tennessean made his position clear to Floridians: "The Supreme Court has spoken. Desegregation is the law of the land." When asked by journalists, Barton explained that "the senator comes from a Southern state, so I figured he would naturally believe in segregation." Kefauver maintained the moderate position that individual communities held primary responsibility for desegregation, so that compliance with the edict would proceed over a set period. Yet, in Florida he announced that while federal troops "ought to be avoided," he was willing to use them in recalcitrant communities "in cases of rebellions and riots when Federal property is involved." He explained the tightrope that he walked on the issue: "Desegregation should be kept in the judicial machinery," but federal marshals could and should enforce court orders.[76] That Kefauver made the declaration in the Deep South reveals his strategy to take bold steps to upset the Illinois frontrunner. The Civil Rights Movement was an issue whose time had come, one that could no longer be ignored in national partisan politics.

Despite their attempts at vacillation, the two candidates clearly offered contrasting viewpoints on civil rights. Speaking before a labor rally in Milwaukee, Wisconsin, Kefauver declared, "I have nothing but criticism to make of the mobs that have come about in connection with the University of Alabama matter." In contrast, Stevenson continued to equivocate, hoping to not estrange his base. "There is a rising tension in the South," Stevenson said, when specifically asked about Lucy. "But it is not enough just to cry out in emotional protest against these things. Our purpose must be to find an answer to the problem, and I suggest that an answer will never be found by cynical politicians who work to gain votes by pitting angry men against each other." In a speech at the University of Michigan in early March, Stevenson further called upon the North to alleviate its own instances of discrimination and cease "pointing an accusing finger at the South."[77]

Indeed, the Civil Rights Movement became the salient issue of the 1956 presidential primary season, which threatened to divide the Democratic Party. The constant struggle to define the meaning of *Brown II*, the pending civil rights bills, the Powell Amendment, and the emerging struggle for black freedom in the South made desegregation the focal point of the congressional agenda and the early presidential campaign. Democratic congressional candidates were thus forced to state a position on the Civil Rights Movement that threatened the Southern Congressional Delegation's control over the party's legislative agenda. Accordingly, the Southern Caucus soon took steps that allowed them to dictate the national debate over civil rights for both the 1956 national elections and years to come.

3. Who Wrote the Southern Manifesto?

The Civil Rights Movement's thrust into American partisan politics made the 1956 presidential candidates acknowledge the struggle for black freedom as a force for positive change. The Powell Amendment's attempt to enforce *Brown v. Board of Education* (1954), combined with the emerging bipartisan coalition supporting civil rights legislation, threatened to destroy Jim Crow and break the South's control over the United States Congress. If the federal government did not enforce *Brown* and pass civil rights legislation, however, the South retained both its seniority in the Congress and its racial caste system. To use the classic analogy of C. Vann Woodward, the Civil Rights Movement made the United States stand before another "two-pronged forked road." The federal government could either enforce *Brown* and enact civil rights legislation, or capitulate to the political defenders of the white South and prolong the modus vivendi established at Redemption.[1]

The Southern Congressional Delegation worked assiduously to block civil rights bills from being released out of committee for formal debate in the second session of the Eighty-Fourth United States Congress. They also tried hard to prevent *Brown*'s full-scale implementation in the forthcoming 1956–1957 school year, which coincided with the national election cycle. If these developments were impeded, civil rights would define neither the summer primaries nor the fall national campaign. The southern strategy to stymie these two fundamental civil rights goals culminated with the promulgation of Jim Crow's most famous and influential *apologia*, the "Declaration of Constitutional Principles," popularly known as the Southern Manifesto.

Most people believe that United States senators Harry F. Byrd, Sr., of Virginia and J. Strom Thurmond of South Carolina were the principal authors of the Southern Manifesto. In this standard interpretation, Byrd and Thurmond became the leaders of the counterrevolution against the Civil Rights Movement that came to be known as Massive Resistance, and then they personally directed defiance of the federal judiciary on both the state and national levels. As the historian Numan Bartley attests, Byrd "originated the term 'massive resistance' and played a crucial role in its evolution in his home state and in the attempt to create a South-wide effort. No man did as much to move the front lines of opposition from the Deep South to Washington, D.C., and the Potomac River."[2]

Bartley's interpretation frames the scholarly consensus toward the Southern Manifesto, but some historians acknowledge that the statement's drafting was more of a collective effort by the entire Southern Caucus. These scholars concur that Thurmond and Byrd initiated the idea for such a statement, but they also note the influence of others, such as Democratic senators Price Daniel of Texas, Sam Ervin of North Carolina, J. William Fulbright of Arkansas, Richard Brevard Russell, Jr., of Georgia, and John Stennis of Mississippi. In this view, these senators still merely played a peripheral role, only editing the statement and toning down the language of Thurmond's initial "fire-eating draft."[3]

The Bartley school reflects contemporary reports by journalists, who depict Thurmond, followed by Byrd, as writing out the basic ideas in the Southern Manifesto, and only later approaching others in the Southern Caucus. In this perspective, many senior southerners initially balked at issuing such a statement, but when Thurmond and Byrd threatened to proceed alone, the rest of the Southern Caucus went along, to try to control the situation and continue the appearance of coherence and uniformity within southern ranks.[4]

Whoever actually wrote and then endorsed the Southern Manifesto ultimately produced a statement that fully articulated the collective mentality of the white South toward the Second Reconstruction in general and *Brown* in particular. The statement achieved a remarkable, nearly unanimous, consensus within the Southern Congressional Delegation that satisfied a large majority of the South's intransigents and moderates. The authors and signers, furthermore, gained a large swath of support among their constituents while profoundly changing the political landscape. The traction gained by the statement affected not just the 1956 elections, but also the larger legislative process towards the Civil Rights Movement in the years to come.

If this traditional interpretation is correct, therefore, then why were Thurmond and Byrd inclined to issue such a statement? Were they, moreover, intellectually and politically capable of writing and promulgating such a document? What was the specific role of other members of the Southern Caucus, and what about that of southerners in the House of Representatives? Where did the arguments in the Southern Manifesto come from, and why was certain language used? Why did the vast majority of southerners sign, and what were their motivations for doing so? What about those southerners who did not sign? Answering these questions illuminates the ways and means in which the white South countered the initial momentum of desegregation and resuscitated Jim Crow after its discriminatory educational foundations were removed from the body of the American common law.

Other than a visceral attachment to states' rights and white supremacy, what were the most immediate motivations for the Southern Congressional Delegation to produce such a statement? Foremost, the Civil Rights Movement directly threatened their careers. If the Democratic presidential nominee formally supported *Brown*'s enforcement and federal civil rights legislation, southern delegates would likely bolt the national convention to form another white supremacist third party, as had occurred in 1948. Hypothetically, this new southern third party could either run its own presidential ticket or try to improve upon 1952's Operation Dixie and support President Dwight D. Eisenhower for reelection. The former strategy had already been tried, failed miserably, and proved counterproductive to the white South's ultimate goal of retaining control of the congressional legislative process. The latter strategy, however, meant endorsing Ike the Republican, who had nominated Chief Justice Earl Warren, called for compliance with *Brown*, and supported congressional civil rights legislation by default. Yet, if civil rights continued to dominate the presidential campaign and was endorsed by both parties, then the white South was largely impotent, unable to sustain its powerful electoral pivot that so far had forced the Democratic Party to compromise on white supremacy to win presidential elections and congressional majorities. Those members of the Southern Congressional Delegation who sought reelection in 1956 potentially faced opposition from both intransigent segregationists that would target them as "soft" on segregation, and newfound Republican challengers. Both potential opponents could exploit the region's antagonism toward the national Democratic Party, while the latter could also push Ike's business-friendly policies, which were particularly attractive in the emergent Sunbelt.

Just how recalcitrant was the white South in early 1956? The Gallup Poll released February 27 of that year, after civil rights confrontations had dominated national headlines for over two months, showed that the South was clearly out of step, if not out of touch, with the rest of the United States. In the former Confederate states, only 16 percent of whites approved of *Brown*, while 80 percent disapproved and 4 percent were undecided. Outside of the South, however, 71 percent of Americans approved of *Brown*, while 24 percent disapproved and 5 percent were undecided.[5]

In this scenario where civil rights became the dominant issue of the 1956 presidential campaign, southern congressional incumbents instead stood before a three-pronged forked road. First, they could maintain allegiance to the Democratic Party and likely be defeated, even if they would actually stay in a party formally committed to civil rights. Secondly, congressional incumbents could help lead a third-party movement devoted to white supremacy and formal defiance of the federal judiciary. This option meant that incumbents faced internecine conflicts within their own state parties and potentially could run in the fall election against a Democratic nominee who would have control over most of the party machinery, a prospect that further threatened their prospects in the general election. Incumbents also forfeited any support—both financial and political—from the national party, often the crucial difference in tight races. In 1948, the vast majority of southern Democratic congressional incumbents recognized the pitfall of this option and neither actively participated in nor formally supported the Dixiecrat Revolt. Thirdly, incumbents could switch parties and run in the fall campaign as Republicans. This option was equally precarious, as the Eisenhower administration was identified with *Brown*, had mildly supported both compliance with the decision and civil rights legislation, and might even come out more forcefully for civil rights in the fall campaign. Incumbents' lifelong party identification, moreover, made it difficult to start from scratch in the GOP, raise money, make contacts, win a primary, and do all of the sundry tasks involved in establishing and maintaining a viable political organization. Regardless, most of the Southern Democrats in the Eighty-Fourth Congress were bred and buttered populists, small "d" democrats whose early careers were spent in the heart of the New Deal. They were raised to idolize Old Hickory, Cleveland, the Commoner, Woody, and FDR. They saw the party of Lincoln as an anathema.

Southern congressional incumbents who took any of these three roads faced direct political and professional costs. All choices threatened their professional livelihoods, but the latter two meant that they would formally abandon the Democratic Party and certainly forfeit their seniority in congressional committee assignments and in the party caucuses. Collectively, all of these choices meant that the last bastions of defense for the southern caste system (Senate Rule Twenty-Two and the congressional committee chairmanships) were lost. Substantial civil rights legislation inevitably passed and destroyed white supremacy. In summary, the Southern Congressional Delegation perceived the antipodal Civil Rights Movement as a zero sum game.

In the winter of 1955–56, civil rights workers became more successful, white supremacists became more desperately violent, and Americans outside of the South became more sympathetic to the cause of black freedom. On January 30, 1956, the home of Rev. Dr. Martin Luther King, Jr., was firebombed while he was away speaking at a meeting of the Montgomery Improvement Association (MIA). His wife, Coretta Scott King, and one of her friends narrowly escaped death as their front room was blown apart. After rushing home, Dr. King—assured that his family was safe and sound—addressed the crowd that had gathered, which included a number of reporters. In an early demonstration of his hallmark composure in the face of violent opposition, King pleaded with MIA members and civil rights workers across the nation to avoid violent retaliation against white terrorism: "We are not advocating violence. We want to love our enemies. I want you to love our enemies. Be good to them. Love them and let them know you love them." Two days later, the home of another MIA leader—E. D. Nixon—was also bombed. Just days before, Montgomery Mayor W. A. Gayle announced that he and other members of the city council were formally joining the local Citizens' Council chapter. Gayle denounced whites who gave blacks rides to and from work, asserting that "the Negroes are laughing at white people behind their backs," and "have made their own beds, and the whites should let them sleep in it."[6]

After the Alabama violence, Dr. King embarked on a series of previously scheduled speaking and fund-raising engagements in Chicago, Nashville, and Atlanta, and further drew national attention to the boycott. While away on February 21, King and 114 other MIA leaders were indicted under an old Alabama antiboycott law. Upon his return to Montgomery, each member of the group posted a three-hundred-dollar bond. Orchestrated by the non-violence advocate Bayard Rustin, the group's release was widely covered in the press. The MIA then held a massive rally that night at the First Baptist Church, where the rejuvenated group vowed to continue the protest. Their courage under fire drew substantial attention from the national press. The *New York Herald Tribune* and *New York Times* carried favorable front-page stories of the boycott, while *Time* published a sympathetic portrayal of the MIA under the charismatic leadership of King. "Gandhi-like passive resistance," the *New Republic* observed, "is leading toward a new national crisis of the magnitude of 1860 but whose character is only dimly seen."[7]

The black freedom struggle moved quickly across the United States. Democratic U.S. Representative Reverend Adam Clayton Powell, Jr., of New York, joined with the National Association for the Advancement of Colored People (NAACP) in calling for a nationwide "National Deliverance Day of Prayer" to be held March 5 in honor of the boycott. Black churches throughout the nation participated and, led by the United Packing Workers of Chicago, a one-hour work stoppage across the United States was planned to protest the arrests of the MIA leaders. Thirteen bishops of the African Methodist Episcopal (AME) Church urged Eisenhower to intervene in what they described as the "tragic persecution" and "police state methods" of Montgomery authorities.[8]

As national attention focused upon Alabama, the NAACP increased the pressure on Congress to pass civil rights legislation. In early March, the NAACP sponsored a three-day "Leadership Conference on Civil Rights" in Washington, D.C., at the Willard Hotel. Autherine Lucy appeared to a rousing ovation before a crowd estimated at eighteen hundred, while conference speakers repeatedly reminded Democrats that they could not count on black allegiance in the fall elections. NAACP Chief Counsel Thurgood Marshall predicted that the legislative fight for civil rights would inevitably be "mean, nasty, and dirty," and that presidential nominees "can holler, scream, beg, and cajole, but there's not a candidate who can get the Negro vote until he can produce something close to civil rights."

The Civil Rights Movement's political power was readily apparent at this moment in history, as both parties actively courted black voters at the conference. The Democrats, however, succored most attendees after Senator Thomas Hennings of Missouri announced to the conference that on March 4, his Senate Sub-Committee on Civil Rights had approved his civil rights legislative package, just as the larger Judiciary Committee was considering the perennial antilynching bill. Both measures ensured that civil rights questions would be front and center in the Eighty-Fourth Congress and dominate news headlines in the midst of the primary campaign season.[9]

As the NAACP conference came in the aftermath of his California debacle, former Illinois governor Adlai Stevenson finally recognized that, as the front-runner for the Democratic presidential nomination, he must endorse *Brown* and acknowledge the emerging Civil Rights Movement. Stevenson's strongest challenger, U.S. Senator Estes Kefauver of Tennessee, won substantial support through his stronger stand for desegregation. The Tennessean was, furthermore, a member of the Senate Judiciary Committee, so was well-positioned to help Hennings push through his civil rights package and directly confront the obstreperous southern chairman, Democratic Senator James Eastland of Mississippi.

On February 25, at the Jefferson-Jackson Dinner in Hartford, Connecticut, Stevenson, hoping to stem his self-inflicted damage, formally endorsed *Brown* and condemned the interposition movement by equating the doctrine with nullification. The Democratic front-runner proclaimed that Andrew Jackson's Nullification Proclamation was "essential Democratic doctrine—and American doctrine—one hundred and twenty years ago. It is essential Democratic—and American—doctrine today." Abandoning his former moderation, Stevenson stated that the "Supreme Court has re-affirmed this essential doctrine of democracy in the school desegregation cases. These decisions speak clearly the law and the conscience of this land." Maintaining that "time for transition and compliance is necessary, time for the adjustments that have to be made," he gave southern Democrats room for maneuver. But, he noted, such did "not recognize or permit repudiation or rejection of these decisions of the court and of the people." He concluded his address with the claim that the party of Jefferson stood for equality, "in terms of the most crucial issue within this beloved land of ours today, equal rights for all—regardless of race and color," and embraced the movement's ultimate goals: "Freedom is unfinished business until all citizens may vote and live and go to school and work without encountering in their daily lives barriers which we reject in our law, our conscience, and our religion." Widely circulated in all sections of the country, Stevenson's remarks were interpreted for the first time as a strong endorsement of *Brown* and the ultimate desegregation of American life.[10]

In turn, intransigent segregationists repeatedly reminded their congressional representatives of the political implications of the Civil Rights Movement. Southern editors, for example, were concerned about presenting the white southern viewpoint to the rest of the nation in the wake of these strategic losses. The Citizens' Councils, furthermore, widely distributed a circular that asked members, "What plans are the Congressmen in your state making to defeat this NAACP inspired movement toward the abolition of state lines, totalitarian government, and a classless society, such as exists in Soviet Russia?" As the Delta planter R. S. McCarter told Fulbright, "In our school district there are 290 white children and 1350 negro children. We <u>can</u> <u>not</u> [*sic*] even consider integration. It would be an immortal sin to even think of such a thing." He warned Fulbright, "In the coming elections, the man who takes a stand for the white citizens will get our votes. Make segregation your first concern—then Russia and 90% parity next. Segregation is what we are interested in now."[11]

At the beginning of the 1956 southern primary campaigns, intransigents had already built the Citizens' Councils into formidable political organizations to challenge any congressional incumbent who did not forthrightly oppose black equality. A crowd of some two thousand squeezed into the high school gym in the small town of England, Arkansas, on February 24 to hear speakers denounce *Brown* and the NAACP. Given standing ovations, speakers included Bob Patterson, executive secretary of the Mississippi Citizens' Councils; editor of the segregationist *Arkansas Faith* and future state supreme court judge Jim Johnson; a Little Rock lawyer and furniture store owner who had declared himself president of White America, Inc., Amis

Gutheridge; the oil tycoon and former Arkansas Democratic governor Ben Laney; and Roy V. Harris, a former Georgia Democratic state senator and editor-in-chief of the *Augusta Courier*, one the South's leading intransigent organs. The delegation that Democratic Governor Orval Faubus of Arkansas sent to study Virginia's Gray Plan also attended. Charging that the NAACP had targeted the state's segregation laws, Gutheridge labeled Arkansas the South's "weakest link." Johnson urged Arkansawyers to pass an interposition resolution. Harris claimed that "the Highway Patrol, the National Guard, and every able-bodied white man in Georgia" would defend segregation and put "the Negroes back in their place" if they tried to attend white schools. Patterson predicted that desegregation would never come to pass in Mississippi. The loudest reception, though, was held for Laney, who made one of his first public appearances since leaving office in 1949. The former Arkansas governor reminded the crowd of his leadership in the Dixiecrat Revolt, and fueled rumors that he would make a political comeback to challenge Fulbright in that summer's Democratic primary. Alluding to the state's junior U.S. senator, the Dixiecrat proclaimed, "We have some sanctimonious politicians in Arkansas who couldn't open their mouths on the issue before," but "after a few more meetings like this they will reconsider." Afterward, England resident Joe Foster advised Fulbright that, for his "own good," he should speak "out and join Senator Eastland in his fight." The segregationist-leaning *Arkansas Recorder* predicted, "Whatever chain reaction sets in will be traceable to that community gathering."[12]

Like Fulbright, United States Senate President Pro Tempore Walter George of Georgia exemplified the predicament of southern congressional incumbents. At seventy-eight years old, George had served continuously in the Senate since 1922 and was the senior member of the Southern Caucus. In the Eighty-Fourth Congress, George chaired the prestigious Foreign Relations Committee, and worked intimately with the Eisenhower White House in the formation of Cold War foreign policy. A legendary campaigner, George famously survived F. D. R.'s 1938 purge after he led congressional opposition to the ill-fated Court-Packing Plan.[13]

In 1956, Georgia's former Democratic governor, Hermann Talmadge, threatened George's Senate seat. Son of the race-baiting populist Governor Eugene Talmadge, Herman formally entered politics in 1947 after his father died shortly after election to another gubernatorial term, but before being sworn in at his inauguration. Dominated by Talmadge partisans, the Georgia Legislature empowered itself to elect Hermann to replace his deceased father, while a vocal minority supported the accession of Lieutenant Governor M. E. Thompson. After a tense standoff, which included units of the National

Guard taking sides, the fiery young Talmadge took the oath of office. While the Georgia Supreme Court ultimately nullified his coup d'état and installed Thompson as governor, Talmadge easily won the next gubernatorial Democratic primary in 1948. Thereafter, he purged black registrants from the voting rolls in the rural counties he controlled. Talmadge then unsuccessfully aligned himself with the Dixiecrats but, largely through Russell's influence, Truman's Democratic ticket carried Georgia in the national election. Serving two gubernatorial terms, Talmadge became even more of a political force than his infamous father. Whereas Old Gene's support came largely from the rural white yeomanry, the younger Talmadge also tapped into the Peach State's urban sophisticates. As a University of Georgia graduate who served as president of the student government and later as a leader in the Law Society, "Hummun" was also a decorated navy officer of the Pacific Theater during World War II. Upon retiring from the governor's office in 1952, Talmadge served a term as president of the University of Georgia Alumni Association, and gained access to professional circles across the state. Indeed, he achieved the distinction that his father could never attain, that of the gentleman's white supremacist.[14]

Because Russell was by then the unassailable leader of Georgia politics, Talmadge sought the elderly George's coveted seat. During the 1952 Democratic National Convention, Talmadge appeared on NBC's *Meet the Press* to defend Jim Crow and denounce civil rights. He later claimed that at the convention, George confidentially told him that he was not going to seek another term in 1956, and encouraged Talmadge to seek his seat. After the Democrats won the 1954 midterm elections and George became chair of the Foreign Relations Committee, however, the senior senator evidently changed his mind. Talmadge's *You and Segregation* appeared in 1955, among the era's most influential intransigent treatises. In a thinly veiled reference to George, Talmadge warned white southerners of "a type of candidate who will make deals, sacrifice principles and sell out, while giving lip-service" on white supremacy. "Beware that candidate! He is the most dangerous," Talmadge warned. "He is the thief in the night, clothed in garments of sweet lip-service, but whose raiment, we know from costly experience, conceals the deadly dagger of treachery."[15]

Talmadge traveled across the South to promote his book, raise cash for his campaign, and gain a regional following. His travels included many stops in the bellwether state of southern public opinion, South Carolina, as well as an address before a joint session of the Alabama Legislature. He often appeared with the South's leading politicians, such as the Palmetto State's Democratic U.S. senator, Olin D. Johnston. Talmadge's tour of Dixie was promoted by

Thomas Waring's star reporter for the *Charleston News and Courier*, William Workman. On the southern hustings, Talmadge employed modern multimedia campaign techniques to promote segregation and defiance of the federal government.[16]

George's congressional seniority and international prestige did not fend off Talmadge's challenge. As one constituent said, George was now "regarded with suspicion by many persons at home. They think he has gone high-hat, or turned Yankee, and forgotten their problems. All they can talk about now is the race problem." George also lost his support from Georgia's powerful business interests. Likely hoping that Eisenhower would intervene with close friend and golfing buddy, Coca-Cola President William E. Robinson, George had lobbied the White House for support. But, with Talmadge's money and access to Georgia's professional class, George had little hope of big business support. Indeed, George's situation only showed senior southerners in the Congress that they now faced the prospect of credible opposition in their reelection campaigns. The counterrevolution against the Civil Rights Movement made it clear to southern congressional incumbents that something had to be done to demonstrate their zeal for white supremacy, reassert their control over electoral politics, and direct the regional defiance of the federal judiciary.[17]

The Southern Congressional Delegation also foresaw the real threat of another Dixiecrat Revolt heading into the 1956 Democratic National Convention. Another third political party of the parochial South would again be led by Thurmond, who had caused trouble for the Southern Congressional Delegation ever since he arrived on the national political scene after World War II. After the 1948 Dixiecrat Revolt, Thurmond served out his gubernatorial term and then challenged the incumbent Johnston in South Carolina's 1950 Democratic primary for the U.S. Senate. In one of the most overtly racist campaigns of postwar America, Thurmond promoted the most vitriolic position and lost the election, largely because of heavy returns for Johnston in enfranchised black wards. In 1952, Thurmond helped Democratic Governor James F. Byrnes direct Operation Dixie in South Carolina, and nearly won this former Democratic bastion for Eisenhower. Two years later, Thurmond became the first person in American history to win a U.S. Senate race with a write-in vote, after South Carolina's senior senator, Burnett K. Maybank, died of a heart attack just two months prior to the general election. With *Brown*'s declaration the previous May, Thurmond and his proven track record of racial antagonism easily bested the hastily selected official Democratic candidate, the doting state Senator Edgar Brown. After Thurmond and his cohorts claimed—disingenuously—that he was a member of the Democratic Party, former President Harry S. Truman unsuccessfully intervened and endorsed Brown as the "genuine" Democratic candidate. Thurmond later boasted that in some areas, voter returns showed that he "received a two-to-one majority in all . . . white precincts. In the all Negro . . . precincts my opponent received" all of the votes. Thurmond bragged, "I didn't get a one."[18]

Upon entering the Senate, the Dixiecrat asserted his independence. At the initial meeting of the Democratic caucus, Thurmond let it be known that, during his Senate race, the Democrats had "spent money against me, so I don't want any Democrat up here to think I owe 'em anything," adding, "but I hope we can work together for the good of the country." He wanted "simply to keep the record straight, no credit is due the Steering Committee for my election." Distancing himself from the Democratic Senate Campaign Committee, Thurmond nevertheless attended the Southern Caucus and aligned with the Democratic majority, despite having severed his formal ties to the party six years earlier. Thurmond generally supported the Democratic legislative agenda during his brief two-year stint in the Senate, such as southern agriculture exports and the construction of federal facilities in South Carolina. He made sure to remind constituents, however, that his voting record in the Eighty-Fourth Congress received a "zero rating" by the Americans for Democratic Action (ADA). Declaring that he would uphold his campaign pledge, Thurmond announced on March 2, 1956, that he would resign his Senate seat as of April 4, the day before the filing deadline, so that he could run in the Democratic primary on June 12. Thurmond's resignation meant that no other senator "won for himself a more enviable position in the respect and confidence of his colleagues," said Byrd from the Senate well. Thurmond would, therefore, be an elected nominee of the Democratic Party in the 1956 general election, but outside the confines of the Senate, and not responsible to any of the party leadership.[19]

Just after Thurmond's announcement, Byrnes declined his election as a delegate to that summer's Democratic National Convention in Chicago. The press immediately began to speculate that Byrnes's refusal meant that he would run against Johnston for the U.S. Senate either in the Democratic primary or later as a Republican in the general election. Byrnes explained his actions by making a direct threat of another Dixiecrat Revolt if both party platforms endorsed civil rights. Thurmond publicly praised Byrnes's stance, and added that neither national political party catered to southern segregation, though he remained committed to serve as a delegate in Chicago. Instead of forming a third party beforehand, Thurmond recommended that to keep their options open, South Carolina Democrats should not adjourn, but only recess, their state convention in late March, then reconvene after the national conventions. In the meantime, Thurmond asked all Democratic convention delegates from the South to work for the return of the two-thirds nominating rule for the party's presidential nominees, to "prevent the nomination of a person who is antagonistic to the views of the South." Thurmond believed this maneuver would give southern Democrats "a strong voice in party matters again and Southern views would be recognized in the party platform." According to Thurmond, "South Carolina must send delegates to Chicago who are prepared to fight against this radical faction of the Democratic Party" that supported *Brown* and federal civil rights legislation.[20]

In this atmosphere, where southern antagonism toward *Brown* was at a fever pitch, only a politician with as much national recognition, as unbound, and as adept at race-baiting as Thurmond possessed the potential to lead the South into another credible third-party movement. He fueled such speculation for months. In the fall of 1955, Thurmond told the *Saturday Evening Post* that "the South must resist integration by every means," so, "if the two major political parties do not respect the wishes and beliefs of large segments of the people, then I can see how a third party can rise again." "For myself," he confessed, "I hope to stay within the framework of the Democratic Party, but I shall not hesitate to do what I think best for my state and my country." Actually, Thurmond was never a loyal Democrat and, unlike so many others in the Southern Congressional Delegation, was not in Congress during the heady days of the New Deal and World War II. Thurmond had led the Dixiecrats in 1948, but the defiant atmosphere of that year paled in comparison to the hysterics arising after *Brown*. Longtime senate aide George Reedy recognized the Dixiecrat's potential for sewing discord in the 1956 elections: "We talk about somebody being more Catholic than the Pope. Well, at that particular point Strom had become more Confederate than Robert E. Lee. He had the power that so often resides in someone who has cut himself off from all political organization, which Strom had really done. He'd cut himself off from everybody." For Reedy, Thurmond "was so deeply involved in the Confederacy that he really had no organizational obligations. And a person like that is capable of coming up with all kinds of weird things that really put people on the spot."[21]

Thurmond's toady reporter, Workman, helped the Dixiecrat keep the Palmetto State at the forefront of any potential third party movement. In a lengthy editorial, Workman threatened that "any attempt to enforce integration in Southern states will produce a catastrophic explosion." Workman called on South Carolinians to follow Thurmond's recommendations and act in concert with Byrd's Virginia to control the Democratic National Convention. For the obsequious Workman, Thurmond was a natural leader of any southern third party, a "soft-spoken Patrick Henry with a deadly sincerity and the eloquence to inspire it in his southern compatriots." If their efforts failed, Workman said that the Old Dominion and the Palmetto State should lead the South out of the Democratic National Convention, for "they are the cavaliers, the aristocrats, who command the allegiance of their sister states even in a time when the world has gone Roundhead. They may not win, but they will interpose a formidable opposition to the orthodoxy of the Supreme Court and to the Stevenson-Kefauver-Harriman Democracy."[22]

Thurmond's obstreperousness, however, was antithetical to Russell's professional goals, political strategy, and personal disposition. As leader of the Southern Congressional Delegation in general and the Senate's Southern Caucus in particular, the Georgian's overriding concern was to maintain hegemony over the congressional agenda and thereby ensure that civil rights legislation did not become federal law. For him, the tactics of Thurmond, Talmadge, Eastland, and other racial demagogues were often counterproductive, especially when they threatened congressional control over the Democratic agenda by promoting a third-party movement. Russell and Thurmond first crossed paths at the 1948 Democratic National Convention, when the Georgian allowed his name to be placed in nomination against Truman in the unsuccessful effort to keep the southern delegations in the Philadelphia convention hall. Russell did not typically intervene in another state's politics, but he formally endorsed Johnston just prior to election day in the latter's narrow win over Thurmond in 1950. Six years later, he sought to control Thurmond and prevent him from threatening the electoral prospects of southern incumbents facing reelection. In his view, the Dixiecrat was a loose cannon, a grandstander who imperiled both his own leadership of the Southern Caucus and the South's domination of the Congress. Russell likely despised Thurmond.[23]

In the 1956 Election, Byrd also used intransigent politics to his advantage. By then, Byrd had ruled Virginia for over thirty years with a political machine that possessed unrivaled control over state and local government policy, including the selection of most officeholders. At the national level, he was a leading opponent of the New Deal and, after World War II, a staunch opponent of organized labor, investigating union ties to the international communist conspiracy. The Virginian, moreover, was a close ally of Eisenhower, as they campaigned together in the Old Dominion in 1952. By the mid-1950s, however, Byrd was slowly but surely losing his grip over his state's politics. The decline began in 1948, when he endorsed the Dixiecrats even as the Virginia General Assembly refuted him and supported the eventually triumphant Truman-Bartley ticket. Byrd helped Eisenhower carry Virginia in 1952, but his once unassailable organization had faced serious yet ultimately failed challenges in both the 1949 and 1953 gubernatorial races, and was certain to do so again in 1957. The Virginian was also getting older and, despite reports to the contrary, did not exert much influence in controlling legislation in the halls of Congress. He certainly enjoyed little respect among Senate staffers and other congressional insiders. Harry McPherson, aide to Senate Majority Leader Lyndon Baines Johnson of Texas, believed that Byrd "was always a kind of croaky-voiced old man in a yellowing-white suit whose main contribution was a quarterly report on nonessential federal expenditures. But he was no force at all. He was someone to be used, someone to try to get by."[24]

Virginia's leadership of the interposition movement provided the aged Byrd an opportunity to reassert control over the state and, once again, be a force in national politics. But, if Byrd did not actively promote defiance of *Brown*, he could also just as easily see his organization slip out from under his control, to become even less than the titular leader of Virginia politics that he had by then already become. After becoming enamored with the editorials of James Kilpatrick's *Richmond Times-Dispatch*, Byrd personally oversaw Virginia's school privatization plan and adoption of interposition legislation. To take Virginia's case to a larger audience, Byrd was highly motivated to seek some sort of action on the federal level.[25]

Thurmond and Byrd, therefore, were certainly capable of bringing the interposition movement onto the national stage. But, does that mean that they actually wrote the Southern Manifesto? The idea that they did is based upon the research of Hayes Mizell, which shaped Bartley's conclusions that, in turn, informs all subsequent scholarship. As a graduate student at the University of South Carolina in the early sixties, Mizell wrote to several members of the Southern Caucus, asking that they dictate their recollections of the drafting process. In his form letter to the senators, Mizell included a summary of his understanding of the drafting process, which he entitled "Origin of the Southern Manifesto." From reading the contemporary accounts in periodicals, Mizell placed Thurmond at the center of the drafting process. Mizell concluded that in order to foster southern unity and persuade wavering colleagues, Thurmond and Byrd threatened to issue their own statement if a meeting was not called, for they wanted to take interposition to the national level and help George win reelection.[26]

The idea that Thurmond was the central figure in the drafting of the Southern Manifesto, however, was largely of his own making. That is, the Dixiecrat successfully manipulated the press and the subsequent historical record to establish this perception. His personal records of the Southern Manifesto, moreover, which also include Mizell's summation, are similarly constructed to show him as intimately involved in every aspect of the drafting process. Similarly, that Byrd's name has long been associated with the drafting of the Southern Manifesto is also a myth that came from the era's journalists, who assumed that the interposition movement and the drafting of the Southern Manifesto were one and the same. The widely accepted belief that Byrd was one of the principal authors of the Southern Manifesto actually has little or no basis in fact.

In response to Mizell's inquiry and attached summation, Russell emphasized that he personally led the effort against *Brown* in national politics. The Georgian proudly recalled that it was he who "was the first Southern Senator to take the Floor of the Senate and denounce the Court for this decision. I did it after Senator Price Daniel of Texas had read one of the briefs he had prepared as Attorney General of Texas. He merely sought to justify the fact that the South litigated the question, whereas I was explicit in my condemnation." After this initial speech, "Two or three of my colleagues who later became very indigent about the decision told me at the time that they thought I was somewhat harsh in my statement." Russell admitted that he was "not absolutely positive in my recollection," but recalled that "a couple of hours later, Senators Harry Byrd of Virginia and Strom Thurmond of South Carolina came up to me, either in the Cloakroom or on the Floor of the Senate, and told me that they thought the Southern Senators should make some kind of statement condemning the decision and that a meeting should be held for that purpose." Was Russell's memory misleading him? Or was the plan for a formal denunciation of *Brown* in the works as early as May 1954? Thurmond did not enter the Senate until December of that year, so either Byrd alone likely approached Russell or the Georgian was confused in his chronology. Nevertheless, there is a distinct possibility that the idea for a formal statement of opposition was discussed within the Southern Caucus at this early date. Indeed, Russell and others understood that for such a statement to have the desired political affect, they would have to calculate the most opportune time for its promulgation.[27]

According to Russell, when he returned to Washington after he was hospitalized with influenza in Miami following a testimonial dinner for U.S. Senator George Smathers of Florida in late January 1956, he and Byrd called upon George, as the senior member of the Southern Caucus, to discuss the proposal. Thereafter, on Monday, February 6 (during which time the Montgomery Bus Boycott and the Lucy riots dominated national headlines), George called a meeting for February 8, 10:00 a.m., in his office, Senate Office Building 342. The next day, Eastland was scheduled to give the keynote address to the Montgomery Citizens' Council rally in the midst of the boycott,

3.1 The United States Senate's Southern Caucus in 1957, the year after the promulgation of the Southern Manifesto. At the head is the acknowledged leader, Democrat Richard Brevard Russell, Jr., of Georgia. From his right are Democrats Allen J. Ellender of Louisiana, Kerr Scott and Sam J. Ervin of North Carolina, John Sparkman, J. Strom Thurmond of South Carolina, George Smathers, James O. Eastland of Mississippi, A. Willis Robertson and Harry F. Byrd of Virginia, Lister Hill of Alabama, Russell Long of Louisiana, Spessard Holland of Florida, Olin D. Johnston of South Carolina, John Stennis of Mississippi, and the newest member, Herman Talmadge of Georgia, who ousted George in the previous year's Georgia Democratic primary. Conspicuously absent are Arkansas Democrats Fulbright and John L. McClellan, as well as newly elected Democrat Ralph Yarborough of Texas. Courtesy of AP Images.

while Georgia Democratic Governor Marvin Griffin appeared on statewide television to endorse the Peach State's interposition resolution. According to Russell, the meeting "was attended by practically all of the Southern Senators who had been active in opposing the various legislative proposals aimed at the southern states." The group also included Democratic Majority Leader Lyndon Johnson of Texas, but not Tennessee's Democratic senators, Estes Kefauver and Albert Gore.[28]

At this first meeting, Thurmond presented an initial statement proposal, a revision of a draft he had written in the previous weeks. According to Thurmond's personal papers, the revised draft (copies of which also appear in other senatorial collections) was the one that was discussed at this meeting. Upon a motion made by Democratic Senator Lister Hill of Alabama, George appointed a committee composed of Russell, Stennis, and Ervin. Russell later recalled that Johnston was also on the committee, but then retracted this assertion. There is no evidence that Johnston was ever an active participant on the first drafting committee. On the floor of the Senate, Johnston gave a lengthy denunciation of the Supreme Court on March 1, 1956, entitled "Politics in the Supreme Court." The timing of the speech may be the reason that Russell's recollection was skewed and why many people later associated Johnston with the drafting process. George instructed all of the southern senators to submit their suggestions to Russell in writing for consideration, and that the committee's report should be completed before the Easter holiday. Why Thurmond was left off the drafting committee, something he later admitted himself, is unknown. But, for the declaration to have even a modicum of respectability, overt race-baiters like Thurmond and Eastland had to maintain political distance.[29]

The composition of this drafting committee reveals much about the project. As the leader of the Southern Caucus, Russell was certain to be a member of any such endeavor. Stennis was also a logical choice. The Mississippian had joined Daniel and Russell, together with Johnston, Maybank, and Russell Long of Louisiana, on the Senate floor the day after *Brown's* declaration to condemn the Supreme Court. A former prosecuting attorney and circuit judge, Stennis had then chided, "I have never seen a group of attorneys before any court with so little straw with which to make brick, as was the case with the attorneys who represented the petitioners on this question as to the historical basis of the [Fourteenth] amendment." Stennis offered his oft-repeated threat toward black southerners: "The problem is now at their doorstep. I pray that they will have the right guidance in making their decision, rather than follow the advice of outside agitators." Mississippi was the most obstreperous state, but Eastland was much too bombastic, and his controversial aura would only diminish the project's credibility to Americans outside the South. Other than Byrd, within the Southern Caucus Russell and Stennis possessed the best understanding of the states' interposition movement. In their respective states, Russell and Stennis were both privy to the negotiations surrounding the adoption of interposition, frequently consulted by state officials on the language and arguments used in the legislative resolutions.[30]

Ervin was also a practical choice for the drafting committee. North Carolina's governor specifically appointed Ervin to the Senate in 1954 as an alternative to the leading candidate, Irving Carlysle, who had advocated compliance with *Brown.* In 1956, Ervin was trying to retain his seat, running in the Democratic primary against Winston-Salem Mayor Marshall C. Kurfees, who also supported compliance with desegregation orders. In contrast,

Ervin was at the forefront of the interposition movement. As former state judges, Ervin and Stennis granted interviews to *U.S. News & World Report* in November 1955, where they outlined the strategies for resistance to *Brown II.* As a graduate of Harvard Law School, moreover, Ervin had crucial ties to the North. On April 28, 1955, just before the proclamation of *Brown II*, Ervin gave an articulate defense of segregation at the annual dinner of the Harvard Law School Alumni Association at New York City's Harvard Club. His speech, entitled "Alexander Hamilton's Phantom," emphasized that no member of the Supreme Court had ever served as a judge of a court of general jurisdiction or appellate court, and that only two had previous experience in the federal judiciary. From this reasoning, Ervin concluded that the Supreme Court "on many occasions during recent years has to all intents and purposes usurped the power of the Congress and the States to amend the Constitution." The speech made headlines throughout the country, with favorable editorials published across the South. Constituent mail flooded into his office praising his condemnation of the court, especially from lawyers and his former colleagues of the North Carolina judiciary.[31]

Ervin was also a member of the Senate Judiciary Committee, and headed the Southern Caucus's strategy against the respective Hennings and Eisenhower civil rights bills. At the time of the Southern Manifesto's drafting, Ervin was preparing the South's opposition to these bills. The Tar Heel closely studied the debates surrounding the bills' passage in the House of Representatives, while his office performed extensive research on the adoption of the Fourteenth Amendment and the 1866 Reconstruction Codes. Ervin's staff conducted copious study of the legislative statutes, as well as federal and state judicial precedents, that anteceded *Brown*, which upheld the "separate but equal" doctrine of *Plessy v. Ferguson* (1896). Until his retirement in 1975, Ervin was the Southern Caucus's expert on constitutional segregation, providing much of the legal framework for the repeated southern filibusters during the civil rights era. While in 1956, Ervin's lack of seniority made him a relatively minor player within the confines of the Senate, by then he had already established an affable working relationship with the Washington press corps, who soon became enchanted with the courtly southern judge, as did the rest of the country. Ervin was already viewed as the foremost authority on the strict constructionist interpretation of the Constitution, and was frequently hired as a public speaker to professional organizations, civic clubs, and alumni associations across the country.[32]

The drafting of the Southern Manifesto was to be a public affair from the beginning, with periodic announcements to the press after important developments. The publicity allowed the Southern Caucus to gain the public's attention and take the initiative away from civil rights workers in the South, as well as to influence and control the nation's perception of interposition. The Southern Caucus was thus able to counteract the influence of civil rights on the national political debate. The publicity also showed the white South that their congressional representatives were working just as hard as state officials to subvert *Brown*. That is, the publicity helped incumbents like George resist challenges from intransigents like Talmadge. Long-entrenched southern senators like Byrd, Russell, and Stennis were similarly able to sustain their influence over state politics.

Immediately after this initial meeting to determine the drafting committee, George briefed reporters, as did Ervin and Stennis. Ervin made sure to criticize the Supreme Court again, telling reporters the purpose of the drafting committee was to "ascertain whether it is possible to keep the states from being destroyed." Russell and Stennis actually kept state leaders abreast of the project's developments, while Ervin openly discussed his role on the drafting committee in his weekly radio program in North Carolina. The publicity quickly drew a sharp rebuke by the NAACP's Clarence Mitchell, who said the meeting "promotes the false hope that there can be a successful defiance of the U.S. Constitution." Mitchell predicted that "wise men will not be deceived by it but hoodlums will regard the meeting as a green light for the kind of mob action that disgraced the University of Alabama."[33]

Weeks before in late January, Thurmond already gave secret inside scoops to his favorite South Carolina reporters, Workman and Frank Van Der Linden of the *Greenville News*. Thurmond informed Workman and Van Der Linden at this early date that he was pushing for a collective effort to oppose *Brown* on the national level. These reporters returned the favor by portraying Thurmond's idea as directly aligned with the southern governors who were, at the very same time, discussing interposition in Richmond, Virginia. Because Byrd was then working with Virginia officials on the state's interposition resolution, his name began to be associated with any such similar plans by the Southern Caucus. The reporters portrayed Thurmond's plan as a response to the Powell Amendment then gaining momentum in the House of Representatives, and alleged that George, as dean of the Senate, would direct any such future action by the Southern Congressional Delegation. During this early stage of the campaign season, therefore, Thurmond's trial balloons publicized his resignation from the Senate and assured that his name would hereafter be identified with any concerted southern action to subvert *Brown*, both in South Carolina and on the national stage.[34]

Byrd's public statements at the time also depicted Virginia interposition as part of a concerted regional effort to subvert *Brown*. In his formal endorsement of the Gray Plan to privatize Virginia's public school system, Byrd announced, "Ten other states are confronted with the same acute problem. These states are all seeking a way to preserve their schools, and it is possible that some form of action can be accepted as a pattern for all." When "developments occur, and the resistance of the South continues," he said, "there can be some degree of coalition between the 11 Southern States which will strengthen the position of the individual state." Speaking before the Richmond Industrial Management Club on February 14, Byrd was asked by a reporter to state his views on interposition. In response, Byrd cited the Southern Caucus's efforts to present a united front against *Brown*. Sounding much like North Carolina Democratic Governor Luther Hodges with his call for "voluntary segregation," Byrd said, "Passive resistance is the best course for us to take." He added, "I am strongly in favor of all the Southern States uniting." Ten days later on February 24, Byrd issued a press release stating that his comments were misunderstood. Instead, Byrd believed that "if we can organize the Southern States for massive resistance to this order, I think that in time the rest of the country will realize that racial integration is not going to be accepted in the South," for "in interposition the South has a perfectly legal means of appeal from the Supreme Court's order."[35]

Byrd thus coined the term "Massive Resistance" at the very same time that Russell, Ervin, and Stennis were drafting the Southern Manifesto. Byrd's statements are the reason, therefore, that both journalists and later scholars mistakenly assume that he was intimately involved in the drafting process and that it directly correlated with Virginia's interposition movement. As he was more intimately involved with his own state's interposition movement than any other U.S. Senator, Byrd was not directly involved in the drafting of the Southern Manifesto. Byrd was actually away from Washington most of that year, tending to his ill wife, when not overseeing state politics. At the time of the drafting, moreover, Byrd was suffering from a hernia. Early the next month, he was hospitalized and had to undergo surgery. The facts show that after helping to initiate the project, Byrd neither played an integral role in the drafting process nor in the promulgation of the Southern Manifesto.[36]

After the first meeting of the entire Southern Caucus on February 8, Russell dictated a preliminary draft at the request of Ervin and Stennis. The Georgian's impassioned, vitriolic four-page-long diatribe is very revealing of his thinking at the time. He worked from a massive amount of preparatory material, including a plethora of background information on Thurgood Marshall, the NAACP, and their legal tactics for the desegregation cases. Russell also requested that the Legislative Research Service of the Library of Congress, the American Law Division, send him information on the cases that

Marshall had lost before the Supreme Court. Thurmond, however, later contradicted Russell's own recollection. According to Thurmond, "I brought in a proposed draft and they followed that to a great extent in the first one. Then in the second one they still followed it to a great extent, but changed some of it."[37]

So who was the real author of the Southern Manifesto? Was it Thurmond, was it Russell, was it a collective endeavor by the committee appointed by George, or the product of the entire Southern Caucus? Russell should actually be considered most responsible for the language used in the statement. But the question as to who is the real author is actually subservient to the fact that three common themes unite each of the drafts of the Southern Manifesto that exist in the southern senators' papers, all of the suggestions from various members of the Southern Caucus, and all of the state interposition resolutions and related legal and constitutional arguments defending Jim Crow states' rights. First, southern segregationists argued that *Brown* was not based upon the concept of stare decisis, and thus was without basis in the American common law. According to this perspective, the Supreme Court justices had both misinterpreted and added to the U.S. Constitution's Fourteenth Amendment. Secondly, segregationists called into question the integrity and capability of the Supreme Court justices themselves, claiming that they were not disinterested judges but subjective partisans whose decrees were based not upon legal principles but unproven scientific theories. Thirdly, and arguably most revealing, segregationists contended that *Brown* destroyed the supposedly harmonious race relations that previously existed, inciting communist-aligned civil rights workers to provoke violence and uproot the southern way of life. Led by Russell, the Southern Caucus succinctly articulated what most southerners believed about the static nature of the federal Constitution, their culture, their black neighbors, and themselves. They also convinced many other Americans about the righteousness of this cause.

4. The Declaration of Constitutional Principles

The two Democratic United States senators foremost responsible for the Declaration of Constitutional Principles, popularly known as the Southern Manifesto, produced similar initial drafts of the statement. Democrat Richard Brevard Russell, Jr., of Georgia certainly read the draft from J. Strom Thurmond of South Carolina before dictating his own statement. These two highly individualistic minds each represented the mainstream of segregationist thought, but from different perspectives. Both Russell's and Thurmond's initial drafts argued that *Plessy v. Ferguson* (1896) was the correct interpretation of the Fourteenth Amendment, firmly established in both legal precedent and legislative statute. They both noted that when the Fourteenth Amendment was adopted, segregated public school systems existed throughout the North, and were subsequently upheld by numerous Supreme Court decisions, not only by *Plessy* but also by *Gong Lum v. Rice* (1927). Russell and Thurmond also emphasized that Chief Justice William Howard Taft, also a former Republican president of the United States, wrote *Gong Lum's* majority opinion. Here, Russell and Thurmond borrowed heavily from Texas Democratic U.S. Senator Price Daniel's brief for the defense in *Sweatt v. Painter* (1950). As the Lone Star State's attorney general, Daniel lost the case that conclusively desegregated public higher education. When he denounced *Brown* on the floor of the Senate in 1954, Daniel had read into the *Congressional Record* the judicial precedent of segregation under the Fourteenth Amendment that served as the defense's argumentative basis in *Brown*. Daniel had also included a lengthy discussion of segregation in the North that began with *Roberts v. City of Boston* (1849).[1]

Russell's first draft of the Southern Manifesto, however, came mostly from the statement he had inserted into the *Congressional Record* during the Southern Caucus's initial condemnation of *Brown* in the Senate in May 1954. Like so many other southern-trained lawyers, Russell had castigated the use of expert witnesses and modern psychological theory used by the NAACP to win the case. Russell also mocked the Eisenhower administration's amicus curiae. "If they are to rely on psychology," the Georgian explained, "then we should either add trained psychologists of recognized ability to the Court, or else we should provide that a Court psychologist of high standing shall attend the sessions of the Court and assist the Attorney General of the United States in bringing the Court to its conclusions." In his earlier Senate speech, Daniel had also specifically condemned U.S. Supreme Court Justice Felix Frankfurter because of his affiliation with the NAACP. Russell thereafter helped the Georgia attorney general investigate as to whether Frankfurter could be charged with a conflict of interest.[2]

Russell continued these themes in his first draft, revealing his contempt for the Supreme Court justices, especially Chief Justice Earl Warren. While contemporary reports and historians' subsequent scholarship denote the viciousness of Thurmond's initial draft, Russell's dictated first draft actually exceeded all of his colleagues in personally attacking individual justices of the Supreme Court. In this respect, Russell was especially nasty. He charged that *Plessy* was "accepted as the law of the land by real lawyers and judges for more than half a century." The Georgian argued that the Supreme Court used *Brown* to "willfully and arbitrarily and illegally undertake to interpose the personal views of the nine members of the Court for the established laws of the land and to willfully, arbitrarily and illegally strike down the established system which was the product of much effort and of the minds of real lawyers." He appealed to other sections of the Union, declaring that *Brown* was "the apparent determination of the present Supreme Court to mold this nation to its liking without regard to precedent, law or the Constitution," requesting that "those who believe in preserving the rights of the states as the last protection of individual liberty of our people, wherever they may live, to join with us in denouncing and reversing the Court's continued encroachment upon the legal systems and governmental functions of the several states."

Throughout his career, Russell framed his defense of the Jim Crow caste system in his conviction of the superiority of what he and others benignly described as the southern way of life. Russell's first draft noted: "Throughout the years the peoples of our States had taxed and bonded themselves per capita more heavily than those of other states in establishing a system of education in compliance" with the *Plessy* doctrine. *Brown* only inflicted "chaos, confusion, disorder and great loss and damage to our States. It has all but destroyed the amicable racial relations between the white and negro races that have painfully created through ninety years of patient effort by the understanding people of both races." On the side of his dictated draft, Russell then penciled in "Planted rancor and hatred and suspicion where there has been friendship and understanding." Daniel had previously warned that the "decisions have sounded the death knell to the public-school systems" and the South's ability to "maintain peace, order, and harmony." Russell concluded that *Brown* "threatens to destroy the system of public education built through so much sacrifice and effort in some of the states."[3]

Russell met with the other members of the drafting committee, Democratic U.S. senators John Stennis of Mississippi and Sam Ervin of North Carolina, at least three times over the next three weeks to discuss revisions. At Ervin and Stennis's request, Russell prepared a final draft, which the committee then approved for circulation within the Southern Caucus. Russell's committee draft evolved into a summary of the various suggestions offered by most of the members of the Southern Caucus. Russell placed these ideas into logical order, establishing the segregationist arguments within the boundaries of legal precedent, traditional American values, and political acumen. Russell drew upon all the ideas offered. Yet again, all of these suggestions were substantially similar in content. In this respect, Russell was less the principal author of the statement and more like editor-in-chief. Russell combined all the ideas of the Southern Caucus to compose a unified statement that articulated the legal arguments of segregationist ideology and the collective mentality of the white South.[4]

For the introduction, Russell built upon his previous speech read into the *Congressional Record* the day after *Brown*. Russell had then declared that the court exercised "a flagrant abuse of judicial power." He had charged that "the Supreme Court is becoming a mere political arm of the executive branch of the Government," because U.S. Attorney General Herbert Brownell was "grasping for more and more power" and "using the Court as a pliant tool to acquire the authority to direct every activity in the life of our people from Washington." The Republican administration was "making mere satrapies out of once sovereign states." For the Southern Manifesto, however, Russell understood that the language must be nonpartisan. For the preface, he evoked lofty ideals to heed the warning:

> The unwarranted decision of nine men, constituting the Supreme Court,
> in the Public School Cases is now bearing the fruit always produced when
> men substitute naked power for established law.[5]

Russell then turned to the eloquent Ervin, who was the most adept at employing historical memory to legitimate discrimination. For Ervin, the statement should evoke the ideals of classical republicanism and the American Revolution. The Tar Heel sought to remind Americans that "the Founding Fathers realized that history teaches this tragic truth: No man or group of men can be safely trusted with governmental power of an unlimited character." Ervin promoted a strict constructionist interpretation, stating that the Founders "framed a written Constitution, which was designed to put the fundamentals of government beyond the control of the varying mood of public opinion and the personal notions of the temporary occupants of public offices." According to Ervin, this interpretation struck at "the very nature of things, the meaning of a written Constitution is fixed when it is adopted, and is not different at any subsequent time when a court has an occasion to pass upon it. If this were not so, a written constitution would be far more worthless than the scraps of paper upon which its words are inscribed." Ervin understood, however, that in order to attract support outside the South, segregationists must concede that the Constitution was not completely static: "The Founding Fathers knew that from time to time new occasions would require changes in the Constitution." Yet, he also knew that regardless of their views toward segregation, most Americans believed that social and legal changes should come within the bounds of the written law. Therefore, Ervin wanted to remind Americans: "For this reason, they inserted in the Constitution Article V, which confers upon Congress and the States exclusively the power to amend the Constitution by joint action on their parts." Russell condensed Ervin's points into the next paragraph with his own rhetorical flair:

> The Founding Fathers gave us a Constitution of checks and balances
> because they realized the inevitable lesson of history that no man or group
> of men can be safely entrusted with unlimited power. They framed this
> Constitution with its provisions for change by amendment in order to
> secure the fundamentals of government against the dangers of temporary
> popular passion or the personal predilections of public office holders.

Russell made certain that the preface stated the South's principal grievance that *Brown* was outside the bounds of the constitutional process. Stennis also advocated mentioning Article V in the statement, even suggesting that they consider recommending legislation that would make it easier for the states to submit and ratify constitutional amendments. From Ervin's and Stennis's suggestions, Russell wrote:

> The decision of the Supreme Court in the School Cases is a flagrant and
> unjustified abuse of judicial power. It climaxes a trend in the Federal Judi-
> ciary undertaking to legislate, in derogation of the powers of Congress, the
> rights of the states and of the people.[6]

The text of Russell's committee draft dealt with segregationists' specific grievances. Here, Russell used Thurmond's recommendations, which, like most segregationist thought, followed John W. Davis's oral arguments in *Briggs v. Elliot* (1952), one of the subordinate cases under *Brown* that concerned segregation in South Carolina. Before the Supreme Court, Davis had argued that when adopted, the Fourteenth Amendment had allowed for segregated school systems. Russell's and Thurmond's initial drafts, as well as all of the subsequent recommendations of the southern senators, had drawn upon Davis's reasoning. From these suggestions, Russell simply put the argument into his own words for the next three points:

> The Constitution does not mention education. Neither does the Fourteenth Amendment. The debates preceding the submission of this Amendment clearly show that there was no intent that this Amendment should affect the systems of education maintained by the states.
>
> The very Congress which proposed the Amendment provided for segregated schools in the District of Columbia.
>
> When the Amendment was adopted in 1868, there were 37 states of the Union. Every one of the 26 states that had any substantial racial differences either approved the operation of segregated schools in existence or subsequently established them by the same law-making body which considered the Fourteenth Amendment.[7]

The next point was the crucible for the legal defense of segregation, and thus the Southern Manifesto. Here, Russell made the oft-repeated charge that *Brown* lacked judicial precedent, a clear departure from the common law standard of stare decisis. He again drew from both Daniel's briefs in *Sweatt v. Painter* (1950) and the Southern Caucus's collective denunciation of *Brown* in the Senate in May 1954. All had noted that the *Plessy* doctrine was reaffirmed repeatedly for sixty years since its declaration, most notably in *Gong Lum*. Once again, all of the senators who made suggestions simply drew from these previous sources. Russell summarized the argument thus:

> Beginning with the case of *Plessy vs. Ferguson*, the Supreme Court expressly declared that under the Fourteenth Amendment no person was denied any of his rights if the states provided separate but equal public facilities. This decision was in essence reaffirmed in 157 other decisions since *Plessy vs. Ferguson*. It is notable that the Supreme Court, speaking through Chief Justice Taft, a former President of the United States, unanimously declared

in 1927 in *Lum vs. Rice* that the principle of separate but equal was '. . . within the discretion of the state in regulating its public schools and does not conflict with the Fourteenth Amendment.'[8]

Russell then turned to the specific suggestions of Thurmond and Stennis. Both of them believed that the statement should depict the South as a beset minority whose cultural identity was under assault. Drawing upon his earlier public statements, Stennis said that segregation should be defended as "a firmly established principle of Constitutional law which established the habits, customs, traditions and way of life of the people." Similarly, Thurmond wrote: "Parents should not be deprived of the right to guide and regulate the lives of their own children." Russell combined these suggestions:

> This interpretation, placed time and again, without exception, became a part of the life of the people of many of the states and confirmed their habits, customs, traditions and way of life. It is founded on elemental humanity and common sense, for parents may not be deprived by a super government of the right to direct the lives and education of their own children.

Stennis was responsible for the language used in the next point. "Without any change of law by the Congress, without any Constitutional Amendments by the people, and without any serious public expression of any kind to change or offset this almost century-old Constitutional principle, the Supreme Court," the usually composed Mississippian furiously complained, "suddenly uprooted, overturned, scuttled, and reversed these settled principles and set up a rule of their own." Barely concealing his fury, Stennis raged: "In Constitutional parlance such an act was illegal in the sense that there was no political, moral, or legal basis for such action, except the naked power of nine men, strategically placed, to substitute their own individual political and social ideas for the law of the land." Russell sanitized Stennis's diatribe, combining the first two sentences, but let the last phrase stand verbatim:

> Though there has been no constitutional amendment or Act of Congress changing this established legal principle almost a century old, the Supreme Court of the United States, with no proper political or legal basis for such action, undertook to exercise the naked power of nine men, strategically emplaced, and substituted their personal, political and social ideas for the established law of the land.[9]

It was now Russell's turn to vent his anger. The next two points are his alone, for they are taken from his own initial dictated draft. The Georgia bachelor often sat alone in his office into the late evening, watching the evening news while relaxing over cigarettes and Tennessee whiskey. There he was, alone in front of the dim light of the television, smoking and sipping his drink, watching civil rights workers fight the historic battles in Alabama, contemplating ways to thwart their efforts. In this paragraph, Russell first alluded to the Montgomery Bus Boycott that increasingly captivated the nation's attention:

> This illegal and unconstitutional seizure of power by the nine men composing the Court is creating chaos and confusion in the states principally affected. It is destroying the amicable relations between the white and negro races that have been created through 90 years of patient effort by the good people of both races. It has planted hatred and suspicion where there has been heretofore friendship and understanding.

With little effort to conceal his true meaning, Russell then referred to the NAACP's legal challenges that forced southern states to comply with desegregation. Autherine Lucy's attempt to attend the University of Alabama earlier that month was surely the focus of Russell's gaze:

> Without regard to the consent of the governed, agitators from afar are threatening immediate and revolutionary changes in our public school systems. If done, it is certain to destroy the system of public education in some of the states.

More than any other contributor, Thurmond was responsible for the statement's conclusion, which was arranged into a stanza. The basic tenets held by the Southern Caucus were enunciated here. Russell changed some of the wording for a more logical flow of argumentation and for calculated effect, but the ideas are mostly Thurmond's. To begin this section, the Dixiecrat offered: "In view of the foregoing:" Working from Thurmond's draft, Democratic Senator A. Willis Robertson of Virginia reworded this phrase to suggest that they use "In light of these facts." Instead, Russell melodramatically wrote:

> With the gravest concern for the explosive and dangerous condition created by this decision:

Russell then kept Thurmond's exact language for the first tenet enunciated, writing:

> We reaffirm our reliance on the Constitution as the fundamental law of
> the land.

For Thurmond's next tenet, "We decry the Supreme Court's encroachment on rights reserved to the States," Russell added a popular phrase learned during his early days in the New Deal:

> We decry the Supreme Court's encroachments on rights reserved to the
> states and the substitution of a government of men for established law.[10]

The next tenet considered the important question as to whether the statement should formally endorse interposition. Both Russell and Thurmond had explicitly endorsed the interposition movement in their initial drafts. Russell had heatedly dictated that interposition was "a solemn protest by a sovereign state of the invasion of its rights and powers by federal government and a notification that the state intends to exercise all of its constitutional powers," as well as a "notice that the state will use all legal and peaceable means to defeat and reverse all illegal encroachments upon its people by a power-mad Judiciary which is answerable to no constituents and the product of political appointment." He considered interposition resolutions as "lawful means and measures calculated to bring about a reversal of this illegal and unconstitutional decision of the Supreme Court." Thurmond was even more emphatic, stating: "We commend as truest patriotism the actions of the States which have adopted these resolutions." The Dixiecrat wanted to "urge other affected States to enact similar resolutions and to present . . . a solid front with their sister States against the illegal and unconstitutional action of the Court." Certainly influenced by the actions of his home state, Robertson had improved on Thurmond's language, suggesting that the statement should read: "We commend the patriotic motives of those states which have adopted resolutions of interposition to assert their determination to resist by every lawful means invasion of their sovereignty resulting from this ill-advised Court decision." Russell simplified the wording of this tenet considerably for the committee's draft. The leader of the Southern Caucus understood that he could not explicitly endorse interposition if he were to get most of the Southern Congressional Delegation to endorse the statement. Although there is no explicit paper trail in these politicians' historical collections, some senators had most likely made their objections known to him previously either at George's meeting or in private consultation. As the unassailable leader of the Southern Caucus, Russell actually omitted the word "interposition" from the statement himself, and he narrowed down the reference to just one sentence:

> We commend the motives of those states which have declared the inten-
> tion to resist this invasion of their sovereignty by the Court by every lawful
> means.

Russell then returned to another theme prevalent in the Southern Caucus's suggestions to his committee: an appeal to other regions of the United States for solidarity with the South. That is, the Southern Caucus evoked senatorial courtesy, appealing to their fellow senators' common sense of self-preservation. Specifically, the Southern Caucus wanted other members of Congress not to push through civil rights legislation that would threaten southerners' electoral prospects. Thurmond asked "colleagues to join us in resisting invasion of the legislative field by the Judicial branch of the Government." In his initial dictation, Russell had appealed to "the people of this Nation whose rights may be next affected by the apparent determination of the present Supreme Court to mold this nation to its liking without regard to precedent, law or the Constitution," and "to consider the imperative necessity of curbing the increasing assumption of legislative and executive power by the nine men who now constitute the Court."

Robertson and Stennis, however, conceived the exact language that developed into this tenet. Robertson had suggested this wording: "We urge States which are not so directly concerned with the school segregation decision to consider whether they should not ally themselves on the side of constitutional principles, because the time may come when on other issues they may become the victims of judicial encroachment." Stennis then improved upon Robertson's language: "We appeal to the States and the people elsewhere to consider the Constitutional principle involved in this case against the time when they too, on other issues, vital to them, may be the victims of judicial encroachment." Stennis wanted the statement to admit, "Even though we presently constitute a minority in the Congress we urge them to join us in our active efforts to create the necessary majority to submit amendments or pass legislation designed to remedy this wrong." Russell slightly changed Stennis's phrasing, drawn from Robertson, and then omitted the Mississippian's last sentence, thus:

> We urge states and people who are not directly affected by the school

segregation decisions to consider the Constitutional principles involved in this case against the time when they, on other issues, may be the victims of judicial encroachments.[11]

Stennis encouraged Russell to use his own concluding remarks from his initial dictation for the conclusion, which read:

> We pledge ourselves to support by any and all lawful means all measures calculated to bring about a reversal of this illegal and unconstitutional decision of the Supreme Court.

Russell then added a call for the white South to maintain law and order, despite what he viewed as direct provocation from outsiders. In order for the white South to convince others of the righteousness of their resistance to *Brown*, Russell knew the statement must channel opposition to civil rights into a nonviolent means of defiance, up through the political process, into the region's most powerful tool of influence, the U.S. Senate. That the entire statement described the federal government as tyrannical, Russell's plea for confining resistance to the legal realm was at best perfunctory, at worst disingenuous. As his generation's foremost political talent, Russell surely understood that a statement primarily designed to undercut public support for *Brown* and permit the South to ignore federal desegregation mandates would surely produce more than its share of violent confrontations between civil rights workers and the white South's unrestrained ruffians. Nevertheless, Russell improved on Thurmond's call for "using every lawful means of resistance against the decision of the Court," by also asking white southerners to support their representatives in the Congress:

> We appeal to our people not to be provoked by the agitators and trouble-makers invading our states and to scrupulously refrain from disorder and lawlessness in this trying period as we seek to right this wrong.[12]

Russell showed the finished committee draft to Stennis and Ervin on the morning of March 1. They all signed this version. Russell then delivered a copy to the senior member of the Southern Caucus and Senate President Pro Tempore Walter George, who also signed. Stennis volunteered to circulate the draft among the Southern Caucus, personally delivering copies that morning throughout the Senate office building. Some senators, including Daniel and Spessard Holland of Florida, evidently requested advance copies of the committee's completed draft once they were finished. Upon delivery,

Stennis asked his colleagues "not to let it fall in the hands of the press or in the hands of anyone else as we were not releasing anything until all the Senators have had a chance to look this over."[13]

The next day, however, Thurmond moved back onto the frontlines. He signed the committee's draft, and then helped Stennis distribute copies to other senators. Thurmond also tried to secure the signatures of senators from the border states, but they refused. Thurmond repeated Stennis's call for confidentiality, and urged them to "give no publicity to it until Senator George releases the statement after everybody has had an opportunity to sign it." The previous day, however, another of Thurmond's toady journalists, Frank Van Der Linden of the *Greenville News*, somehow obtained a copy of this committee draft, and then reported on some of its finer details. Van Der Linden quoted a "senior southern senator who is a leader in the movement," which clearly had to be Thurmond. All circumstantial evidence points to the Dixiecrat as the source of this leak. He included the article, for instance, with the copy of the committee's draft that he sent to his senior Democratic senator from South Carolina, Olin D. Johnston. Van Der Linden reported that his anonymous senator confided (in typical Thurmond language) that the goal of the project was to make "the Supreme Court pause and take a second look at its decisions," for "if the integrationists could pick us off, one by one, they would have an easier time of it. But they will find that we mean business."[14]

The series of events that ensued is a matter of dispute. Russell later recalled to the University of South Carolina graduate student Hayes Mizell that "several Senators including Senators Fulbright, Holland and Daniel thought that the language I had originally suggested was . . . 'too bitter' and these Senators made some revisions, changing a few words to a softer meaning but not altering the substance of the declaration." Ervin, however, told Mizell that all the senators in the Southern Caucus were regularly consulted during this initial drafting process, and then the committee met again "and approved such final draft, which was the draft signed by other Senators and which was then read . . . on the Senate Floor."

Despite the apparent contradictions, the two narratives are reconcilable. Ervin's and Russell's recollections of some of the finer details were sure to have been somewhat unclear, given that they were remembering events six years beforehand. Ervin may not have been privy to the protests of these senators, who may have made their objections known only to Russell, Stennis, and maybe Thurmond. Nonetheless, Ervin was correct that all of these senators played an active part in the drafting process. All members of the Southern Caucus would, at least in the short term, benefit from such a statement of protest. Every member of the Southern Congressional Delegation, moreover, sought some way to stop civil rights legislation from being considered in the Congress during this election year. All southerners agreed that a unified course of action was the best way to accomplish that goal. A strongly worded protest of *Brown* was the best means to that end. The Southern Manifesto provided unity and, hence, safety.

Russell and Stennis wanted as strong a denunciation of *Brown* as possible. "There is a wide divergence of opinion between the Southern Senators," Russell complained to a Georgia state official during the drafting process, "some even favor the decision." Stennis later told Mississippi newsmen that "I favored as strong a statement as possible within the limits of reason and sound logic, and I stressed the necessity of unity among those from the South, because in union there is strength." While their statements could be taken at face value, Russell and Stennis also wanted to deflect charges by intransigent segregationists that the Southern Congressional Delegation was not doing enough on the national level to oppose *Brown*. Despite the fact that they were constitutionally incapable of overturning *Brown*, these Senate leaders were still subject to a hostile electorate. They thus sought to place blame upon some of their colleagues, thereby deflecting some of the intransigents' criticism. Russell admitted, "I am trying desperately to get something respectable that most of our Southern Senators can sign, but when you run into 5 or 6 who are unwilling to denounce the decision as illegal and unconstitutional it is discouraging. I think it would be better not to have anything than a feeble, watered-down gesture of protest." During the drafting process, Stennis similarly informed Speaker of the Mississippi House of Representatives Walter Sillers that the committee stood "in favor of a very strong statement, but getting one to which most of them [southern senators] will subscribe is a difficult problem." When Sillers inquired as to whether interposition was achievable on the national level, Stennis demurred, "I do not think we are in a position to raise that issue now at the legislative level when we have only about twenty votes we can count on" for such legislation.[15]

As many scholars note, Russell, Stennis, Ervin, and the rest of the senators who made suggestions did not offer any overtly racist arguments for consideration. They followed a trend seen both in the defenses' arguments in the collective *Brown* cases as well as the state interposition resolutions. Russell and the Southern Caucus, however, realized that to offer any overtly racist statements would inevitably estrange most if not all potential allies outside the South, both within the Congress and the American public at large. Overt racism would, furthermore, undermine any credibility that may be achieved with the statement before the court of world opinion. They defended the southern caste system with the traditional interpretation of the

Fourteenth Amendment, so their arguments rested on solid legal precedent and in a place that most of the Southern Congressional Delegation found common ground. Racist arguments were omitted because the politico-legal defense of segregation had the wholehearted support of the entire Southern Congressional Delegation (not to mention many people outside the South). Maintaining unity through constitutional arguments made it relatively easy for the vast majority of the Southern Congressional Delegation to endorse the statement.

Following contemporary accounts, previous studies of the Southern Manifesto portray the next stage of the editing process as an agonizing and divisive series of events, during which personal and professional relationships were strained to the breaking point. According to this view, moderate senators courageously objected to the more inflammatory language used by the drafting committee to frame their arguments. The moderate senators insisted that the language be weakened or they would not endorse the project. Consequently, Russell, Thurmond, and the other hardliners capitulated in the quest for unity. The most influential contemporary account comes from the journalist Elizabeth Carpenter of the *Arkansas Gazette*, who based her report upon a confidential source that was likely Arkansas Democratic Senator J. William Fulbright's secretary, John Erickson. "Although the final doctrine still denounces the Court decision and encourages lawful resistance," Carpenter reported, "it is a far cry from the original piece of paper." In this standard interpretation, after the initial committee draft was circulated, Daniel, Fulbright, and Holland offered an alternative statement that was fundamentally weaker than the initial drafts of Russell and Thurmond. The entire Southern Caucus met again, and appointed an entirely new drafting committee consisting of Russell, Stennis, Thurmond, Fulbright, and Daniel, which then wrote the final ameliorated version.[16]

Ervin and Russell refuted this narrative of the sequence of events. "I never heard anything to the effect that the original committee . . . was superseded by a new committee," wrote Ervin. Russell thought it mistaken to label the revisions an actual "Holland- Daniel-Fulbright draft," for "I do not think they rewrote it but merely made alterations on the original" committee draft. Russell later told Mizell, "No new committee was ever appointed insofar as I was ever advised, nor was there any indication of 'continued opposition' by some members of the Southern group other than to the text of the document that I finally drafted."[17]

The historical record actually supports the recollections of Russell and Ervin. The changes to the committee draft were largely cosmetic. The substance of Russell's committee draft remained mostly unaltered and the following revisions only added weight to the fundamental arguments of the statement. The standard narrative of the second stage of the editing process of the Southern Manifesto, therefore, is inaccurate. In summary, a combination of omission, mistaken authorship, as well as both a conscience distortion and slapdash reading of the historical record, results in a problematic depiction of the entire second drafting process.[18]

To date, the most in-depth narrative of the second stage of the editing process is based on personal interviews with both Fulbright and one of his staffers, J. H. Yingling. Based on these interviews, historians recognize that the Southern Caucus's moderates were advocates for continued segregation. But, like contemporary accounts, reliance upon Yingling's highly questionable recollections results in the portrayal of Fulbright as torn over the decision as to whether or not to endorse the Southern Manifesto. In Yingling's account, he and Erickson urged Fulbright not to sign. After discussing the issue with them at the office, however, Fulbright drove out to George Washington's Mount Vernon with his wife, Elizabeth. After much contemplation, the couple decided that he must participate in order to ameliorate a potentially dangerous situation. By participating, the Arkansawyer could simultaneously satisfy his constituents, retain influence within the Southern Caucus, and move the campaign against *Brown* into a peaceful, more rational direction. After returning to the capital, Fulbright called Daniel, as well as Democratic senators Lister Hill and John Sparkman of Alabama and convinced them to join him in his quest to diffuse this dangerous situation.[19]

Yingling and others within Fulbright's office, therefore, created a myth that was employed by moderates and accepted by the journalists who covered the story. This myth became the standard interpretation not only of the drafting of the Southern Manifesto, but of liberal southern Democrats who supported segregation in general. Erickson or someone else within Fulbright's office was the likely source for Carpenter's inside scoop on the drafting process. Fulbright and his aides thus had the opportunity to make the historical record portray the Arkansawyer as a voice of reason amidst a sea of troglodytes. During his career in the Senate, Fulbright's reputation as a liberal internationalist deflected criticism surrounding his active role within the Southern Caucus. Afterward, *Harper's* acknowledged, for instance, that his signature on the Southern Manifesto "shattered his chances" for a presidential candidacy, but they still described Fulbright's record as "not the blatant anti-Negro position of many of his fellow southerners."[20]

Fulbright considered his position carefully. His office wrote a memorandum (likely the document that Yingling remembered) stating objections to the wording of Russell's committee draft. Most scholars view this statement as a clear indication that Fulbright was not going to sign if the intransigent seg-regationists prevailed. The memorandum's language, however, is sufficiently equivocal to make his reservations clear without taking an absolute position until he was finally required to do so. Fulbright's memorandum, rather, recommended how the Southern Manifesto might be framed in such a way as to appeal to Americans outside the South. In this manner, the statement would be as beneficial to the Southern Congressional Delegation's three short-term objectives: prevent *Brown*'s implementation, bury civil rights legislation, and keep the South within the Democratic Party. In order to attain their preeminent goal of reelection, these aims must be achieved simultaneously. So, in this instance (as in almost every other), Fulbright and other southern moderates used racial demagoguery to their advantage, successfully defending Jim Crow before the court of world opinion, just as much as their supposed more intransigent colleagues. These southern moderates were not driven by their intransigent colleagues to adopt a more obstreperous position. Rather, they achieved professional success within a political economy based upon a racial caste system. They never advocated desegregation. They just made Jim Crow appear at best more benign, at least more palatable, to white Americans outside of the South.[21]

Fulbright began this memorandum with the hallmark equivocation of a sagacious politician: "Although I agree with much of the statement, I cannot conscientiously subscribe to all of it." While he held reservations, Fulbright assured his fellow southerners that he remained loyal to Dixie. He recognized "the dangerous and potentially explosive situation which has arisen in the South" after *Brown*. The decision was especially troublesome for him and fellow strict constructionists in the Congress "who have resisted punitive federal legislation over the last decade—attempts to use the police power of the national government to usurp the rights of the states and bring federal force to bear upon the traditions and customs of our people." Fulbright stressed that the only way that they successfully blocked civil rights legislation in the past, and would thereafter continue to do so, was "to convince many persons of good will in the rest of the nation that we ourselves have been making rapid progress in the improvement of race relations and in the welfare of the negro minority in the South." Because these "problems arising from the Supreme Court decisions are serious and grave in the extreme—beyond comprehension of anyone lacking the historical perspective of the Southerner," he exclaimed, "I find myself unable to subscribe to the statement."

Fulbright explained his specific objections to the committee draft. *Brown* was the law of the land, so as written, "the statement will not appeal to the good sense, understanding and, indeed, compassion of non-southerners—with whom we have lived in relative peace since Reconstruction days." He repeatedly emphasized that allies were needed for their cause "if we are to resist successfully the full power and force of the federal government." For this reason alone, he objected to the committee's use of the terms "illegal" and "unconstitutional" to describe *Brown*. Such language "holds out the false illusion to our own southern people that there is some means by which we can overturn the Supreme Court's decision." For Fulbright, "Our duty to our own people in their hour of travail is one of candor and realism. It is not realistic to say that a decision of the Supreme Court is 'illegal and unconstitutional,' and to imply, thereby that it can be overturned by some higher tribunal." Fulbright also took issue with the committee draft's mild endorsement of interposition, primarily because his own state had not yet acted on such a resolution. He wanted to avoid all such language "recalling of the ghost of nullification." As a principled strict constructionist and defender of states' rights, moreover, Fulbright argued, "It is quite beyond our powers and prerogatives to suggest to the state governments that they should or should not take any action."

Fulbright recommended that the best possible course of action for the South to take after *Brown* was to do absolutely nothing. In language very similar to that employed by the southern moderate governors, Fulbright said that the South should "give to its local communities and school boards, the widest possible discretion to do what they wish and what they can. For this is a problem which is peculiarly local in the strictest sense of that word. Locally autonomous school boards can deal with it far more wisely and effectively than can we, the Congress, or perhaps even the states." Fulbright likely looked to his hometown as a prime example of where this policy had succeeded. As the seat of the state's land grant university, the Fayetteville citizenry prided themselves as a progressive community whose board of education (under the direction of Fulbright's brother-in-law Hal Douglas) in 1955 became the first school district in the entire former Confederacy to comply with *Brown*. Previously, the district's small number of black students were bussed weekly to Fort Smith for matriculation. They traveled some sixty miles over the Boston Mountains on a winding, hilly, deeply rutted, treacherous road pass misnamed Highway 71. Fulbright, however, also had a good personal example of when and how a do-nothing policy could result in disaster. The previous year in the small Delta town of Hoxie, the school board unanimously voted to desegregate in order to save money by avoiding duplicate purchases of

4.1 Arkansas's Democratic United States Senators Fulbright and McClellan, with the latter's secretary, Harriette Story. Courtesy of the University of Arkansas Mullins Library, Special Collections.

education materials. Arkansas's peddling Jim Crow mongers promptly drove to the small town, stirred racial discord, and intimidated the community into rescinding the school board's previous resolution.[22]

Fulbright's memorandum concluded by reminding his confreres that he "fought with them against attempts to bring federal force to bear on this problem of race relations," and "I expect to fight with them again, for we are even now threatened by some with federal force." With utmost clarity, Fulbright laid bare their primary object of mutual concern. In his most persuasive tone, he warned that if the Southern Caucus became irreparably isolated, if not estranged, from their fellow senators, Rule Twenty-Two was doomed: "Our last weapon in this fight has been and probably will be the right of unlimited debate in the Senate. We shall need all the non-southern support we can muster to maintain this right." "It is a false assumption," the Arkansawyer noted, "that the nation will support us in defiance or castigation of the Supreme Court." To think otherwise would only "give aid and comfort to agitators and trouble makers within and without the South."[23]

Fulbright was foremost a southern segregationist senator whose primary goal in 1956 was reelection. He was, however, also a senior campaign adviser and close confidante to Adlai Stevenson. The junior senator from Arkansas recognized, and made perfectly clear to Russell and the rest of the Southern Caucus, that regardless of how despicable it seemed, the South's control of the Congress was inextricably tied to the electoral prospects of the Democratic presidential nominee. In the perspective of both moderate and intransigent segregationists, neither the national Democratic Party nor the Southern Congressional Delegation materially benefited from a breech. Fulbright from his vantage point best understood this reality. Stevenson was forced to formally denounce interposition, so he would inevitably have to distance his candidacy from any such endorsement. Fulbright's memorandum made clear that if the Southern Manifesto formally endorsed interposition, the South's congressional incumbents who signed the statement would thereby be committed to using the issue in their campaigns, making an internecine fight at the Democratic National Convention and another southern walkout that much more likely. Indeed, Fulbright's memorandum convinced Russell and the others that moderation was more to the advantage of the Southern Caucus, the larger Southern Congressional Delegation, their control of Congress, the national Democratic Party, and the perpetuation of Jim Crow.

As the drafting of the Southern Manifesto was a public affair, some letters actually arrived in Fulbright's and Holland's offices urging them to sign before the final statement was released. Fulbright's standard reply to constituents asking him to sign reminded them that "the decision of the Supreme Court is not subject to control by the Congress," and "the Supreme Court is an independent branch of Government, and there was no possible way that the Congress could control or . . . change that decision directly." Unhappily, Holland similarly lamented that "we Southern senators and we Southern white people are a minority—I think the finest group in the nation, but still a minority." Nevertheless, Fulbright believed that there were "alternative policies which we may follow and which are being examined by all of the Southern Senators and Congressmen, in an effort to find some answer to this very difficult problem." He added: "As you know, the decision does not require immediate integration, so that we have a reasonable time at least to find some alternative."[24]

The persistent presence of former Arkansas governor and leading Dixiecrat Ben Laney, who was then being courted by the state's leading intransigent segregationists to run against Fulbright in that summer's Democratic primary, made the incumbent senator bolster his segregationist credentials. A prominent West Memphis attorney informed Fulbright: "Some down here thought after the meeting on integration at England and the speech that Laney made that he had desires to run against you. One of my old friends recently contacted us over here and asked how he'd do against you. We gave you all the votes here and none to Laney, even though he was an old friend." Surveying the political landscape for Fulbright's primary campaign, Erickson found similar sentiments. Using the *Gazette*'s Carpenter as a medium, Erickson sent feelers out to a Laney confidante, Sam Harris, as to the Dixiecrat's intentions for the upcoming campaign. In a confidential memorandum, Erickson told Fulbright that Harris "does not think Laney is giving any consideration at this time to a race for the Senate. He says that Laney has a hard core of about 40,000 votes and knows that he can't add much to that unless he starts early and has a good issue. As to the issue, Sam thinks that your signing the Manifesto pretty well takes care of Laney."[25]

After Russell's committee draft was circulated throughout the Southern Caucus, a group consisting of at least Daniel, Fulbright, Sparkman, and Democratic Senator Russell Long of Louisiana met for an early lunch in Long's office on March 6 to consider their response. According to Carpenter's narrative of events in the *Gazette*, Long had by then already signed Russell's committee draft, but upon hearing of the other senators' reservations, decided to participate. After lunch, Fulbright joined Stennis in the Senate cloakroom, where together they approached Holland and Democratic Senator George Smathers of Florida to gauge the statement's ramifications. This was Holland's first day back in the Senate after being incapacitated for over a week with a harsh cold that turned into a serious sinus infection. After a brief discussion, the three informed Stennis that they could not endorse the committee draft as written. The Mississippian was swayed by their arguments and, apparently without prior authorization from Russell, gave them copies of the committee draft to revise before the Senate Caucus met again to formally approve the statement.

As a former governor who knew firsthand about the Sunshine State's race troubles, Holland also weighed his options carefully. He agreed with Fulbright about the language used in the committee draft. On his personally edited copy, Holland wrote five specific objections: "1. Some statements incorrect. 2. Some statements unduly inflammatory. 3. Our affirmative case not stated as strongly as we would like. 4. Our appeal for fair play from others. 5. The state references." Immediately upon his return to his office at 1:30 p.m., his telephone rang with a call from Daniel, who told Holland that he too was not going to sign the statement as written. The word on Capitol Hill spread quickly, for his fellow Florida Democrat, U.S. Representative Robert Lee Fulton Sikes, also called Holland to inquire about the committee draft. All that afternoon, Holland debated the political implications of his endorsement. He twice called Bobby Baker, talking with the personal secretary to Lyndon

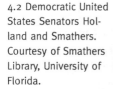

4.2 Democratic United States Senators Holland and Smathers. Courtesy of Smathers Library, University of Florida.

Baines Johnson of Texas off and on for nearly two hours about the majority leader's response and sound out the ramifications for Senate Democrats. Holland then telephoned another close Florida contact in the Congress, U.S. Representative Albert Sydney Herlong, Jr., to measure the implications for House Democrats in the coming primaries. Just after he hung up with Herlong, Daniel called again, for the group of revisionists had still not reached a consensus on how to proceed.

The next morning, Wednesday, March 7, Holland rose early, for he and some other congressional leaders had an 8:15 a.m. breakfast scheduled at the Pentagon with the army brass to discuss sundry military matters. Upon his return to the office midmorning, Holland took care of some home state chores, but then Stennis called again, just before the Senate opened at high noon, inquiring as to whether he and the others had made a decision. By this time, Holland and the others had clearly decided to participate, so he likely told Stennis to give his group a little more time to present their recommendations. After the close of the Senate that afternoon, Holland received yet another call from Daniel, who informed him that the entire Southern Caucus was to meet early the next morning to formally consider the statement. They must get busy. For the next two hours, Holland and Fulbright each edited their own copies of the committee draft in the confines of their private offices, swapping phone calls so that they could read their edits to one another. After they finished, Holland called Smathers to check with him about the exact wording of the revised statement. At 5:15 p.m., as the afternoon sunlight waned in the dusk of the late winter day, Daniel, Fulbright, Holland, and Smathers gathered in the well of the Senate to complete their revisions.[26]

The best way to measure the group's impact on the drafting process is to compare Russell's committee draft with the final statement. Their revisions collectively made the Southern Manifesto focus more upon denouncing *Brown* in and of itself, and engage less in Russell's personal criticism toward the individual Supreme Court justices themselves. Their influence is clearly marked on the final published draft, for it succeeds in addressing their primary concern of making the statement more credible to white Americans outside the South. Fulbright and Holland in particular—both of whom enjoyed national constituencies beyond their states' borders—successfully transformed the Southern Manifesto into a statement that did not estrange, and maybe even gained, the potential allies that were needed to maintain Democratic unity, while still satisfying the majority of the Southern Caucus's white constituents. The idea that the revisionists somehow diffused or ameliorated the statement does not completely address all of the effects of their editing. The revisionists' foremost goal was to make Russell's committee draft more acceptable, if not appealing, to a wider audience and thus more influential. That was the path for southern incumbents to return to Congress.[27]

At Holland's suggestion, the final version's preface omitted the phrase "nine men, constituting," to state: "The unwarranted decision of the Supreme Court in the public school cases is now bearing the fruit always produced when men substitute naked power for established law." Other than describing the supposed "lesson of history" as "inescapable" rather than "inevitable," Fulbright let Ervin's second paragraph stand verbatim. Fulbright, Holland, and Daniel then made some stylistic changes that bolstered their arguments. For example, Holland made it more a statement of opinion by simply adding the phrase "We regard" to the first sentence of the third paragraph, then replaced the phrase "flagrant and unjustified" with the simple adjective "clear" to describe the alleged "abuse of power" by the Supreme Court. The declaration now read: "We regard the decision of the Supreme Court in the school cases as a clear abuse of judicial power." Daniel changed the language from "to invade the legislative field" to "undertaking to legislate." Fulbright maintained their established basis of argumentation when he changed the second sentence's phrasing from "in derogation of the powers of Congress, the rights of the states and of the people" to "in derogation of the authority of Congress, and to encroach upon the reserved rights of the States and the people." Fulbright, Holland, and Daniel also reinforced the strict constructionist doctrine, making it clear that "the original Constitution does not mention education. Neither does the Fourteenth nor any other Amendment."

After Fulbright and Holland made a few more stylistic changes, Daniel's already profound influence became more apparent in the revised draft. The Texan suggested that they should reiterate his argument made in *Sweatt v. Painter* (1950), which he repeated the day after *Brown* in the well of the Senate. Russell evidently thought this was a good idea, for it only strengthened the statement's reliance on precedent, succored solidarity within the Southern Congressional Delegation, and appealed to other sections of the Union, especially areas of Democratic strength. On the paragraph submitted for consideration by Daniel, the Georgian scribbled, "Good will—To sustain—Motives of the States we should welcome all state constitutions—State Constitutions—States rights weakening ways of looking at it." Accordingly, Daniel's paragraph was inserted almost verbatim except that the phrase "changed to integrated systems" was altered to read "changed their school systems."

4.3 Democratic United States Senator Price Daniel of Texas. Courtesy of Sam Houston Regional Library.

> As admitted by the Supreme Court in the public school case (Brown v. Board of Education), the doctrine of separate but equal schools 'apparently originated in Roberts v. City of Boston . . . (1849), upholding school segregation against attack as being violative of a State Constitutional guarantee of equality.' This constitutional doctrine began in the North—not in the South, and it was followed not only in Massachusetts, but in Connecticut, New York, Illinois, Indiana, Michigan, Minnesota, New Jersey, Ohio, Pennsylvania and other Northern States until they, exercising their rights as States through the constitutional processes of local self-government, changed their school systems.

The revisionists replaced specific details with generalities. Instead of arguing that *Plessy* "was in essence reaffirmed in 157 other decisions" the final draft said it "has been followed in many other areas." Rather than profess that *Plessy* was an "established legal principle," they said it was a "constitutional legal principle" that was overturned. The Southern Caucus's goal was to avoid theory as much as possible, so that subsequent arguments over specific details would neither drown out the overlying message of the statement nor diminish its impact. Instead of Stennis's accusation that the Supreme Court "undertook to exercise the naked power of nine men," Fulbright changed it to "undertook to exercise their naked judicial power," which sounded more persuasive (and less homoerotic).[28]

The revisionists also addressed the most contentious language used in the concluding passages. Russell had charged in the committee draft, "This illegal and unconstitutional seizure of power by the nine men composing the Court is creating chaos and confusion in the states principally affected." Fulbright's memorandum had specifically objected to this phrase. According to Carpenter, Daniel also objected, declaring at one juncture: "You can't call any action of the Supreme Court unconstitutional or illegal." The former Texas attorney general, who ranked among the principal architects of the modern legal defense of segregation, protested, "That just isn't true and I won't sign it." As was their role, the revisionists found a middle way. Robertson first suggested the phrase "unwarranted construction of the Constitution" be substituted for this passage, but was judged not forceful enough. They then conceived a phrase that avoided personalities yet was also acceptable to intransigents: "This unwarranted exercise of power by the Court, contrary to the Constitution, is creating chaos and confusion in the States principally affected." The slick phrase "contrary to the Constitution" was acceptable to all within the Southern Caucus. It labeled *Brown* outside the law without using overt terms of denunciation.[29]

The revisionists then strengthened the language of the last section of the Southern Manifesto. They recommended that the words "and enlarged by outside meddlers" be added to the committee draft's call: "With the gravest concern for the explosive and dangerous condition created by this decision." Russell liked the idea, but tweaked it a bit further, using Daniel's language, so that the final draft read: "With the gravest concern for the explosive and dangerous condition created by this decision and inflamed by outside meddlers." The revisions continued to make the statement avoid direct personalities, repeating the unique turn of phrase. They changed the third principle enunciated in the last section to "we decry the Supreme Court's encroachments on rights reserved to the States and to the people, contrary to established law and to the Constitution." The revisionists originally wanted the phrase to read "contrary to established law and to the intent of the Constitution," but evidently Russell did not agree that "intent" should be included in any articulation of strict constructionist doctrine.

The committee draft's relatively minor endorsement of interposition was diluted further, to the point where it no longer recognized the legality of the resolutions. Holland evidently wanted to strike out all of the neo-Confederate language, but Daniel and Fulbright again found the middle ground, instead affirming the Southern Caucus's solidarity with interposition as such: "We commend the motives of those States which have declared the intention to resist forced integration by any lawful means."

Fulbright and Holland concurred with Thurmond's and Stennis's argument that the statement should make overtures to nonsoutherners, actually the critical component of the revisionist agenda. Russell had originally omitted from the committee draft Stennis's admission that the South was a political minority in the Congress. But, with Fulbright's insistence, the gist of Stennis's argument returned, rewritten to appeal to the entire American public rather than just to their colleagues on Capitol Hill: "Even though we constitute a minority in the present Congress, we have full faith that a majority of the American people believe in the dual system of government which has enabled us to achieve our greatness and will in time demand that the reserved rights of the States and of the people be made secure against judicial usurpation."

Fulbright again condensed, then substituted, his own turn of phrase for Russell's oath: "We pledge ourselves to use all lawful means to bring about a reversal of this decision which is contrary to the Constitution and to prevent the use of force in its implementation." He then kept Thurmond and Russell's languid plea for nonviolence.[30]

5. The Signatories

On Thursday, March 8, 1956, at 10:00 a.m., the United States Senate's Southern Caucus met in the office of Senate President Pro Tempore Walter George of Georgia to sign the final draft of the Declaration of Constitutional Principles. The declaration's editor-in-chief, Senator Richard B. Russell of Georgia, met with reporters the next morning to announce the completion of the project and to inform them that George was scheduled to read the statement into the *Congressional Record* on the following Monday morning, March 12. This schedule gave the Southern Caucus the weekend to confer with colleagues in the House of Representatives and secure signatures. Russell decided that his colleagues would be allowed to endorse the statement until the close of legislative business on Monday evening, just before the *Congressional Record* was edited and printed. When asked by journalists, Russell dubbed the statement with the name known to history. "We might call it a manifesto," he proclaimed, but would "have to look that word up in the dictionary."[1]

This early announcement was clearly calculated for effect. By speaking with reporters prior to the Southern Manifesto's promulgation, Russell prevented any prospective dissenters within the Southern Congressional Delegation from using the excuse that they did not know about the statement before its formal appearance. Furthermore, the early announcement took press coverage away from an extensive investigative report by the *New York Times* covering the South's compliance with *Brown v. Board of Education* (1954) in their Sunday edition. Most importantly, however, the early announcement allowed the Southern Caucus to dominate the weekend's headlines, and steal press coverage away from the upcoming New Hampshire presidential primary the next Tuesday, March 13. The front-runner for the Democratic presidential nomination, former governor Adlai Stevenson of Illinois, did not compete in New Hampshire because it was still a "preferential" primary, with the state's delegates not bound to uphold the voters' preference at the national conventions. His foremost challenger, Senator Estes Kefauver of Tennessee, was running alone in this first primary. Stevenson first learned of the manifesto when his press secretary, Harry Ashmore, read a copy that was leaked to the press on Friday, March 9. Ashmore read the statement to Stevenson via telephone, just before the Democratic front-runner appeared on stage at a campaign rally with Governor G. Mennan "Soapy" Williams of Michigan. According to Ashmore, the Stevenson campaign viewed the statement as a "conspiracy" against his renomination.[2]

The procurement of signatures in the House of Representatives proceeded smoothly. During the next three days, the only noted controversy occurred when a young Democratic congressman, Ross Bass of Tennessee, signed the statement, then told reporters that he overheard Russell, who was evidently securing signatures in the House's cloakroom, telling colleagues that the manifesto was primarily designed to reelect George. Angrily telling reporters that the Southern Caucus's motives were genuine, Russell emphatically denied the allegation. While he likely did not design the document specifically to protect his senior colleague, Russell was certainly concerned about the general threat coming from widespread Democratic primary challengers and a national party split. Russell sought to protect southern congressional seniority and the Democratic majority, threatened by candidates like George's primary opponent, former Georgia governor Herman Talmadge. While Talmadge's segregationist credentials may have made him at least grudgingly acceptable to the Southern Caucus, retaining seniority and the congressional committee chairmanships was the principal concern of both Russell and other incumbents in the Southern Congressional Delegation.[3]

From this perspective, most incumbent southern congressmen signed the Southern Manifesto for political expediency. To stave off challenges by race-baiting intransigent segregationists, moderates had to endorse the statement. As U.S. Senator Lister Hill of Alabama rhetorically asked a friend about a fellow politician, "Do you want him to stick his neck out and get beat, or stay here and get something done?" In this view, these moderate politicians personally disagreed with much of the language used in the statement; if given their druthers, the vast majority of them would not have signed. Extremists on both sides of the issue had pushed them into their position.[4]

Some scholars, though, accept the moderate participants' explanations as genuine. That is, moderates who signed the statement ameliorated a potentially dangerous situation. The revision process and endorsement by the overwhelming majority of the Southern Congressional Delegation turned the manifesto into a relatively benign legal brief that defended states' rights, and thereby kept opposition to *Brown* mostly confined to the legal and political realms, rather than allowing it to be controlled by violent extremists.[5]

Regardless of their motivations or subsequent explanations, all of the moderates who signed the Southern Manifesto were fully committed—intellectually, socially, and politically—to the preservation of segregation. Their primary motivation for signing was to prevent *Brown*'s implementation during the following school year when they were campaigning for reelection. Circumstantial evidence suggests that Democratic U.S. Representative Brooks Hays of Arkansas, for example, probably had better inside information about the drafting process than any other House member. As mentor and close confidante to his junior U.S. senator, J. William Fulbright, Hays was likely privy to some of the negotiations over the revisions. In contrast to other southerners in the House, Hays evidently saw the first committee draft and expressed his reservations concerning the more inflammatory language. He also probably sounded out other southerners in the House for Fulbright and the other revisionists. Hays later explained that he "joined with a number of other members of Congress who refused to sign the document unless it removed all mention of the doctrines of nullification and interposition. In this way, the Southern moderates hoped to preserve the Constitutional guarantee of the right to dissent without advocating measures which might do violence to the Constitution."[6]

That weekend, Arkansas Governor Orval Faubus came to Washington, D.C., to confer with his delegation and other members of Congress. While there, Faubus lobbied hard for the Southern Manifesto. After he learned that Hays and Democratic U.S. Representative James Trimble planned not to sign, Faubus accompanied both Hays and intransigent Arkansas segregationist U.S. Representative Oren Harris to the ill Trimble's bedside in the Bethesda Naval Hospital. That entire Saturday afternoon, the men discussed the situation. After a heated lengthy discussion, Trimble relented and signed. Hays, though, later remembered that he "was about ready to dig in and refuse." He "was tortured by this thing because there was some validity to what Faubus was saying." Faubus's reasoning epitomized moderate doctrine, and he told his congressmen, "Gentlemen, if you don't do this, the feeling in Arkansas is such that our whole political establishment will be turned over to the White Citizens' Councils and Ku Kluxers and the rabid, extreme kind of segregationists. You ought to do this to save the state from that kind of political leadership." Given this option, Hays reluctantly signed. As he finished, Hays gazed up at his governor and lamented, "What will some of my good friends say to me now?" In later years, Hays confessed that his signature did not spare Arkansas from the turmoil of desegregation, seen just over a year later during the Little Rock Central High crisis. "I can see that I shouldn't have done it because it did not spare us much," he recalled. "I think we could still have saved the state from those extremists, but the threat was powerful enough that I was influenced."[7]

5.1 Democratic United States Representative Brooks Hays of Arkansas. Courtesy of the University of Arkansas Mullins Library, Special Collections.

Hays's posthumous regret contrasts with his stated opinion before the death of Jim Crow. Beforehand, Hays justified his actions by supporting the intent, language, and message of the manifesto:

> I signed this declaration as a proper statement of the South's objections to the overthrow of the *Plessy v. Ferguson* decision and violation of the *stare decisis* principle in Constitutional law. While it contained items which to me would have been better omitted and expressed some sentiments in language not to my liking, I believed the declaration was an honest reaction to the injury the South believed had been done to its way of life.

Hays always maintained that his endorsement prevented violence. Desegregation promised "an upheaval that would be pretty severe. And I don't mean just office-changing." If desegregation was fully implemented there would be widespread "discontent and the loss of confidence in the congress and in the state leadership of the Southern states."[8]

Like Hays, many who endorsed the manifesto later expressed regret. Bill Cochrane, aide to Democratic U.S. Senator Kerr Scott of North Carolina, claimed that, after thinking over the weekend about his decision to sign, Scott instructed him on Monday morning to see if he could withdraw his endorsement. Cochrane, however, informed Scott that copies had already been distributed to the press, and that to withdraw his endorsement then would only exacerbate his problems. "I was already sad that we couldn't get his name off there," he maintained. "Senator Scott never had any problem with black people and he never went in for that kind of strong stuff." As just another staffer with the perspective of hindsight, Cochrane failed to remember that Scott had always been a committed segregationist, and never encouraged the Tar Heel State to comply with *Brown*.[9]

As self-interested seekers of reelection, most southern House members were of similar disposition as Hays. They generally accepted the basic premises of opposition to the Supreme Court. With the possible exception of Hays, they did not participate in any of the drafting sessions of the statement (there is scant evidence in any of the era's southern congressmen's papers that any House members were privy to the negotiations). Indeed, there existed little if any communication between southern congressmen and the Southern Caucus regarding legislative defiance of *Brown*. The southern members of the House simply took the manifesto as a logical statement of protest to desegregation, as the best way to satisfy their constituents and keep their seats. In the end, seventy-seven House members joined their nineteen Senate colleagues from the eleven states of the former Confederacy to endorse the Southern Manifesto. The signatory parties included the entire delegations of seven states: Alabama, Arkansas, Georgia, Louisiana, Mississippi, South Carolina, and Virginia. With the exception of Texas, the majority of the Florida, North Carolina, and Tennessee delegations also signed, including four Republicans. The alacrity with which southerners in the House signed only demonstrated the unanimously satisfactory document that their colleagues in the Senate drafted. The vast majority of the Southern Congressional Delegation readily endorsed the statement, without the moral crisis of conscience that many would thereafter claim and that contemporary journalists, and later scholars, accepted.[10]

The same professional self-interest is generally true for those members of the Southern Congressional Delegation who did not sign the manifesto. The most famous nonsigners were Kefauver and his fellow Tennessean, U.S. Senator Albert Gore, Sr. While both senators never participated in the Southern Caucus, Kefauver's reasons for not signing are obvious. The one distinct issue defining Democratic presidential candidates in 1956 was their position on civil rights. There was no chance that Kefauver, whose campaign was increasingly identified with immediate compliance with the federal judiciary, would endorse the statement. During the weekend that the Southern Caucus secured signatures, Kefauver sat for a nationally televised interview on Sunday in the capital. He emphasized that his position on *Brown* was "constitutionally correct," and added, "I see no justification now for changing my views on the manifesto. I am not going to sign and I've told them so." When asked the following day to elaborate on his position, Kefauver lost patience with reporters, snapping, "I just don't agree with it," turning the conversation to less controversial issues.[11]

During the drafting process, Kefauver positioned himself as the presidential candidate most committed to *Brown*'s implementation. He told a predominantly white Nashville audience that *Brown* was "the law of the land and should be obeyed," and that southerners "could not secede from the Supreme Court." While desegregation should be first implemented "at the local level," the Southern Manifesto, "however conscious the objectives, can only result in an increased bitterness and hard feelings and add confusion to an already difficult situation." "My position may have cost some political support in the South," Kefauver admitted, "but I think it is right and that is that." To answer critics of his refusal to sign, he employed some of the manifesto's own language: "It is far better if we keep so-called manifestos and harsh words on both sides to a minimum and work instead toward assuring good will between the races which has been a product of hard and understanding effort by many leaders of both races throughout the years."[12]

The reasons for Gore's decision not to sign are more obscure. In his memoirs, Gore described the *Plessy* doctrine as "pernicious," and labeled the manifesto as "a bit of low doggerel which hardly lived up to its high-flown title" that served only as a "dangerous, deceptive propaganda move which encouraged Southerners to defy the government and to disobey its laws, particularly orders of the federal courts." His refusal to sign was based on principle alone. The Southern Manifesto "(what an irritating and pretentious name!)" was "the most unvarnished piece of demagoguery" that he "ever encountered." His fellow southerners in Congress "were deliberately and callously misleading the people, and that nothing but tragedy and sorrow could come of this open defiance of the law, this cheap appeal to racism."[13]

Gore's panegyrics were a change of heart from his earlier career position. After the first drafting session was announced in the press, constituents urged Gore to attend the meetings of the Southern Caucus. He initially told constituents that the meeting to consider the question of interposition had not yet been called. After the first meeting was held, Gore explained that he had a previously scheduled meeting of the Rules Committee at the same time. After the final draft of the Southern Manifesto was complete, reporters pressed Gore as to whether or not he would sign, but he refused to comment. After failing to sign, Gore finally explained, "I found myself in agreement with some parts of the statement but unable to sign the full document."

Thereafter, Gore argued that the statement had no force behind it, and would only cause further impediments to finding a solution to the civil rights controversy. For Gore, the statement "could serve no particular good" because it threatened to divide the national Democratic Party in an election year and prevent the Congress from passing other necessary legislation. His equivocation evidently encouraged U.S. Senator J. Strom Thurmond of South Carolina to cajole him to sign. As such, Gore and Thurmond produced a (likely preconceived) mutually ostentatious public confrontation of political theater that helped with each of their respective constituencies. The following week, during a Senate session in the well directly below the press gallery, Thurmond sauntered up to Gore and thrust a copy of the Southern Manifesto into his face, a gesture to which the Tennessean replied with an emphatic "No!"[14]

Theatrics aside, Gore stood on firm political ground. *Brown* was generally not a divisive issue in eastern Tennessee, a traditional Republican bastion. The region's two Republicans, U.S. Representatives Howard Baker of Knoxville and B. C. Reece of Johnson City, did not endorse the manifesto. Neither did Democratic U.S. Representative J. Percy Priest of Nashville. Priest's seat was fairly secure, and he usually received support from Davidson County's black community. His only potential rival was Nashville Mayor Ben West, also a self-described moderate. In reply to constituents who criticized his stance, Gore reiterated his public support for the Supreme Court, and stressed that the manifesto "might make the situation worse instead of better." The strongest criticism of Gore's and Kefauver's refusal to sign came from west Tennessee, the region based upon the Delta's plantation economy and, not incidentally, generally outside their electoral bases of support. Both Kefauver and Gore were initially elected to the Senate by defeating incumbents backed by the faltering Crump political machine. Given that the once powerful Memphis political boss partly based his power on a tightly controlled black voting bloc, one that by 1956 was a potential means of support, Gore's and Kefauver's electoral prospects were not improved by returning Tennessee to the Southern Caucus. Just after *Brown* in 1954, Tennesseans sent Kefauver back to the Senate despite the challenger's overt race baiting. Gore's refusal to sign was the savvy political move in the Volunteer State.

Like his senior colleague, Gore too had presidential ambitions. He sought the vice presidential nomination at the 1956 Democratic National Convention (where he solicited and received the formal endorsement of Senator James O. Eastland of Mississippi), as well as in 1960. Gore realized that endorsing the manifesto excluded him from any higher aspirations for national office. He ultimately supported the 1957 and 1960 Civil Rights Acts but, when faced with a strong Republican opponent in the general election, he voted against the 1964 Civil Rights Act, the one bill that specifically outlawed segregation. The next year, he supported the 1965 Voting Rights Act. Gore perhaps had sincere moral qualms about the manifesto, but he also recognized its political implications. Writing to his close friend Jennings Perry of Nashville, a lobbyist for the Tennessee Valley Authority, Gore thanked him for his "commendation on my declination of the opportunity of signing the so-called manifesto. What a misnomer. Stump speech would have been more appropriate."[15]

Other members of the Southern Congressional Delegation who refused to sign maintained that they could not endorse a statement that questioned the legality of a Supreme Court decision. Democratic U.S. Representative Dante B. Fascell of Florida asserted that the Southern Manifesto was "a denouncement of the Supreme Court, which is a cornerstone of our American Government." Democratic U.S. Representative Thurmond Chatham of North Carolina professed, "I, personally, will not sign anything that will tear down the power and prestige of the court as the final arbiter of justice. We sometimes forget that, in a country ruled by a dictator, the courts are destroyed first."

Nonetheless, nonsigners also made sure to defend their records as staunch segregationists. Like the revisionists, many nonsigners understood that inflammatory acts of defiance could do more harm to Jim Crow than anything else could. As Democratic U.S. Representative W. R. Poage of Texas explained:

> I'm for segregated schools, but the way to retain it is not by going around
> yelping like a band of coyotes on a midnight hill. If we sit tight and tend
> to our business we will be more help in maintaining the status quo than
> by inviting a lot of people to come into our area. We don't want to divide
> Congress into two extreme camps. For one thing, if we do that, the South-
> erners are outvoted.[16]

The best expression of this viewpoint came from Democratic U.S. Representative Harold Cooley of North Carolina, the powerful chair of the House Agriculture Committee. From the outset, Cooley took personal offense because southern House members were not consulted during the drafting process. But, as did so many of his colleagues, Cooley carefully weighed his response. When Cooley received the copy of the completed statement, he read each sentence line by line, then checked off beside each paragraph whether he either agreed (Y), disagreed (N), or did not understand (?) each point. Cooley supported the opening stanza with its evocation of the Found-

5.2 Democratic United States Representative Harold Cooley of North Carolina. Photo, collection of the U.S. House of Representatives.

ers and hard-won American liberty, and with the manifesto's interpretation of the Fourteenth Amendment and support for *Plessy*, marking "Y's" beside each of these paragraphs. He did not believe, however, that Fulbright's revisions went far enough in moving the criticism away from the Supreme Court justices themselves to attacking *Brown* specifically. Cooley found the Southern Manifesto's description of *Brown* as "a clear abuse of judicial power," that possessed "no legal basis," and an "unwarranted exercise of power by the court" much too distasteful, and wrote "N" beside each of these paragraphs. Lastly, Cooley thought Thurmond's closing stanza vague and confusing, but agreed with the finale's call for law and order. At the bottom of his personal copy, Cooley scribbled "8 agree = more ½, 3 Dis = ⅕, 4? = ⁴⁄₁₅." From this simple calculation, Cooley determined that, while he agreed with more than half of the statement, he certainly disagreed with 20 percent of it, and found nearly another third unclear enough to dissuade him from endorsement.

Thereafter, Cooley informed his constituents: "I am now and always have been definitely and positively in favor of our present system of segregated schools. I am certain that the thinking people of both races appreciate fully the mutual advantages of our present segregated school systems and I believe that they will try honestly and sincerely to solve all of the problems presented." Much as Gore's official statement did, Cooley said that the Southern Manifesto was "a dangerous document, calculated to aggravate the situation and inflame the minds and intensify the feelings of many people in many parts of our country. The document is also calculated to bring all of the courts of our country into disrepute." Cooley supported the manifesto's call for civil rights to be resolved at the local level, as well as its description of the Constitution as inherently perfect. Yet, he continued, "Neither as a member of Congress nor as a lawyer do I know of any way to reverse the unanimous decision" of *Brown*. Alluding to Thurmond's final stanza that he found so confusing, Cooley noted that none "of the distinguished authors of the 'manifesto' even suggest or offer a remedy by which the decision of the highest court of the land may be reversed." For Cooley, the statement only held "out the false hope that there are legal means through which the Supreme Court decision can and may be reversed," and thus he "did not approve of either the form or substance of the document."[17]

The most important members of the Southern Congressional Delegation not to sign were Texas's Senate Majority Leader Lyndon Baines Johnson and Speaker of the House Sam Rayburn. Both of them explained that, as the Democratic leaders of the Congress, they could not give the appearance that the statement was official party policy. Many scholars, however, disagree on Johnson's and Rayburn's actual motivation for failing to endorse the statement. They generally agree that Johnson's presidential ambition was the chief motivating factor for them not to sign the Southern Manifesto. Some, though, argue that Johnson's and Rayburn's declinations were sincere disagreements with the principles espoused, and that the statement only threatened to divide the Democratic Party in an election year. Their refusal, moreover, reflected their general displeasure with absolutist political stands. Hence, Johnson especially despised segregation and other anachronistic traits of the South, the defense of which only delayed much-needed economic progress. Others depict Johnson's decision not to sign in a more pragmatic light, by emphasizing his own insatiable presidential ambitions. Johnson's decision only distanced him further from association with the Southern Caucus and made him appear more of a national figure before the American electorate.[18]

Johnson's and Rayburn's decision not to endorse the manifesto was determined both by the 1956 presidential election and the throes of Texas politics. That year, Johnson and Rayburn were in a pitted contest with Governor Alan Shivers for control of the Texas Democratic Party. Shivers emerged as the leader of the states' rights segregationist faction of the Texas Democracy in the wake of the 1944 Texas Regulars and 1948 Dixiecrat Revolt, both of which unsuccessfully tried to lead independent movements in the Lone Star State. In 1952, Shivers headed the successful "Operation Dixie," which abandoned the Stevenson-Sparkman ticket to endorse Eisenhower and Nixon. Texas was the most important state campaign and won much of the South for the GOP that election year. With the desegregation controversy compounded by natural gas deregulation and offshore oil deposits, Texas was the focal point of controversy over federal/state relations. By the time of the manifesto, Shivers had already declared his intention to work for Eisenhower's reelection and gain a permanent foothold for the GOP in both the Lone Star State and across the former Confederacy. Johnson and Rayburn tried to find a way to win control of the state machinery for the national party, and thereby ensure that Texas remained within the Democratic fold.

By not endorsing the manifesto, Johnson and Rayburn aligned themselves with both the Texas majority and the national Democratic Party. The episode marked Johnson's formal departure from the Southern Caucus. He was thereafter depicted as the leader of the national Democratic Party. Ironically, by not signing he also ensured his control over both Texas and the South at large because he now was a southerner accepted by the rest of the nation. Johnson's and Rayburn's refusals to sign ultimately assured that southern incumbents were not defeated, and ensured a Democratic congressional majority and southern control over the chairmanships. Johnson successfully blocked civil rights legislation from being debated by the Congress, from being formally supported by the Democratic Party, and from becoming the pivotal issue for the 1956 election.

Johnson's decision not to sign helped him with a majority of his constituents. Immediately after the manifesto's promulgation, Johnson called for the abolishment of poll taxes, and declared that he would work to push the proposed constitutional amendment out of the Judiciary Committee. The quest to end poll taxes was supported by both civil rights advocates and many moderates. Johnson thus turned the focus of civil rights debates off desegregation. Texas Hispanics, furthermore, were considered among Johnson's most loyal constituencies. Most of the south Texas county machines built upon the Hispanic vote certainly wanted more voters out on election day, so the abolishment of the poll tax helped Johnson in this regard. Furthermore, Texas's Hispanics advocated desegregation even more than the Lone Star State's black community did. In the 1955 Texas Poll, 77 percent of Hispanics supported compliance with *Brown*, with 30 percent advocating gradual compliance and 47 percent urging full-scale desegregation immediately. These percentages were even higher than among African Americans, who supported gradual desegregation 22 percent and immediate compliance 40 percent, for a total of only 62 percent. Furthermore, an astounding 42 percent of Texas Anglos said that they supported some form of desegregation, 31 percent advocating gradualism, while 11 percent supported immediate compliance with *Brown.* These statistics stand in stark contrast to those of other regions of the South. Indeed, other than Democratic U.S. Senator Price Daniel, only four of the twenty-one members of the Texas congressional delegation signed the statement. "The question certainly arises whether politicians such as Governor Allan Shivers," the Austin-based *News Bulletin* observed, "actually represent the feelings of the *majority*—not just of the so-called 'White' population—but of the *entire* population of Texas."[19]

Contemporaries disagree as to whether or not Russell asked Johnson to sign. Nevertheless, thereafter Russell explained, if not defended, the majority leader's position to the other members of the Southern Caucus. In his official

5.3 Democratic Speaker of the United States House of Representatives Sam Rayburn of Texas. Photo, collection of the U.S. House of Representatives.

press release, Johnson said that he had not been asked to sign and had not even seen the document before it was released. Southern senators did not request his endorsement, Johnson explained, because "they did not want their statement to be construed as an attempt to formulate Senatorial or Democratic Party Policy." He staunchly defended the Southern Caucus; he claimed the statement was issued "with the fervent hope of helping in the solution of this great problem which involves the principle of equal rights under the law, in which we all believe, and the traditions, feelings, and way of life of a large part of our country." Johnson then echoed the presidential candidates, moderates, and segregationists alike, for "the solution of the problem cannot be found on the Federal level, for it involves basic values reflected in the sovereignty of our States. It's my hope that wise leaders on the local levels will work to resolve these differences." To a Texas constituent who still questioned his southern loyalty by not signing, Johnson explained:

> Ever since I came to Congress 19 years ago, I have voted consistently for legislation designed to protect the rights of the states. I have stated forcefully and repeatedly that I am against any forced integration. I believe my feeling on this matter is the one you would expect to find in a man who has lived in the South all of his life, whose ancestors have lived in the South, and both of whose grandparents fought on the Confederate side in the War Between the States.[20]

The South immediately reciprocated Johnson's gesture of solidarity. Many of the South's most important national leaders quickly endorsed Johnson for the Democratic presidential nomination. A few weeks beforehand, Rayburn postponed consideration of the Powell-amended McClellan Bill until mid-March. The speaker's delay was, more than likely, to allow the manifesto to be promulgated first, and thus counter the momentum of the Powell Amendment. Rayburn also publicly launched his campaign to have the Texas State Democratic Convention nominate Lyndon Johnson for president as a "favorite son" candidate, a nomination which would give these two congressional leaders control of the Texas delegates to that summer's national convention in Chicago. Outside the Lone Star State, Russell led Johnson's campaign for southern support. The same day of the promulgation, Russell declared, "I will support Johnson 100 percent if he wants to run." Similarly, Daniel portrayed Johnson as a national statesman with "the greatest ability of any man in our party to bring dissenting factions together," because "he would be more than a sectional candidate" and claim support "in all sections of the country." Thurmond weighed in too. The Dixiecrat announced that Johnson would prove to be "an attractive candidate" in South Carolina.[21]

Johnson thus positioned himself directly in the middle of the civil rights/states' rights debate, between the northern and southern wings of the Democratic Party. As the key endorsements for president combined with Johnson's staunch advocacy of natural gas deregulation and state control of offshore oil deposits, the majority leader was the leading defender of both Texas's and southern states' interests. By not signing the manifesto, Johnson also projected himself as a national Democrat, a progressive who stood apart from white southern parochialism. The political leverage he acquired by not signing proved to be a powerful tool. According to Democratic U.S. Senator Hubert H. Humphrey of Minnesota, "When he'd get in an argument with Paul Douglas or Herbert Lehman or Estes Kefauver or any of these people that he thought he couldn't quite manage or that were resisting him," Johnson would "let them know." As Humphrey explained:

> Every so often he'd drop that little atom bomb; that when it was all said and done, "Boys you've got some boys over here that you're sleeping with day in and day out, like Bill Fulbright, but I wasn't there when they signed that Southern Manifesto. I said no, and your hero said yes. Now how do you justify that?" See, he'd put them on the defensive. He used these things. He was so adroit.[22]

In its final version, the Southern Manifesto appealed to intransigent and moderate segregationists alike. The former demonstrated their commitment to oppose implementation of *Brown*, question the legitimacy of the Supreme Court, and lead the interposition movement. Similarly, the latter who signed displayed their zeal for segregation but did not estrange their more progressive supporters because they promoted the perception that they were forced to sign for political reasons. Indeed, most observers concluded that by engaging in the drafting process, moderates vitiated a project with dangerous potential. Nonsigners also benefited in this regard. They were able to demonstrate to the nation that they were not staunch intransigents. They recognized the supremacy of the Supreme Court, but they were nonetheless sympathetic to white southerners.

By convincing the vast majority of their colleagues to sign, the authors of the Southern Manifesto ensured that the entire Southern Congressional Delegation was sufficiently committed to the preservation of segregation. These particular senators helped direct the interposition movement throughout the South. But the interposition movement also pushed them to act. Nearly every member of the Southern Congressional Delegation was motivated to seek some sort of regional response to desegregation in order to assure his self-preservation. The moderates' participation in the drafting process allowed the Southern Manifesto to be palpable to and beneficial for all the southern Democrats who signed. The statement provided unity and hence safety.

6. The Promulgation

On March 12, 1956, at 8:00 a.m., the Southern Congressional Delegation began their assault against *Brown v. Board of Education* (1954) and the Civil Rights Movement. At this time, Democratic United States Senator Spessard Holland of Florida appeared on NBC's *Today* show, where he explained to a nationwide audience the purpose of the forthcoming declaration. As Holland later told constituents, "After intensive study of the subject, and three moderating revisions of the original suggestion," he and his colleagues "felt that we should take a strong and united stand for it and thus appeal for understanding outside the South for avoidance of violence at home, and against any use of force in the implementation of the decision." Holland hoped "that the appeal to reason that the declaration contains will have a wholesome effect upon those who are not in sympathy with and have little, if any, understanding of southern racial problems."[1]

The Floridian's television appearance had its intended effect. A Rhode Island resident, for instance, informed Holland that his interview was "a credit to the South." He and the rest of the Southern Caucus also conveyed this message to their constituents back home. "What especially appealed to me," a Miami constituent informed Holland about his nationally televised interview, "was your laying down a middle-of-the-road program which will evoke sympathetic response, I am sure, for all of the Americans regardless of whether they are from the north or south, and tend to eliminate the lunatic fringe on both sides of this very explosive question."[2]

Three hours later that morning, the U.S. Senate opened in the Capitol. The Senate gallery was already packed with tourists who, together with an unusually large number of journalists, staffers, and senators' spouses, arrived early enough to gain admittance. On a workday typically given to mundane procedural business, the Senate was forced to consider some highly controversial matters that appeared on the day's docket. Included was the reading of two state resolutions: South Carolina's request that the U.S. attorney general place the National Association for the Advancement of Colored People (NAACP) on the list of subversive organizations, and Mississippi's recently passed interposition resolution. Senator Everett Dirksen of Illinois chose that morning, furthermore, to introduce the Republican civil rights bill (S. 3415), which would create a bipartisan congressional commission to study *Brown's* effects and make recommendations for its implementation. After these documents were read, the Senate's presiding officer, Vice President Richard M. Nixon, asked if there was any further business pending for consideration. As many senators were lingering in the cloakroom, Democratic Majority Leader Lyndon Baines Johnson of Texas requested that the chief clerk initiate a quorum call. Johnson's signal spurred most of the senators to quickly appear and sit down at their desks, so that the roll call halted before it was finished.

Because of Holland's opening strike, as well as the past week's incessant press coverage, everyone in the Senate chamber already knew what lay next on the docket. With the chamber now at full capacity, attention turned to the front row of senators' desks, where sat the president pro tempore, Walter George. At seventy-eight years old, the Georgia Democrat still ranked among the Senate's most notable orators. George slowly rose from his desk and began to speak without recognition by Nixon, showing to his audience that the forthcoming series of events was already planned. He began:

> Mr. President, the increasing gravity of the situation following the decision of the Supreme Court in the so-called segregation cases, and the peculiar stress in sections of the country where this decision has created many difficulties, unknown and unappreciated, perhaps, by many people residing in other parts of the country, have led some Senators and some Members of the House of Representatives to prepare a statement of the position which they have felt and now feel to be imperative.

When Nixon asked George if he needed more than the usual two minutes allotted under Senate rules, the courtly Georgian informed his audience that his address would be brief. Nonetheless, this "declaration has not been hastily taken," but "has been carefully considered for some 4 or 5 weeks." George's comments directed toward "proposed legislation now before the Senate" and "perhaps some other important legislative matters which may be immediately considered," clearly referred to both of the pending Republican and Democratic civil rights legislation. George's provocative preamble provoked uproar within the chamber, as the gallery droned with whispers while northern senators audibly grumbled on the floor. Republican Senate Minority Leader William Knowland of California hastily arose and called for order, prompting Nixon to gavel for silence.

George then began to read the statement of opposition to *Brown* promulgated by the former states of the Confederacy. The statement was formally labeled the Declaration of Constitutional Principles, but by then was already known by its nom de guerre, the Southern Manifesto. Capitol Hill's old-timers surely recognized the irony of George reading the South's *profert* against the federal judiciary, nineteen years after he led the Senate's defense of the Supreme Court against President Franklin Roosevelt's infamous "court-packing plan."[3]

After two minutes of reading, the elderly Georgian's slow steady cadence had finished but three of the opening paragraphs; he paused, out of breath. Sensing impending disruption, Johnson stood to request that George be allotted an additional three minutes. "Is there objections?" Nixon quickly asked, impetuously declaring, "The Chair hears none." Democratic Senator Herbert Lehman, however, used the interval to thrust himself into the complicit proceedings. Lehman informed his colleagues that he did not object to George's remarks; he only wanted to speak after the Georgian was finished. The interruption angered Johnson, for he and Lehman had spoken beforehand. "I have assured the Senator from New York twice, and I assure him the third time," the majority leader snapped, "that he will be recognized before the morning hour is over, insofar as I can assure him, and that he will be allowed to speak for as long as he may choose." Lehman thanked Johnson and sat back down in retreat, aware of the futility of challenging the scripted political theater.

Nixon then made certain that the South dominated that day's legislative stage. The vice president announced that "the Chair has received an additional request for recognition" after George finished. Accordingly, he recognized not Lehman, but Senator J. Strom Thurmond of South Carolina. Nixon also assured Lehman that the day was still early and that he would be allowed to speak before the end of the morning's business, though after Thurmond concluded his own remarks. George then continued from the place where he was "interrupted" and finished reading the final draft of the Southern Manifesto into the *Congressional Record*, which included the list of congressional members who endorsed the statement.

As George sat down, Thurmond upheld senatorial courtesy and offered to "yield, first, to the distinguished Senator from New York." Lehman accepted, but did not have a formal speech prepared. So, he announced that he simply sought to "recognize and respect the right of any Member of Congress, as any other citizen of our country, to hold and express such views as he may approve," but he did not want a "failure to make immediate reply to the proclamation" to mean an "acceptance of the views expressed therein." He was "wholly in disagreement" with the manifesto and "would have more to

6.1 United States Senator J. Strom Thurmond and Mrs. Jean Crouch Thurmond in their staged photograph distributed to journalists the weekend before the promulgation of the Southern Manifesto. Courtesy of the J. Strom Thurmond Institute.

say on this subject at an early date." The New Yorker yielded the floor back to Thurmond, who stood up to reiterate the standard segregationist arguments already encapsulated in the South's official statement. Thurmond offered nothing new but, as was his demeanor, was more acrimonious toward black civil rights workers themselves. He described the National Association for the Advancement of Colored People (NAACP), for instance, as a cast of "professional racist lawyers" that used their tax exempt status toward their ultimate goal of "the mixing of the races."[4]

Despite its lack of substance, Thurmond's addendum was the culmination of his efforts to establish the perception that he was the Southern Manifesto's originator and principal author. In an extensive interview to the Associated Press over the weekend, he related the narrative of the drafting process that placed him at the center of the project and, by implication, leader of the southern campaign against *Brown*. He also assured the American people that he supported South Carolina Democrats if they chose to bolt that summer's Chicago national convention and form another Dixiecrat Revolt. Thurmond consummated his propaganda campaign by distributing a photograph to the journalists present, which showed him dictating the statement to his wife, Jean Crouch. Appearing on the front pages of newspapers across the country, the picture implied that the Thurmonds were typing up the statement's final draft.[5]

Thurmond was obsessed with the idea that he alone was the great champion of Jim Crow. The news magazine *Time* recognized the Thurmonds' phony picture as merely a publicity stunt, and reported that when the Dixiecrat's initial "arm-waving call for nullification" was presented on February 8, the Southern Caucus "pushed Thurmond aside, ordered the paper rewritten by more temperate Senators," and rightly identified Democratic Senator Richard B. Russell of Georgia as the principal author. Incensed, Thurmond informed the editor that "the word nullification was not in the draft I presented," and disingenuously claimed that "there was no such implication" therein. He repeated the mendacity that he had "served on the final drafting committee at the request of Senator George, who acted as chairman of the caucus." The damage control succeeded; his personally manipulated narrative of the drafting process is still widely accepted by both scholars and the general public. Thurmond should not be given undue credit, though, for the worst episode of racial demagoguery in modern American political history.[6]

After the loquacious Thurmond finished speaking, the Senate's civil rights advocates came to the support of the retreated Lehman. Next recognized by Nixon, Senator Wayne Morse of Oregon agreed with George that "the hour is indeed historic," but proclaimed that the Senate was considering a different "great constitutional question," which was "whether or not there was to be equality of justice for all Americans, irrespective of race, color, or creed." Morse refuted the South's criticism toward the federal judiciary: "A unanimous Supreme Court, which includes in its membership men with the tradition of the South in their veins, has at long last declared that all Americans are equal, and that the flame of justice in America must burn as brightly in the homes of the blacks as in the homes of the whites." He dismissed gradualism, for "the South has had all the time since the War Between the States to make this adjustment.

"How much more time is needed," Morse asked, "in order that equality of justice may be applied to the blacks as well as to the whites in America?" The Southern Manifesto was only a clandestine endorsement of interposition, which "means nothing but nullification," said Morse, "and a determination" by white southerners "to put themselves above the Supreme Court and above the Constitution." He alleged that the statement's thesis was disingenuous. "If the gentlemen from the South really want to take such action," the Oregon Independent challenged, "let them propose a constitutional amendment that will deny to the colored people of the country equality of rights under the Constitution, and see how far they will get with the American people." Morse concluded, "You would think Calhoun was walking and speaking on the floor of the Senate." To which, in the Senate gallery, George's wife, Lucy Heard,

6.2 Memphis *Commercial Appeal*, March 14, 1956, p. 14. Courtesy of the *Commercial Appeal*.

leaned over to Jean Crouch and explained that the comparison to the antebellum statesman was the utmost compliment.[7]

Democrats Hubert H. Humphrey of Minnesota and Richard Neuberger of Oregon followed Morse. They agreed that the manifesto endorsed interposition and thus nullification, but also stressed that opposition to *Brown* was detrimental for American attempts to win allies in the Cold War. Humphrey especially defended *Brown II*, asserting that its timetable for implementation was "an order based upon reason, knowledge, and understanding." Their speeches included the sycophantic references to Johnson typical from Senate Democrats (the majority leader picked up a number of key presidential endorsements from his colleagues in the coming weeks). Most notably, Neuberger proclaimed that Johnson's abstention from signing the manifesto was "one of the most courageous political acts of valor I have seen take place in my adult life." The Texan "deserves credit and commendation for a political act of the highest bravery and the highest courage."[8]

On the other side of Capitol Hill, the House of Representatives opened at high noon, just as the promulgation was concluded in the Senate. In the lower house, the powerful head of the Rules Committee, Democrat Howard Smith of Virginia, read the Southern Manifesto into the *Congressional Record.* Smith enjoyed a much smaller audience than his counterparts in the Southern Caucus, as the media's attention was focused almost exclusively upon the Senate. Still, as the acknowledged southern leader in the House and cosponsor of the pending Kelly Bill (HR 3305), the Virginian stood at the forefront of congressional efforts to subvert *Brown.* "In the life of a nation there come times," Smith said, employing the rhetoric of interposition in his own preamble, "when it behooves her people to pause and consider how far she may have drifted from her moorings, and in prayerful contemplation review the consequenc-

6.3 Democratic United States Representative Howard W. Smith of Virginia. Oil on canvas, Victor Lallier, 1961, collection of the U.S. House of Representatives.

es that may ensue from a continued deviation from the course chartered by the founders of that nation." "The temporary occupants of high office of the judicial branch deviate from the limitations imposed by the Constitution," he charged, were "reversing long established and accepted law," and made decisions "based on expediency at the sacrifice of consistency."[9]

When asked about the Southern Manifesto, the Eisenhower administration initially said there would be no comment from the president. But, as there was already a news conference scheduled for that Wednesday, March 14, Ike would surely be pressed by journalists on civil rights. For White House Executive Assistant E. Frederic Morrow, the manifesto would only "add fuel to the already raging fires, and reporters can bombard the President with questions as to his attitude." Accordingly, the White House executive staff met that morning to prepare his notes for the press conference. Morrow's colleague, Jerry Persons, lightened the mood of the otherwise intense discussion with the wisecrack that, after reading the manifesto, he thought the statement "did not seem too bad, for Alabama!"

In the 1956 election year, Ike's staff pushed a moderate response to the Southern Manifesto. They recommended that the president acknowledge the right of members of Congress to make pronouncements and, as chief executive, he did not want to interfere with another branch of government. He should avoid refuting the constitutional arguments made in the statement and, most importantly, imply that *Brown* would not be enforced with federal troops. As he stood for reelection, therefore, recalcitrant southern state and local officials could just ignore *Brown* indefinitely, without fear of federal intervention or punition.[10]

At his press conference, held in the Executive Office Building next to the White House, Ike heeded counsel. Standing before reporters amidst the gilded opulence of the Indian Treaty Room on the third floor (which reporters dubbed the Cupid Room for its four winged cherubs that each adorn a corner of the room), the president defended the manifesto's thesis. "They say they are going to use every legal means. No one in any responsible position has talked nullification," he reminded journalists. The commander in chief dismissed the idea that southerners had called upon their constituents to defy the federal judiciary. "I don't believe they expressed their defiance," Ike declared. "I believe they expressed their belief that it was in error, and they talked about using legal means to circumvent or get it, whatever the expression they have used." He maintained that gradual desegregation was working: "More than a quarter of a million Negro children in the border and some Southern states have been integrated in the schools, and except for certain areas in which the difficulties are greatest, there has been some progress." "The people who have this deep emotional reaction on the other side were not acting over these past three generations in defiance of the law," he said, talking past reporters' interruptions, "they were acting in compliance with the law as interpreted by the Supreme Court of the United States under the decisions of 1896." For Ike, "Now that has been completely reversed, and it is going to take time for them to adjust."

On other civil rights issues, the president stayed the course. When asked about the Montgomery Bus Boycott and the arrest of Dr. Martin Luther King, Jr., Ike called for "the South to show some progress," but also asked Americans for "understanding, for really sympathetic consideration of a problem that is far larger, both in its emotional and even in its physical aspects than most of us realize." "Let's don't try to think of this as a tremendous fight that is going to separate Americans and get ourselves in a nasty mess," he recommended. "Let's try to think of it of how can we make progress and keep it going and not stop it." Ike dismissed the proposal to host a meeting of black and white leaders to discuss *Brown*. He instead referred back to his State of the Union proposal that had since evolved into the Dirksen Bill. A temporary bipartisan congressional commission would prove more effective because it would possess subpoena power and make specific recommendations for *Brown*'s implementation. The president refused to comment on the Powell Amendment to the Kelly Bill, maintaining that he would not interfere with another branch of government. Democratic U.S. Representative Adam Clayton Powell, Jr., of New York had previously announced that if the president would restrict federal funds from school districts that openly defied *Brown*, he would withdraw his amendment from consideration. Ike, therefore, tacitly assured the South that he was not likely going to adopt such a policy.

Ike's response to the manifesto showed in other ways too. At the full cabinet meeting of March 23, Attorney General Herbert Brownell introduced for discussion the administration's complete civil rights legislative package to be introduced to Congress. The legislation did not deal with desegregation, only with extending federal jurisdiction to secure voting rights for individual citizens. Gauging the topic's unpopularity with those in the room, Brownell offered a tepid introduction for the legislation. Almost unanimously, the cabinet opposed the bill. They argued that such provisions would only further antagonize the South and usurp Dirksen's bill. Presiding over the meeting personally, Ike acknowledged the deep hostility of white southerners to any mention of federal coercion, but he agreed with Brownell that there was no other way to give him the authority to enforce the law and protect black southerners' right to vote. With nearly his entire cabinet in opposition, Ike dropped the matter and moved on, telling Brownell that they would discuss the bill later in private.[11]

For the rest of Ike's first term in office, his administration worked outside official channels to find a modicum of compliance with *Brown*. A few weeks later, Brownell gave the keynote address to the annual convention of the states' attorneys general in Phoenix, Arizona. After his speech, Brownell quietly summoned the southern generals to his hotel suite for a private off-the-record meeting. There, at midnight, Brownell appealed to their sense of duty as fellow law enforcement officers to get their states to comply with *Brown*. The southerners unanimously protested, claiming it was politically impossible to take any steps toward compliance.

The meeting convinced Brownell that the only way left open to implement *Brown* was through the federal courts. Afterward, he sought to appoint sympathetic judges in southern districts "who would uphold the Constitution and who had not publicly opposed the desegregation decision." Such jurists, however, were approved by a U.S. Senate controlled by the Southern Caucus, particularly Judiciary Chairman James Oliver Eastland of Mississippi. Even if they got to the federal bench, the judges would rule on individual suits from thousands of school districts, a scenario both intransigent and moderate segregationists already envisioned.[12]

The front-runner for the Democratic presidential nomination, Adlai Stevenson, followed Ike's lead on the Southern Manifesto. Stevenson said that he did "not agree" with the statement "that the Supreme Court exceeded its authority in its rulings on school segregation," but still defended the signatories as "distinguished, responsible leaders of a great region of our country," whose actions were "a reflection of the gravity of the racial tensions that have arisen" therein. "It is very important to recognize" the former Illinois governor said, "that these Southern leaders urge that violence and extreme measures be avoided" to rectify the situation.[13]

Despite Ike's and Stevenson's attempts to diminish the Southern Manifesto's impact, most observers thought that the promulgation initiated the national debate on civil rights and irrevocably divided the Democratic Party in the 1956 elections. In this perspective, the statement forced southern moderates to endorse interposition and, in turn, made northern Democrats vulnerable to charges that they were not strong enough for civil rights initiatives. Congressional candidates now had to promote either interposition or civil rights in their campaigns, lest they lose their seats. An internecine fight at the Democratic National Convention in Chicago and another southern walkout were now inevitable. The election would certainly be thrown into the House of Representatives, where the South possessed inordinate influence. On both sides of Mason and Dixon's Line, *Newsweek* concluded, "a Democrat who counsels moderation is risking his political life."[14]

As everyone understood that the manifesto was designed to prevent Democrats from formally endorsing *Brown* in their party platform, northern Democrats disparaged the Southern Congressional Delegation for crippling Stevenson's campaign. The pundit Thomas L. Stokes charged that thereafter, "a contest for the Democratic Presidential nomination seemed a somewhat futile activity. For what can that nomination be worth with the party more hopelessly split asunder than in nearly 100 years, and a substantial part of the party in defiance of the law?" Democrats thus had to embrace a strong civil rights agenda and cease to placate their party's geographic base. Describing the manifesto as a "declaration of war" and a "non-emancipation proclamation," the *New York Post* rebuked Johnson's leadership, for his "formula has simply meant surrender of liberal principle to the dictates of the Southern wing."[15]

Civil rights advocates in particular recognized that the promulgation gave the Southern Congressional Delegation the means to prevent both civil rights legislation and *Brown's* full-scale implementation. According to the historian C. Vann Woodward (who helped draft the plaintiff's brief in *Brown*), "The South now possesses formidable weapons of resistance," most notably a "hundred representatives in Congress" who exert a "powerful voice in one of the major political parties and can no longer be ignored by the other." "Gradualism," for Woodward was "the approved approach," but "that definition has been just as clearly rejected by responsible spokespersons of millions of our people." "Little wonder," he concluded, that "the optimism of 1954 has given way to the prevailing pessimism of 1956." In this new reality, NAACP lead counsel Thurgood Marshall announced that he would devote his entire $250,000 yearly budget to bring suit against every school district in the South. "Sure, it'll take time," Marshall admitted. "It's a step by step business," he explained. "Yet get segregated counties circled, little by little," he predicted, "and sooner or later they fall of their own weight. We'll win in the end."[16]

Most Americans shared the view that *Brown* was now protracted in the federal courts, but many also sympathized with the Southern Manifesto. These Americans respected the statement's call for legal redress, peaceful resistance, and near unanimous endorsement by the Southern Congressional Delegation. "The document, while sharp in its criticism of the court, is otherwise moderate in tone in that it calls for a damper on outright rebellion and defiance," opined the *Christian Science Monitor.* "Nearly everywhere there is advocacy of patience and gradualism." In a lengthy critique of *Brown* in the *New York Times*, the Princeton law professor Alpheus T. Mason commended the Southern Manifesto, for it "at the very least, is calculated to give the Court and the country pause." According to the *Wall Street Journal*, the Southern Manifesto employed language that "was not inflammatory; there was a tone of restraint throughout and a cautious admonition to extremists on both sides of the segregation question."[17]

Some political observers, however, refuted the idea that by participating, southern moderates vitiated a potentially dangerous statement. Rather, they predicted that their participation would have the opposite effect. The influential Carey McWilliams of the *Nation* argued that the "gallused demagogues of the South were delighted with the Manifesto; it provides official sanction for their rough stuff." "It will aggravate tensions. It may well lead to violence.

IS CONGRESS DISSEMBLED?

And it will encourage evasion if not outright defiance of the Supreme Court's decision," McWilliams presciently predicted, "for obviously there is no lawful way to disobey the law." In this perspective, moderate signatories had lost any measure of credibility with civil rights advocates. According to the *New Republic*, black southerners "will not object to 'going slow' once there is agreement in the South that the Court's decision will prevail." Meanwhile, "the objective itself is repudiated, not only by extremists but by all the beleaguered moderates in Congress" who signed. For Marshall, the lines were now irrevocably drawn, "between two extremist groups—the White Citizens Councils, the Klan, the signers of the Manifesto, all of those are on one side—and on the other side you have the Constitution of the United States, the NAACP and other organizations that believe in it."[18]

Many observers from outside the South thought that the Southern Manifesto possessed little substance. According to Peter Edson of the *Washington News*, the manifesto was sufficiently "toned down" by southern moderates, and thus "not being taken too seriously here in Washington," as it was simply a "campaign document issued largely for home consumption in the South."

The statement was directed straight toward the Stevenson campaign, but its language, Edson noted, did not completely estrange northern Democrats, who were convinced that if southern incumbents were defeated, "they would be replaced by extreme reactionaries" in the next Congress. Mistakenly, the legal scholar Alexander Bikel believed "the negotiated ambivalence and the euphemisms" encapsulated in the statement were "supported by a legal argument so naïve that it is difficult to charge the able and experienced lawyers among the signers with genuine confidence in it." For the pundit Gerald Johnson, the statement was beset by a "superficial aspect" that "bears some resemblance to the famous bill introduced by a legislator of the last generation which provided that in the state of Missouri the value of *pi* should be 3, instead of the conventional, but inconvenient, 3.1416."[19]

The Southern Congressional Delegation nevertheless employed the Southern Manifesto as a pliant political tool. The signatories immediately sought to control the statement's public image and, in turn, lead the interposition movement. They quickly issued press releases to distribute the statement throughout their states and districts, used the manifesto as the bases of their reelection campaigns, and traveled widely to promote resistance to desegregation. The signatories proclaimed that not only were they now united to fight against desegregation, but they also had articulated the South's position to other parts of the United States, thereby gaining allies to reverse *Brown*. As Democratic Senator Allen Ellender of Louisiana informed his constituents, the manifesto "served notice that the people of the South, both white and negro are not going to be used as either political whipping boys or political pawns in order to fulfill the Supreme Court's new doctrine of sociological justice." For Democratic Senator Sam Ervin of North Carolina, the signatories "formed a solid phalanx, and have shown that serious, conservative level headed Southerners—not just a hot-headed few—are opposing the court's decision in a cool, deliberate manner." From Washington, D.C., Russell bragged that "many Northern Democrats here are completely angry and somewhat stunned" by the statement. "I am of the opinion," the Georgian observed, "that they are likewise afraid of what may happen."[20]

With the Southern Manifesto, the signatories reestablished their hegemony over Dixie's politics. The white South, that is, interpreted the statement in much the same way as the rest of the nation, but from its own perspective. By and large, white southerners believed that the statement strengthened their position in the upcoming presidential election. They now could block both *Brown* and pending federal civil rights legislation. Many also stressed the statement's moderate tone that would restrain both Democrats and Republicans on civil rights. In contrast to most other Americans, however, white southerners perceived the statement as a victory for constitutional law rather than an ignominious defeat.

Most of the white southern press corps adored the Southern Manifesto. The *Atlanta Journal* described the statement as "a reasoned and carefully considered document," while the *Nashville Banner* claimed that the manifesto "effectively, eloquently, diagnoses the record which it indicts. It does not appeal to emotions or to prejudices, but to the law." According to the Memphis *Commercial Appeal*, the statement "epitomized the South's solidarity and its determination to resist the usurpation of legislative prerogatives by the judiciary." For *The South*, an industrial trade magazine, "never had a more forceful statement against the judicial branch been issued by any comparable group." The *Pine Bluff Commercial* predicted that the manifesto would be "recognized by civil rights champions as a sincere expression of a democratic privilege to question the constitutionality of a court opinion." North Carolina's *Lumberton Post* asserted that the congressmen "who signed it as true-blooded Southerners should," were to be congratulated. In sum, John Temple Graves II of the *Birmingham News* observed, "The total of Southern respectability, power, range and long-standing has not been matched since the Confederacy."[21]

Most of the white South's professional class loved the Southern Manifesto. Civic groups passed supporting resolutions, while businessmen, educators, lawyers, and physicians wrote to their congressmen en masse to express approval. For instance, the Albert Pike Chapter of the United Daughters of the Confederacy of Texarkana, Texas, "voted unanimously to express commendation to the senators and congressmen who took a stand for segregation and against integration." Staunch praise also came from businessmen, particularly the South's great industrialists. "The statement is couched in language to which no one can object, except those responsible for creating the reprehensible conditions," said E. J. McMillen, president of the powerful Southern States Industrial Council. Thereafter "the South is unanimous, except for a few dissidents, in its love for those fundamental rights and liberties so clearly enunciated in the Constitution." Educators were especially thankful that they did not have to enact desegregation in the upcoming fall semester. As the superintendent of public schools in Vicksburg, Mississippi, predicted, "The country will be impressed by this historic document," which "has done more to awaken the country to the crisis precipitated by the ill-advised Supreme Court Decision than anything that has happened." Southern lawyers roundly supported the manifesto too, but they generally failed to comment on the statement's legality. The best counsel that Mississippi attorney J. G. Colson could offer his senior Democratic U.S. senator, John Stennis, was "that when the stalwart and majestic pines are removed from our lands, the scrub oaks take over. We must not let that happen to our race." Similarly, the physician Dr. Frank S. Littlejohn asserted in a congratulatory circular letter to the signatories that desegregation was "the most important question before the people today. The less segregation you have the more miscegenation you have with a Negroid nation in the offing. God deliver us from such a calamity."[22]

The Southern Congressional Delegation in general and the Southern Manifesto's drafting committee in particular reaped widespread political support from the promulgation. The Chicago financier Charles H. Schwab II thanked Russell for the "fine, courageous stand against the Supreme Court's stand on integration." Schwab was "in full accord with the Southern point of view regarding segregation!" He asked Russell to continue the "good work and save America for Americans! God Bless You!" Similarly, Ervin's role on the drafting committee catapulted him to widespread fame as the Congress's foremost expert on constitutional law. He also gained strong support within North Carolina as he stood for election later that year. According to the *Asheville Citizen-Times*, "Ervin has been given the recognition which most frequently comes to Senators, if at all, after they have been seasoned by long experience." His role on the drafting committee was "a cause of gratification to Tar Heels regardless of partisan politics." Likewise, a resident of the Mississippi Delta told Stennis that his role on the drafting committee "has brought forth much favorable comment locally," as the manifesto was "one of the finest statements I ever read. You and your committee are to be congratulated for drafting such an instrument."[23]

The signatories also secured the loyalty of the Citizens' Councils. The chairman of a South Carolina council informed U.S. Senator Olin D. Johnston that his chapter was "one hundred per cent for your manifesto," and was "with you, for you, and will back you in all your undertakings." Intransigent segregationists saw the Southern Manifesto as a product of their influence; their political pressure, moreover, had encouraged southern moderates to endorse the statement. As Georgia's Roy V. Harris claimed in his *Augusta Courier*, "Formation of these councils, the activities of white citizens throughout the South, the thumping vote in Virginia and the running of Autherine Lucy out of the University of Alabama have caused these pussy footers to wake up." The statement did not mention interposition per se, but intransigents viewed the statement as an endorsement of their cause. "Now," Harris maintained, signers "agree with us" that "the Supreme Court decisions are illegal and they are not binding on any citizen of this country." The manifesto, however, was just the start of Massive Resistance. The head of the Louisiana Citizens'

Councils, Democratic state Senator Willie Rainach of Shreveport, informed his congressional delegation that "the people are organizing from the grass roots to the skyscrapers throughout the South. We are confident that within a relatively short period we will be in position to take our case to the nation and win it on its merits."

According to plan, the weekend after the promulgation some ten thousand people gathered in New Orleans at a segregationist rally, with Harris and Georgia Attorney General Eugene Cook as the keynote speakers. The Georgians called upon their audience to halt the desegregation of their state, warning them that the national political parties, President Eisenhower, and the media all sought to destroy the southern way of life. Two months later, Georgia Governor Marvin Griffin also came to the Crescent City to lead a segregationist parade of some four thousand people along Canal Street that ended with a rally at Pelican Stadium. Louisiana soon became the sixth state to adopt interposition.[24]

In contrast, members of the Southern Congressional Delegation who did not endorse the Southern Manifesto faced harsh criticism. A Nashville constituent told Democratic Senator Albert Gore, Sr., of Tennessee that by not signing he was aligned "with the Communist infiltrated NAACP," as well as "the Carpet-baggers" and "the brain washed do-gooders." Gore's critics charged that as most Tennesseans favored his signature, his decision did not reflect the will of the people. As such, numerous civic groups passed resolutions urging Gore to either endorse the statement or be defeated in the next election. As a friend warned him, "This is the most important issue of your life," for "it can make or break you."[25]

Gore answered his critics. "Do you seriously suggest," he rhetorically asked, "that I, as a United States Senator, sign and endorse a political statement which I seriously believe to be unsound and unwise, merely for the sake of political expediency?" "At the time I was called upon to make this decision," he explained, "not one single citizen from Tennessee had communicated to me his or her sentiments with respect thereto. In fact, so far as I was advised, not one of the more than three million people in Tennessee had read the contents of the statement or knew of its existence." Gore told constituents that the manifesto was "preposterous," and "more calculated to worsen than to improve an already delicate and dangerous situation," annoyed as the incessant solicitation for him to reconsider continued for months. "Frankly, I do not know where the document is at this time," he admitted later that year. "The time to sign it, or not sign it, was then," he explained, "it is as dead now as last year's newspaper." As future electoral victories proved, Gore had followed both his senior senator and governor's lead and successfully navigated the treacherous political issue of Tennessee desegregation.[26]

Johnson also faced criticism, but events soon proved that he too made the right move by not endorsing the manifesto. After his decision to not sign became known, vigilantes burned a cross outside his ranch in the Texas hill country. More legitimately, however, Johnson's foremost rival for control of the Texas Democracy, Governor Allan Shivers, charged that Johnson's neglect to sign the statement prohibited him from heading the Texas delegation to the Democratic National Convention. "Let me make clear that no criticism of Senator Johnson is implied because he did not sign the 'Southern Manifesto' on interposition," the governor mocked. "His position and duties as Senate Majority Leader made it undesirable for him to become involved in a controversy at Washington." Despite his vitriol, however, Shivers neither played a prominent role in Washington, D.C., nor, as was proven later that summer, did he lead Texas Democrats. In the 1956 election year, Shivercrats were not powerful enough to sway Johnson (or the other Texas congressmen who refused) to endorse either the Southern Manifesto or interposition.[27]

While most of the country predicted that the Southern Manifesto would inevitably produce another Dixiecrat Revolt, the Southern Caucus had successfully designed the statement to keep the South within the Democratic Party. Most southern leaders, therefore, worked diligently in the coming weeks to discourage any speculation about another walkout in Chicago. Many state officials (including most of those who had adopted interposition) quickly dismissed the threat, seeing the logic behind Russell's strategy. "Public sentiment will not be strong enough until after the August conventions," explained Fielding Wright, "which will be too late." The former Mississippi governor (who had served as Thurmond's vice presidential running mate on the 1948 Dixiecrat ticket) still believed, however, that "realignment of the political parties is badly needed; we need a conservative party and a liberal party."[28]

Although most of the white South opposed another revolt, Thurmond remained undeterred. Encouraged by his successful manipulation of the press, Thurmond fueled speculation that he would lead another walkout. He called upon each southern state to send delegations to Chicago that either pledged to a favorite son candidate or to no specific candidate at all, thus holding open as much freedom of action as possible at the convention. That Thurmond had already mentioned Johnson's name as a potential nominee of the South only added further credence to the majority leader's candidacy. So that neither the Democrats' presidential candidate nor their platform endorsed *Brown*, Thurmond asked southern Democrats to hold second state conventions after returning from Chicago, thereby leaving open the threat of another southern party. His machinations did much to disrupt Democratic harmony, as northerners confronted the possibility that another southern walkout would not only produce Eisenhower's cakewalk reelection, but also their likely defeat as well as the loss of Congress if their party disintegrated over civil rights.[29]

Thurmond's lieutenants fought the Lost Cause. At their state convention in Columbia on March 21, South Carolina Democrats adopted a resolution to recess, rather than adjourn, until after the national convention, and then to reconvene to determine their course of action for the November election. Democratic Governor George Bell Timmerman, Jr., amended the resolution so that it also called on the state parties of the former Confederacy to meet prior to the national convention in order to determine a unified course of action.[30]

Despite the white South's overwhelming support for the Southern Manifesto, there was a small but vocal voice of indigenous dissent. From various angles, these critics denounced both the statement's thesis and its promulgation. A few intransigents, for instance, thought the manifesto did not go far enough. A Louisiana councilor told his congressional delegation that while he was "heartily in accord with the idea of resorting to only legal means to enforce our Southern traditions," he warned that "things might get out of hand if non-segregation for our schools is to come." Still others accused the Southern Caucus of just passing the buck for electoral advantage. A Texan pointed out that of the sixteen signers who served in the Senate at the time of Chief Justice Earl Warren's appointment, none voted against his confirmation. The manifesto, he believed, was merely "attempting to shift the blame," for "neither the judiciary nor the executive branches of government would usurp unauthorized powers if the Senate did not abdicate its own Constitutional rights and duties." Other critics believed that the statement departed from the moderate course. From the Arkansas Ozarks, the *Baxter Bulletin* praised *Brown II* and disagreed that desegregation would cause "anarchy" in communities. Still, "extreme caution is required. Politicians should consider their statements carefully, and Negro leaders shouldn't be too eager to expedite compliance with the court decree." Some, though, condemned outright the statement's anachronistic constitutional arguments. The *Raleigh Times* (one of the very few white southern newspapers to formally denounce the manifesto) described the statement as "a pathetic document." The federal Constitution did not mention "highways, hospitals, flood control, hurricanes, hydroelectric dams, crop supports or Social Security. Yet we haven't noticed Southern congressmen up in arms over these projects." A few white southerners even based their criticisms upon a direct concern for the civil rights of their black neighbors. "Mrs. Comer and I are both white, by accident of birth," Gilbert M. Comer of Parks, Arkansas, informed his junior senator, J. William Fulbright, "but we love all people regardless of race. We can see no reason for your action, other than vote counting." Likewise, another southern magazine editor defended *Brown* as the correct interpretation of the Fourteenth Amendment because "citizens black or white or any other color must have an even start so far as it is possible for the Government to provide it." For this editor, the Southern Congressional Delegation's defense of *Plessy* was disingenuous. "They pretend great regard for the Founding Fathers," he charged, "but shout bloody murder when the Supreme Court moves to put the ideas of the Fathers into practice in today's world."[31]

Amidst white southerners, the strongest criticism of the Southern Manifesto came from self-identified Christians. Those self-identified white Christians who may have supported the promulgation, conversely, generally failed to offer their support to the Southern Caucus or invoke scripture to condemn *Brown*. White southern Christians generally sympathized with the directive of *Brown II*, but believed that the promulgation ended any promise of peaceful and gradual implementation. The dean of Southern Baptist College in Arkansas, John Steely, was proud of the efforts toward compliance in his state, but "it is extremely disappointing to learn that our elected representatives

6.6 John Steely, dean of Southern Bap-   6.7 Reverend Donald Campbell. Cour-
tist College. Courtesy of Williams Baptist   tesy of the Presbyterian Church of
College.   Crossett.

in Washington have not kept up with us and appear not to intend to keep up. We would have expected leadership rather than hindrance." Another Arkansawyer, the Presbyterian minister Rev. Donald K. Campbell, condemned the Southern Manifesto for emphasizing precedent over morality. "The only standard I have for knowing right from wrong is Jesus Christ," he informed Fulbright, "who was blind to racial differences, and whose Apostle said that the 'dividing wall' between races was broken down in Him." Campbell condemned *Plessy v. Ferguson* (1896) for being "based not upon the teachings of Christ but upon public opinion in the 1890's. I see nothing sacrosanct about a decision which was inherently evil."[32]

The South's white Christians routinely reminded their congressmen that the vast majority of their denominations had already gone on record supporting desegregation. Another Arkansas Presbyterian minister, W. W. Johnson, admitted that "the Church has been more of a vehicle of the traditions of the South than the mandate of Scripture, but we know we're wrong and don't try to justify our sin with any Manifesto." Similarly, a Louisiana priest defended his archbishop's desegregation edict as he chastised U.S. Representative Hale Boggs for his signature. "It behooves all good Catholics," he reminded Boggs, "soldiers of Christ by the sacrament of confirmation, to stand behind him. True it is hard to shed prejudice acquired in childhood, but a true soldier may not evade hardships."[33]

Like the manifesto's critics in the Senate's Civil Rights Caucus, some white southerners denounced the statement as detrimental to American efforts in the Cold War. A constituent informed Holland that the "Communists are gleefully, and unfortunately, with much success, returning to their original line, that capitalism, colonialism, and color bars are inseparable." For this Floridian, "our statement of the issue as a free world versus communism is false because we do not grant freedom to our colored community." "Should we not take into account," he rhetorically asked, "that, except for the Boers in South Africa, our forced school segregation is weakening our international position throughout the World." Similarly, a Virginian informed her junior Democratic U.S. Senator, A. Willis Robertson, that her first experience with southern hospitality after moving to the Old Dominion thirty years before "was an occasion when a southern white man kicked a colored man in the face for asking him for a match." "The real issue," she informed Robertson, was "whether men shall have equal dignity, whether they can mix socially with courtesy and respect, or whether a white minority of decadent colonialism shall have the special privileges, making a farce of Christianity and democracy."

The self-identified progressives of the white South were also disappointed by the Southern Manifesto, but they were not alienated from voting for the signatories or supporting their other policy concerns. "We of our state who stay in the vanguard of progress for social justice, have to count on you in Washington for leadership in such high causes, as we have no one else to turn to," an Arkansas Methodist minister's wife from Hot Springs told Fulbright. Likewise, an El Dorado woman condemned Fulbright's signature because "segregation is against Christian principles." Nonetheless, she and her kind "cannot afford to have you defeated in the coming election. We do not feel that you are an extremist on this issue and you are very much needed in the place you are now serving." They asked southern moderates to return to the fold. As a Little Rock Methodist minister warned Fulbright, "If people of your reputation and magnitude take a regressive, defeatist stand, our schools and state will be left in the hands of unprincipled opportunists." Holland even gained support for his supposed amelioration of the committee draft. A Sarasota woman commended Holland for "the action you took in preventing the publishing of an inflammatory document."[34]

The Southern Caucus initially responded to the Christian-based criticism by evoking the principles of the separation of church and state and a strict construction of the Constitution. "It is obvious that our views diverge," Ervin's standard reply to such criticism asserted, "because you think that the Constitution of the United States ought to be interpreted to conform to the precepts of religion while I think it ought to be interpreted to conform with the principles of Constitutional law." Such explanations, however, failed to satisfy the devout, who saw no difference between legal principles and religious duty. As a constituent informed Democratic U.S. Senator John L. McClellan of Arkansas, "Segregation is basically a moral question growing out of our belief in God as we have him revealed to us through our Judae-Christian heritage." When pressed with this moral appeal, the Southern Caucus emphasized the statement's call for nonviolent legal redress. Fulbright explained that the manifesto was "a moderate statement, somewhere between the two extremes advocating nullification on the one hand and the use of troops to enforce the decision on the other." According to Holland, the statement would appeal to nonsoutherners through its "moderate but firm tone," its insistence upon "law and order," as well as "patience and time" as opposed to the "too aggressive and inflammatory tendencies of the NAACP." For these moderate signatories, the statement only reflected the emerging national consensus that abhorred the prospect of federal troops enforcing *Brown*, and would help prevent the destruction of the public school system in the South.

Nonetheless, as a consequence of the incessant religiously inspired constituent criticism, southern moderates grudgingly recognized the moral imperative of desegregation and the extension of first-class citizenship to black southerners. "I do not disagree with you as to what will be the ultimate and final development in this field," Fulbright wrote in response to yet another appeal to his moral conscience, "but I do disagree with you as to the best means to move in this direction." After this barrage of condemnation by white southern Christians, that is, most moderate signatories understood that they erred on the wrong side of history.[35]

Similarly, some black southerners expressed displeasure with the manifesto but nevertheless offered their continued support to moderates within the Southern Congressional Delegation and the national Democratic Party. When Democratic U.S. Representative Brooks Hays of Arkansas began his primary campaign that year, he met with a group of forty black ministers in Little Rock. On this occasion, most of the ministers (who had previously viewed Hays as an ally) chastised him for his signature. Hays explained to them that his decision was based upon political expediencies and asked their forgiveness, quoting the apostle Paul to "let your moderation be known to all men." Hays and the ministers departed amicably, as one of the ministers said that he simply would tell his congregation, "I've seen you slip before and then get back on the right track."[36]

Most African Americans, however, expressed outright condemnation toward the manifesto. Memphis's black oriented *Tri-State Defender*, for instance, declared that the signatories "no longer have any usefulness as legislators," and were "so blind with racial prejudice and hatred that they cannot consider any proposed piece of legislation with the balance required of a lawmaker." The manifesto was a "brazen announcement of their traitorous intentions" and a "blow to American prestige." In this perspective, black voters should abandon the Democrats and support Eisenhower for reelection. Before a predominantly black audience in Chicago on April 11, NAACP Executive Secretary Roy Wilkins charged that, combined with Eastland's appointment as Senate Judiciary Chairman, the manifesto should be sufficient cause for African Americans to abandon the Democrats. "Up here we can strike a blow in defense of our brothers in the South," Wilkins asserted, "if necessary by swapping the known devil for the suspected witch. It could be that the witch, if freed of the political necessity of teaming up with the devil, just might do better by us. Certainly, with Eastland on our necks, and with every southern politician yelling that we won't get our rights until doomsday, we cannot be any worse off than we are now." In contrast, the black journalist James L. Hicks argued that instead of employing Wilkins's strategy, northern Democrats should rather call the Southern Congressional Delegation's bluff and dare them to walk. "When you look at it closely," he exclaimed, "this 'manifesto' turns out to be the dumbest move we have ever seen smart people make." "Where will they go?" Hicks rhetorically asked, among the very few nonsoutherners who perceived that the interests of the white South were best served within the Democracy. "They'll tuck their tails and go crawling back to the Democratic Party where their bread is buttered by the powerful committees they head in the Congress." The *Chicago Defender* proclaimed that the signatories in particular should be subjected to ethnic cleansing. "By removing them from general society to the company of their own kind," the newspaper asserted, "the highest form of segregation would be achieved."[37]

Like their intransigent antagonists, African Americans immediately worked to define the Southern Manifesto's political ramifications. For example, black Texans in general and the NAACP in particular were arguably the decisive factor in Johnson and Rayburn's defeat of Shivers for control of the Texas Democrats. Two days after the promulgation, the NAACP's Houston chapter announced that it would lead a boycott of Alan Shivers's speech at the upcoming inaugural of the new president at historically black Texas Southern University. According to the chapter's leader, Francis I. Williams, they protested "the choice of Gov. Shivers as the inaugural speaker because he is an avowed enemy of integration." Addressing the NAACP's Texas state convention soon afterward, Washington Bureau Chief Clarence Mitchell asserted that "Texans will note with pride that Senator Lyndon Johnson did not sign the so-called Southern Manifesto which was a bugle call to defiance of the Supreme Court."[38]

The limitations of southern dissent, however, were readily apparent in North Carolina, where three of the twelve-member House delegation had refused to endorse the manifesto. A sympathetic media initially portrayed Democratic U.S. Representatives Thurmond Chatham, Harold Cooley, and C.B. Deane's refusal to sign as great acts of courage, a perception which the representatives themselves promoted. For his stance, Cooley initially received some eighty letters of support but only seven letters of criticism. Chatham and Deane, however, were both defeated later that year in the Democratic primary, in campaigns in which their refusal to sign was the most salient issue. When Cooley's decision not to sign became public, the Raleigh attorney Pou Bailey quickly declared his candidacy against the powerful incumbent. In his announcement, Bailey declared, "Every Southern representative in Congress, including Mr. Cooley, has a duty to join in" the manifesto. "The time has come," the challenger asserted, "when all who believe in Jeffersonian principles of constitutional government must stand together to preserve these principles."[39]

Cooley responded to the challenge by bolstering his own segregationist credentials. He asked for and received a public endorsement from Eastland for his reelection bid in the Democratic primary. Cooley ran as a staunch supporter of Democratic Governor Luther Hodges's school voucher privatization plan and call for "voluntary segregation." In correspondence with constituents, Cooley emphasized that he "always favored and now favor segregation in our schools." Self-described "as a person who has consistently supported complete segregation and as a person who supports every legal method to assure that continued segregation is maintained," Cooley survived Bailey's primary challenge by convincing his constituents that "there was no man or woman in North Carolina who would do more than I to keep our schools separate and segregated."[40]

As in the former states of the Confederacy, there was also substantial support for the Southern Manifesto in the border states. Some border communities, for instance, were sufficiently encouraged by the promulgation to avoid compliance with *Brown*. On March 15, 1956, the Delaware State Board of Education (which had formally adopted a policy of gradual desegregation) denied a NAACP petition that requested eight state school districts to desegregate immediately. A few border residents wrote to their representatives in Congress, asking them to sign, while a few border newspapers also supported the statement. Agreeing that the manifesto was promulgated by "sober and responsible men," the *Baltimore Sun* nevertheless claimed that "the main hope of the signers is delay," for "gradualism, by whatever name it be called, will be the inevitable course of events."[41]

The greater response in the border states, however, was condemnation. "This attitude, as you well know," an Oklahoma Baptist preacher lambasted Democratic U.S. Representative Wright Patman of Texas, "is not earning many friends in the world for our country. This attitude will continue to slaughter our finest on the blood-soaked battlefields of the world." This minister would not "support nor exert any influence in any way for any candidate for any public office who is a rabble rouser in this respect." "Serious as is interposition's flouting of the unanimous desegregation decision," the *St. Louis Post-Dispatch* asserted, "the manifesto of the Southern Members of Congress is far worse," because they had "put themselves in defiance of the law of the land." Despite the mixed reaction in the region, public opinion was sufficient to ensure that no member of Congress from the border states (all of whom possessed some degree of Jim Crow segregation) endorsed the Southern Manifesto or engaged in the various forms of Massive Resistance that later convulsed all of the former states of the Confederacy.[42]

In the wake of the manifesto, the emergent consensus on both sides of Mason and Dixon's Line was a general call for caution in *Brown*'s implementation; that is, for moderation. As the *New York Times* counseled, "Patience, restraint, and moderation are required on both sides—as much as in New York as in Alabama." Even the manifesto's harshest northern critics called for moderation to be thereafter the guiding policy. Overt race-baiters like Thurmond and Eastland "should be benched," according to Illinois's *Moline Dispatch*, "while the wiser heads of Sens. Russell, George, Lyndon Johnson, handle this man's job."[43]

Indeed, the promulgation achieved the Southern Caucus's goals. As the consensus of American public opinion embraced moderation, *Brown*'s full-scale implementation was delayed indefinitely or, at the very least, until after the 1956 elections. The precedent was set; the statement quashed any concerted thrust for meaningful public school desegregation in the first full school year after *Brown.* As the South Carolina NAACP's Robert A. Brooks lamented, the battle for desegregation in the Deep South was essentially over for the foreseeable future. "Meanwhile," Brooks explained, "we have other battles to fight—getting more economic opportunities, participating more in civic affairs, getting a better break in housing."[44]

The manifesto determined America's immediate political response to *Brown* and the Civil Rights Movement. That is, Massive Resistance was *made* in two ways. First, a regional program for concerted, nonviolent obstruction of both *Brown*'s implementation and federal civil rights legislation was firmly established under the direction of the Southern Caucus. Secondly, for the 1956 elections, this program of obstruction was, if not deemed legitimate, at least tacitly condoned by both major political parties, the president of the United States, and the American public writ large. For the foreseeable future, the white South won both the political and practical debate over desegregation.

Conclusion: The Long Stride Toward Freedom[1]

March 12, 2006, marked the fiftieth anniversary of the promulgation of the Southern Manifesto. Notably absent was any acclaim for the statement's anniversary that was apparent two years before, when America recognized the same anniversary of *Brown v. Board of Education* (1954). The Southern Manifesto is now but a distant memory, both for the American public and most professional historians. There were no academic forums in the leading historical journals, C-SPAN broadcasts of scholarly discussions, or round-tables for audiences to ponder the Southern Manifesto's legacy. Conversely, the voices of the Civil Rights Movement continue to be a part of everyday American life. The ideas of civil rights workers are rightly celebrated as part of the canon of United States history, helping Americans to live up to our national principles enunciated in the Declaration of Independence and federal Constitution. The struggle for black freedom continues to provide an irreplaceable source of inspiration for marginalized groups and victims of discrimination throughout the world. In 2008, a majority of Americans asserted that the election of President Barack Hussein Obama marked the culmination of the movement's long-term goals, initiating a new era of politics, a so-called postracial society. The triumph of the Civil Rights Movement is the American experiment at its best, while the Southern Manifesto was politics at its worst.

So, what is, or should be, remembered about the Southern Manifesto? Truly, the Southern Manifesto provided momentum for Massive Resistance. The manifesto gave state and local intransigent segregationists the political cover to momentarily stifle the Civil Rights Movement within their communities across the South. In turn, the Southern Caucus achieved nearly unanimous support from their electorate with the manifesto which, in turn, provoked a moderate national consensus toward *Brown*. The complete implementation of desegregation was effectively halted for years, as was meaningful federal civil rights legislation. As leader of the Southern Caucus and principal author of the manifesto, U.S. Senator Richard Brevard Russell, Jr., of Georgia enclosed copies of the statement in his constituent mail for the next several years and, until passage of the 1964 Civil Rights Act, pushed newly elected members of the Congress from the South to formally endorse the statement upon their arrival in Washington, D.C.

More immediately, the Southern Manifesto's greatest impact was upon national partisan politics, particularly the 1956 elections, which in turn drove southern politics for the near future. At the epicenter of the emerging revolution, Alabama Governor James Folsom was defeated by an intransigent segregationist candidate in the May Democratic primary, seen as not only complicit with desegregation, but also unable to sustain law and order in the Heart of Dixie. The Virginia General Assembly became even more emboldened, and passed bills that withdrew state funds from any integrated district, and gave the governor broad powers in pupil placement as well as for closing any school that desegregated with local funding. As Democratic United States Senator Harry F. Byrd presciently explained to one of his colleagues, "What we have done is a strong defiance of the Supreme Court, and I do not think integration will occur anywhere in the State."[2]

Before the promulgation of the Southern Manifesto, however, southern moderates never offered a viable means of implementing *Brown* and complying with the federal courts. No southern governor, or any other moderate public official in the South, unequivocally supported compliance with *Brown*. When so-called moderate governors like Tennessee's Frank Clement preached for local control of *Brown*, or North Carolina's Luther Hodges called for "voluntary segregation," they consciously removed their offices from the controversy. If Clement, Hodges, and others such as Arkansas Governor Orval Faubus were moderates before the Southern Manifesto, then surely they and their kind were inextricably tied to the concerted defense of the status quo. Faubus actively encouraged his congressional delegation to endorse the Southern Manifesto on the grounds that, if they did not, intransigent segregationists would quickly overtake the state government, with riotous violence to follow.

What did moderation really offer as an alternative? With the Eisenhower administration sending a clear signal that it was not about to enforce *Brown* in the next election cycle, the South's moderates and intransigents alike thought that they could just ignore the decision indefinitely. Ike's political ally, Democratic Governor Alan Shivers, even used his Texas Rangers to directly block federal desegregation orders in Mansfield at the beginning of the 1956 school semester, and the president did nothing. Faubus simply miscalculated the following year when Daisy Bates and the Little Rock Nine attempted to implement another direct order of the federal court. That is, the biggest mistake that Faubus made was simply that he took Ike at his word.

Following Shivers's precedent, former judge and Democratic U.S. Senator John Stennis's reasoning, and the pusillanimity of the 1956 Democratic presidential campaign (in which his great antagonist Harry Ashmore played an integral part), Faubus assumed that he could openly defy *Brown* because, as a southern governor, he possessed free reign in his state to do as he wished, and could freely block federal orders without fear of interference from the Eisenhower administration. At the insistence of Eisenhower himself, moreover, the Republican Party had denounced the use of force or compulsion in the implementation of *Brown* in their official party platform for the 1956 election. A born and buttered, tried and true social democrat who was both loyal to and stood squarely in the ideological mainstream of his party, the Man from Greasy Creek simply could not fathom that the political winds shifted after Ike's reelection and after the summer's debates over the 1957 Civil Rights Act. Combined with the international embarrassment of the Little Rock fiasco, these developments compelled the Eisenhower administration to act much differently to southern intransigence.[3]

The public perception of moderates may have changed after the promulgation of the Southern Manifesto, but their policies remained unaltered. Liberal Democratic members of the Southern Congressional Delegation, such as Arkansas's Brooks Hays and J. William Fulbright, or Alabama's John Sparkman and Lister Hill, could readily sign the Southern Manifesto and continue to vote against any and all civil rights legislation. They could simultaneously advocate compliance with the federal judiciary, quietly denounce the interposition movement, and call for compromise, peace, and understanding between civil rights workers and their white southern opponents. As committed segregationists, the Southern Congressional Delegation's moderates could just as easily continue to be identified with most aspects of the New Deal coalition's legislative agenda of the postwar period.

Public perception, however, is important. Those southern moderates who did not participate in the promulgation were thereafter identified as reasonable politicians, as bridges of understanding from the South to the rest of the United States who could help to finally bring Dixie back into the Union. Allegedly, these nonsigners allowed the former states of the Confederacy to enjoy the bounties of economic growth and be a part of, rather than separate from, the modern United States. Nevertheless, most of the nonsigners never became formal supporters of the Civil Rights Movement. Like their moderate colleagues who signed, most of those members of the Southern Congressional Delegation who did not, such as Democratic United States Representative Harold Cooley of North Carolina, made sure to display their zeal for Jim Crow when they stood before the electorate. But southern moderates who did not sign the Southern Manifesto and survived the 1956 elections gained political capital as a result, especially within the national Democratic Party in general and amongst African Americans in particular. Foremost, nonsigners were now the good guys; they no longer had the scent of magnolias about them. Senate Majority Leader Lyndon Baines Johnson's neglect to sign made him closer to presidential timber than any other factor. The Texan's refusal strongly influenced the black community's positive attitude toward him. In contrast, the black press strongly criticized southern Democratic liberals like Hays and Sparkman for their signatures. Johnson thereafter stood apart from the Southern Caucus and was clearly acceptable to the national Democrats as a viable presidential candidate.[4]

Leftover moderates who had distanced themselves from the Southern Caucus by not signing the Southern Manifesto did not thereafter promote the cause of black freedom. In the weeks and months after the promulgation, Johnson enthusiastically secured endorsements for the Democratic nomination from the white South's most important intransigent segregationists. When Democratic Senator Estes Kefauver of Tennessee upset Adlai Stevenson in the Minnesota Democratic primary just over a week after the promulgation, civil rights promised to be the focus of debate in the primaries. Johnson thereafter initiated the Democrats' southern strategy. That summer, he and Speaker of the House Sam Rayburn took control of the Texas State Democratic Party, effectively removing Shivers and the intransigent segregationist forces from power in the state. Johnson then secured the support of the key southern state delegations prior to the Democratic National Convention. He funneled money into the campaigns of southern supporters, and extended favors so as to ensure that another southern third party did not emerge. Most importantly, Johnson frequently corresponded with Senator Strom Thurmond of South Carolina throughout the 1956 campaign, and the majority leader promised the Dixiecrat that he would help him retain his committee assignments when he returned to the Senate after his resignation. Likewise, South Carolina leaders led a concerted effort to keep Palmetto State Democrats within the national party and support the national ticket. Across the South, moreover, Democratic congressional candidates successfully portrayed the Republicans as the party of *Brown.* At the behest of Democratic leaders such as Eleanor Roosevelt, Johnson and Rayburn refused to allow either the Democratic or Republican civil rights bills to be considered during the summer congressional session, thereby removing the issue from the public debate prior to the national conventions. With the help of Senator Russell, Johnson took the southern delegations into the Democratic National Convention in Chicago and pledged them to Stevenson, repeating the com-

7.1 The 1956 Democratic presidential ticket, United States Senator Estes Kefauver of Tennessee and former governor Adlai Stevenson of Illinois. Courtesy of the University of Tennessee–Knoxville Libraries.

promise of four years earlier, again to stifle Kefauver's insurgent campaign. Brooks Hays, Sam Ervin, and other southern moderates dominated the convention's platform committee, producing a watered-down civil rights plank which endorsed neither *Brown* nor broad civil rights legislation. Clement was conspicuously selected to formally nominate Stevenson; both the Tennessean and the Illinoisan gave loquacious addresses, filled with the usual platitudes and banalities, offering nothing substantial when either pending congressional civil rights legislation or the emerging southern social revolution were concerned.[5]

In the 1956 presidential election, the Republicans were different from the Democrats in degree, but not in substance. After the Southern Manifesto, the Eisenhower administration did not confront Johnson's and Rayburn's obstruction of their civil rights legislation in Congress, so as not to make the struggle for black equality a salient issue in the national debate. The Republicans, nonetheless, actively campaigned for the support of black voters, noting the accomplishments of the previous four years. Vice president Richard M. Nixon led the way, making frequent campaign stops in Harlem while touting the administration's accomplishments in the civil rights field. He also campaigned extensively in border states such as Kentucky, which underwent wide-scale desegregation in the fall school year. Always linking the Civil Rights Movement to the Cold War, Nixon informed a Louisville audience that Americans could not "afford the economic, moral, or international cost of segregation," in the struggle with the international communist conspiracy. He succinctly summarized his administration's incremental approach in the waning days of the campaign, optimistically predicting that "most of us here will live to see the day when American boys and girls shall sit, side by side, at any school—public or private—with no regard paid to the color of their skin. Segregation, discrimination, and prejudice have no place in America," Nixon said.[6]

The Republicans' moderate program secured the endorsement of important segments of black America's senior leadership, including the Reverend Martin Luther King, Sr., Clarence Mitchell of the National Association for the Advancement of Colored People, U.S. Representative Adam Clayton Powell, Jr., of New York, and longtime Arkansas Republican and civil rights lawyer Harold Flowers. The black-oriented *Louisville Defender* articulated this African American support of Republicans, declaring that "a vote for the Democrats is a vote for the 101 Southern Manifesto signers." Overall, the Republican ticket won the largest percentage of black voters since the Great Depression, capturing 39 percent, sustaining a majority in ten northern and twelve southern cities. The GOP endorsed the ambiguous timetable of *Brown II*, but did not make immediate and unequivocal compliance a campaign issue. Instead of breaking up the New Deal coalition, Ike set the ominous precedent that begat the prolonged violence of desegregation in the years to come. Republican lethargy, furthermore, allowed astute politicians like future presidents Kennedy and Johnson to successfully succor African Americans into the Democratic coalition for at least the next four generations.[7]

Faced with the near certainty of Eisenhower's 1956 reelection, Johnson and Russell still ensured Democratic congressional majorities and southern domination. Ironically, Johnson's ability to lead a Democratic majority in the Senate in the 1950s by stifling civil rights legislation meant that he later received most of the credit for the passage of the 1957 Civil Rights Act, that of 1960, and for the monumental legislation passed during his presidency. Johnson often invoked the words of the prophet Isaiah, "Come, let us reason together." But were such compromises ultimately conducive to national values, in the face of such blatant discrimination toward a significant number of American citizens? Both Kennedy and Johnson built their presidential coalitions partly upon the support of southern moderates, continuing the spirit of compromise and expediency without ever completely embracing the Civil Rights Movement.

The Democrats and Republicans agreed upon a moderate policy toward civil rights, but such compromises produced a potent dose of skepticism within the Civil Rights Movement toward the legislative process, whose vanguard thereafter worked, and succeeded, mostly outside the boundaries of national partisan politics. In the words of the south Florida civil rights activist Isaac C. Gregory, southern moderates' participation in the promulgation of the Southern Manifesto only produced "bitterness" as well as "an undermining of faith in our institutions." Indeed, the political machinations that resulted in the Southern Manifesto were part and parcel of the same dynamics that showed African Americans that the struggle for black freedom would be won not so much through the electoral process but through passive resistance, direct confrontation, sit-ins, freedom rides, and marches before the court of world opinion. As the prominent journalist and civil rights leader James L. Hicks of the *New York Amsterdam News* argued, in the wake of the manifesto, "the only course of action for the Negro people in this war is full speed ahead with no delay. And as we pick up that speed we must be willing to run over any Negro leaders, or any of our so-called white friends, who stand in our way and say 'Go slow.'"[8]

The entire generation of Americans who came of age in the sixties was afflicted by this ennui. The sociopolitical divide in American life became manifest in the coming years, as seen in the Civil Rights Movement's ultimate embrace of Black Power, the New Left's contempt for the formal political process, the neoconservatives' disdain of bureaucracy, and the counterculture's embrace and disdain of everything. If so many Americans of this generation lost trust in their government and civic institutions, a large part of this denouement came from such political episodes, of which the promulgation of the Southern Manifesto is the most infamous example.

The person who most poignantly understood the intellectual climate that permitted the Southern Manifesto was the individual who was soon recognized as the leader of the emerging nonviolent revolution. In the immediate aftermath of his victory in the Montgomery Bus Boycott, Dr. Martin Luther King, Jr., articulated his interpretation of what he described as the "liberal dilemma." King recognized that "the enlightened white southerner, who for years had preached gradualism, now sees that even the slow approach has revolutionary implications." Yet, episodes like the Southern Manifesto only showed that these very same white southerners "have no answer for dealing with or absorbing violence. They end in begging for retreat, lest things get out of hand and lead to violence." King developed this theme throughout the boycott. On March 18, 1956, the day before he was to stand trial for violating Alabama's antiboycott law, King's sermon in the pulpit of the Dexter Avenue Baptist Church was aimed directly toward the University of Alabama for the expulsion of Autherine Lucy, but alluded to the past week's so-called Declaration of Constitutional Principles. King condemned "an inept trustee board succoming to the whims and caprices of a vicious mob," but also addressed the larger challenge to "a deadening status quo." King maintained that the

7.2 The Reverend Doctor Martin Luther King, Jr., in the pulpit of the Holt Street Baptist Church, Montgomery, Alabama. Courtesy of AP Images.

veneer of calm that prevailed "was a peace that had been purchased at the price of capitulating to the forces of darkness. This is the type of peace that all men of goodwill hate. It is the type of peace that is obnoxious. It is the type of peace that stinks in the nostrils of the almighty God."[9]

In his *Letter from Birmingham Jail*, King famously addressed the problematic relationship between moderation and the Civil Rights Movement, between compromise and the attainment of true social harmony and justice. Though speaking directly to local white clergymen, King's arguments bespoke larger truths about white progressives' continual reluctance to embrace fundamental social change. King spoke of his own "painful experience that freedom is never voluntarily given by the oppressor; it must be demanded by the oppressed." "For years now," King wrote, "I have heard the word 'Wait!' It rings in the ear of every Negro with piercing familiarity. This 'Wait' has almost always meant 'Never.'" King's frustration with southern moderates depicted them as just as much or more a part of the problem as intransigent segregationists:

> I had hoped that the white moderate would understand that law and order
> exist for the purpose of establishing justice and that when they fail in this

purpose they become the dangerously structured dams that block the flow of social progress. I had hoped that the moderate would understand that the present racial tension in the South is a necessary phase of the transition from an obnoxious negative peace, in which the Negro passively accepted his unjust plight, to a substantive and positive peace, in which all men will respect the dignity and worth of human personality.

Through his years of experience, King learned to distrust southern moderates' rhetorical pleas for patience and gradualism. Yet, even at this late date, languishing in his jail cell, King admitted that he still had not learned the lesson strongly enough. "I suppose I should have realized," he lamented, "that few members of the oppressor race can understand the deep groans and passionate yearnings of the oppressed race, and still fewer have the vision to see that injustice must be rooted out by strong, persistent, and determined action."[10]

As he wrote this famous treatise in the spring of 1963, King had memories of over eight years of hard-fought battles within the Civil Rights Movement to draw upon. During the Montgomery Bus Boycott in the spring of 1956, King directly faced southern moderation. Here, at the beginning of the most important social revolution in modern history, he and others in the struggle had only to look at the daily newspapers, or watch the evening news broadcasts, to find the clearest example of southern moderates' active support of Jim Crow. Civil rights workers observed Alabama's two U.S. senators and other noteworthy southern liberals not only endorse the Southern Manifesto, but also reap direct political benefits from its promulgation. They watched Alabama's supposedly progressive governor, Democrat James Folsom, go fishing while the state's flagship university descended into anarchy, its broad-minded board of curators expelling a black woman student for attending classes. Soon afterward, Folsom asked his state legislators to change his oath of office so that Alabama governors no longer had to swear allegiance to the federal Constitution. Civil rights workers, furthermore, saw both national political parties, as well as the president of the United States, capitulate to blatant southern disregard for the U.S. Supreme Court, and allow needed civil rights bills to be buried in congressional committee. Indeed, at the beginning of the Civil Rights Movement, these workers for freedom learned their lessons early about the boundaries of southern moderation.

Appendix 1:
The Southern Manifesto (Committee Draft)

The unwarranted decision of nine men, constituting the Supreme Court, in the Public School Cases is now bearing the fruit always produced when men substitute naked power for established law.

The Founding Fathers gave us a Constitution of checks and balances because they realized the inevitable lesson of history that no man or group of men can be safely entrusted with unlimited power. They framed this Constitution with its provisions for change by amendment in order to secure the fundamentals of government against the dangers of temporary popular passion or the personal predilections of public office holders.

The decision of the Supreme Court in the School Cases is a flagrant and unjustified abuse of judicial power. It climaxes a trend in the Federal Judiciary undertaking to legislate, in derogation of the powers of Congress, the rights of the states and of the people.

The Constitution does not mention education. Neither does the Fourteenth Amendment. The debates preceding the submission of this Amendment clearly show that there was no intent that this Amendment should affect the systems of education maintained by the states.

The very Congress which proposed the Amendment provided for segregated schools in the District of Columbia.

When the Amendment was adopted in 1868, there were 37 states of the Union. Every one of the 26 states that had any substantial racial differences either approved the operation of segregated schools in existence or subsequently established them by the same law-making body which considered the Fourteenth Amendment.

Beginning with the case of *Plessy vs. Ferguson*, the Supreme Court expressly declared that under the Fourteenth Amendment no person was denied any of his rights if the states provided separate but equal public facilities. This decision was in essence reaffirmed and has been followed in many other areas since *Plessy vs. Ferguson*. It is notable that the Supreme Court, speaking through Chief Justice Taft, a former President of the United States, unanimously declared in 1927 in *Lum vs. Rice* that the principle of separate but equal was ". . within the discretion of the state in regulating its public schools and does not conflict with the Fourteenth Amendment."

This interpretation, placed time and again, without exception, became a part of the life of the people of many of the states and confirmed their habits, customs, traditions and way of life. It is founded on elemental humanity and common sense, for parents may not be deprived by a super government of the right to direct the lives and education of their own children.

Though there has been no constitutional amendment or Act of Congress changing this Constitutional principle almost a century old, the Supreme Court of the United States with no proper political or legal basis for such action, undertook to exercise the naked power of nine men, strategically emplaced, and substituted their personal political and social ideas for the established law of the land.

This illegal and unconstitutional seizure of power by the nine men composing the Court is creating chaos and confusion in the states principally affected. It is destroying the amicable relations between the white and negro races that have been created through 90 years of patient effort by the good people of both races. It has planted hatred and suspicion where there has been heretofore friendship and understanding.

Without regard to the consent of the governed, agitators from afar are threatening immediate and revolutionary changes in our public school systems. If done, it is certain to destroy the system of public education in some of the states.

With the gravest concern for the explosive and dangerous condition created by this decision:

We reaffirm our reliance on the Constitution as the fundamental law of the land.

We decry the Supreme Court's encroachments on rights reserved to the states and their substitution of a government of men for established law.

We commend the motives of those states which have declared the intention to resist this invasion of their sovereignty by the Court by every lawful means.

We urge states and people who are not directly affected by the school segregation decisions to consider the Constitutional principles involved in this case against the time when they, on other issues, may be the victims of judicial encroachments.

We pledge ourselves to support by any and all lawful means all measures calculated to bring about a reversal of this illegal and unconstitutional decision of the Supreme Court.

We appeal to our people not to be provoked by the agitators and troublemakers invading our states and to scrupulously refrain from disorder and lawlessness in this trying period as we seek to right this wrong.[1]

Appendix 2
The Southern Manifesto (Published Version)

The unwarranted decision of the Supreme Court in the public school cases is now bearing the fruit always produced when men substitute naked power for established law.

The Founding Fathers gave us a Constitution of checks and balances because they realized the inescapable lesson of history that no man or group of men can be safely entrusted with unlimited power. They framed this Constitution with its provisions for change by amendment in order to secure the fundamentals of government against the dangers of temporary popular passion or the personal predilections of public office holders.

We regard the decision of the Supreme Court in the school cases as a clear abuse of judicial power. It climaxes a trend in the Federal Judiciary undertaking to legislate, in derogation of the authority of Congress, and to encroach upon the reserved rights of the States and the people.

The original Constitution does not mention education. Neither does the Fourteenth nor any other Amendment. The debates preceding the submission of this Amendment clearly show that there was no intent that this Amendment should affect the systems of education maintained by the states.

The very Congress which proposed the Amendment provided for segregated schools in the District of Columbia.

When the Amendment was adopted in 1868, there were 37 states of the Union. Every one of the 26 states that had any substantial racial differences either approved the operation of segregated schools already in existence or subsequently established such schools by action of the same law-making body which considered the Fourteenth Amendment.

As admitted by the Supreme Court in the public school case (Brown v. Board of Education), the doctrine of separate but equal schools "apparently originated in Roberts v. City of Boston . . . (1849), upholding school segregation against attack as being violative of a State Constitutional guarantee of equality." This constitutional doctrine began in the North—not in the South, and it was followed not only in Massachusetts, but in Connecticut, New York, Illinois, Indiana, Michigan, Minnesota, New Jersey, Ohio, Pennsylvania and other northern States until they, exercising their rights as States through the constitutional processes of local self-government, changed their school systems.

In the case of Plessy vs. Ferguson in 1896 the Supreme Court expressly declared that under the Fourteenth Amendment no person was denied any of his rights if the states provided separate but equal public facilities. This decision has been followed in many other cases. It is notable that the Supreme Court, speaking through Chief Justice Taft, a former President of the United States, unanimously declared in 1927 in Lum vs. Rice that the "separate but equal" principle is ". . . within the discretion of the state in regulating its public schools and does not conflict with the Fourteenth Amendment."

This interpretation, restated time and again, became a part of the life of the people of many of the States and confirmed their habits, customs, traditions and way of life. It is founded on elemental humanity and common sense, for parents should not be deprived by government of the right to direct the lives and education of their own children.

Though there has been no constitutional amendment or Act of Congress changing this established legal principle almost a century old, the Supreme Court of the United States, with no legal basis for such action, undertook to exercise their naked judicial power and substituted their personal, political and social ideas for the established law of the land.

This unwarranted exercise of power by the Court, contrary to the Constitution, is creating chaos and confusion in the States principally affected. It is destroying the amicable relations between the white and negro races that have been created through 90 years of patient effort by the good people of both races. It has planted hatred and suspicion where there has been heretofore friendship and understanding.

Without regard to the consent of the governed, outside agitators are threatening immediate and revolutionary changes in our public school systems. If done, this is certain to destroy the system of public education in some of the States.

With the gravest concern for the explosive and dangerous condition created by this decision and inflamed by outside meddlers:

We reaffirm our reliance on the Constitution as the fundamental law of the land.

We decry the Supreme Court's encroachments on rights reserved to the States and to the people, contrary to established law and to the Constitution.

We commend the motives of those States which have declared the intention to resist forced integration by any lawful means.

We appeal to the States and people who are not directly affected by these decisions to consider the constitutional principles involved against the time when they too, on issues vital to them, may be the victims of judicial encroachment.

Even though we constitute a minority in the present Congress, we have full faith that a majority of the American people believe in the dual system of government which has enabled us to achieve our greatness and will in time demand that the reserved rights of the States and of the people be made secure against judicial usurpation.

We pledge ourselves to use all lawful means to bring about a reversal of this decision which is contrary to the Constitution and to prevent the use of force in its implementation.

In this trying period, as we seek to right this wrong, we appeal to our people not to be provoked by the agitators and troublemakers invading our States and to scrupulously refrain from disorder and lawless acts.[2]

Notes

INTRODUCTION

1. Numan V. Bartley, *The Rise of Massive Resistance: Race and Politics in the South During the 1950s* (Baton Rouge: Louisiana State University Press, 1969); Neil McMillen, *The Citizens' Council: Organized Resistance to the Second Reconstruction, 1954–64* (Urbana: University of Illinois Press, 1971); Matthew D. Lassiter, *The Silent Majority: Suburban Politics in the Sunbelt South* (Princeton: Princeton University Press, 2006); George Lewis, *Massive Resistance: The White Response to the Civil Rights Movement* (London: Hodder, 2006) and *The White South and the Red Menace: Segregationists, Anticommunism, and Massive Resistance, 1945–1965* (Gainesville: University Press of Florida, 2004); Anders Walker, *The Ghost of Jim Crow: How Southern Moderates Used Brown v. Board of Education to Stall Civil Rights* (New York: Oxford University Press, 2009); Clive Webb, ed., *Massive Resistance: Southern Opposition to the Second Reconstruction* (New York: Oxford University Press, 2005); Brent J. Aucoin, "The Southern Manifesto and Southern Opposition to Desegregation," *Arkansas Historical Quarterly (AHQ)* 55, No. 2 (Summer 1996): 174–189; Anthony J. Badger, "The Southern Manifesto: White Southerners and Civil Rights, 1956," in Rob Kroes and Eduard van de Bilt, eds., *The U.S. Constitution After 200 Years* (Amsterdam: Free University Press, 1988), 94; "Fatalism, Not Gradualism: The Crisis of Southern Liberalism, 1945–65," in Badger and Brian Ward, eds., *The Making of Martin Luther King and the Civil Rights Movement* (New York: New York University Press, 1996), 67–95; "The Forerunner of Our Opposition: Arkansas and the Southern Manifesto of 1956," *AHQ* 56, No. 3 (1997): 353–360; "Southerners Who Refused to Sign the Southern Manifesto," *Historical Journal* 1999 42, No. 2 (1999): 517–534; "The South Confronts the Court: The Southern Manifesto of 1956," *Journal of Policy History* 20, No. 1 (2008): 126–142; Timothy S. Huebner, "Looking Backward: The Southern Manifesto of 1956," *Historically Speaking* 7, No. 5 (May/June 2006): 36–39.

2. David Mayhew, *Congress: The Electoral Connection* (New Haven: Yale University Press, 1974); William S. White, *The Citadel: The Story of the U.S. Senate* (New York: Harper, 1957), and George Reedy, *The U.S. Senate: Paralysis or Search for Consensus?* (New York: Crown, 1986) and *Lyndon B. Johnson: A Memoir* (New York: Andrews & McMeel, 1982); Dorothy G. Scott, *When the Senate Halls Were Hallowed* (Los Angeles: Corillon Press, 2000); Barbara Sinclair, *The Transformation of the U.S. Senate*

(Baltimore: The Johns Hopkins University Press, 1989); Herman E. Talmadge, with Mark Royden Winchell, *Talmadge: A Political Legacy, A Politician's Life, A Memoir* (Atlanta: Peachtree Publishers, 1987); Gregory J. Wawro and Eric Schickler, *Filibuster: Obstruction and Lawmaking in the U.S. Senate* (Princeton: Princeton University Press, 2006); Keith M. Finley, *Delaying the Dream: Southern Senators and the Fight against Civil Rights, 1938–1965* (Baton Rouge: Louisiana State University Press, 2008); Lewis L. Gould, *The Most Exclusive Club: A History of the Modern United States Senate* (New York: Basic Books, 2005); Lawrence K. Pettit and Edward Keynes, eds., *The Legislative Process in the U.S. Senate* (Chicago: Rand McNally, 1969); Donald R. Mathews, *U.S. Senators and Their World* (Chapel Hill: University of North Carolina Press, 1960); Hugh Bone, "An Introduction to the Senate Policy Committees," *The American Political Science Review (APSR)* (June 1956); Sarah A. Binder, "The Partisan Basis of Procedural Choice: Allocating Parliamentary Rights in the House, 1789–1990," *APSR* 90, No. 1 (March 1996): 8–20; C. Lawrence Evans, "Legislative Structure: Rules, Precedents, and Jurisdictions," *Legislative Studies Quarterly* 24, No. 4 (November 1999): 605–642; Richard L. Hall, "Empiricism and Progress in Positive Theories of Legislative Institutions," in Shepsle and Weingast, *Positive Theories of Congressional Institutions* (Ann Arbor: University of Michigan Press, 1995), 273–301; Keith Krehbiel, *Information and Legislative Organization* (Ann Arbor: University of Michigan Press, 1991), 1–103, 247–266; Matthew D. McCubbins and Thomas Schwartz, "Congressional Oversight Overlooked: Police Patrols versus Fire Alarms," *American Journal of Political Science* 28 (1984): 165–179; Terry M. Moe, "An Assessment of the Positive Theory of 'Congressional Dominance,'" *Legislative Studies Quarterly* 12, No. 4 (November 1987): 475–520; Nelson W. Polsby, "The Institutionalization of the U.S. House of Representatives," *APSR* 62, No.2 (June 1968): 144–168; Eric Schickler, "Institutional Change in the House of Representatives, 1867–1998: A Test of Partisan and Ideological Power Balance Models," *APSR* 94, No. 2 (June 2000): 269–288; Thomas A. Becnel, *Senator Allen Ellender of Louisiana: A Biography* (Baton Rouge: Louisiana State University Press, 1995); John L. Bullion, *Lyndon B. Johnson and the Transformation of American Politics* (New York: Pearson Longman, 2008); Karl E. Campbell, *Senator Sam Ervin, Last of the Founding Fathers* (Chapel Hill: University of North Carolina Press, 2007); Robert Caro, *Master of the Senate* (New York: Alfred Knopf, 2002); Nadine Cohodas, *Strom Thurmond and the Politics of Southern Change* (New York: Simon & Schuster, 1993); Dick Dabney, *A Good Man: The Life of Sam Ervin* (Boston: Houghton Mifflin, 1976); Robert Dallek, *Lone Star Rising: Lyndon Johnson and His Times, 1908–1960* (New York: Oxford University Press, 1991); Stanford Phillips Dyer, "Lyndon B. Johnson and the Politics of Civil Rights, 1935–1960: The Art of 'Moderate Leadership'" (dissertation, Texas A&M University, 1978); Rowland Evans and Robert Novak, *Lyndon B. Johnson: The Exercise of Power* (New York: The New American Library, 1966); Gilbert C. Fite, *Richard B. Russell, Jr., Senator from Georgia* (Chapel

Hill: University of North Carolina Press, 1991); Charles L. Fontenay, *Estes Kefauver: A Biography* (Knoxville: University of Tennessee Press, 1980); Joseph Bruce Gorman, *Kefauver: A Political Biography* (New York: Oxford University Press, 1971); Ronald L. Heinemann, *Harry Byrd of Virginia* (Charlottesville: University Press of Virginia, 1996); Kyle Longley, *Senator Albert Gore, Sr.: Tennessee Maverick* (Baton Rouge: Louisiana State University Press, 2004); Robert Mann, *Legacy to Power: Senator Russell Long of Louisiana* (New York: Paragon House, 1992) and *The Walls of Jericho: Lyndon Johnson, Hubert Humphrey, Richard Russell, and the Struggle for Civil Rights* (New York: Harcourt Brace, 1996); Merle Miller, *Lyndon: An Oral Biography* (New York: G.P. Putnam's Sons, 1980); David Daniel Potenziani, "Look to the Past: Richard B. Russell and the Defense of White Supremacy" (dissertation, University of Georgia, Athens, 1981); Lee Riley Powell, *J. William Fulbright and His Time: A Political Biography* (Memphis: Guild Bindery Press, 1996); Bruce J. Schulman, *Lyndon B. Johnson and American Liberalism: A Brief Biography with Documents* (Boston: Bedford/St. Martins, 1995); Virginia Van der Veer Hamilton, *Lister Hill: Statesman from the South* (Chapel Hill: University of North Carolina Press, 1987); William A. White, *The Professional: Lyndon B. Johnson* (Boston: Houghton Mifflin, 1964); J. Harvie Wilkinson III, *Harry Byrd and the Changing Face of Virginia Politics, 1945–1966* (Charlottesville: University Press of Virginia, 1969); Jeff Woods, *Richard B. Russell: Southern Nationalism and American Foreign Policy* (Lanham: Rowan & Littlefield Publishers, Inc., 2007); Randall B. Woods, *Fulbright: A Biography* (New York: Cambridge University Press, 1995) and *LBJ: Architect of American Ambition* (New York: Free Press, 2006).

3. Joseph Crespino, *In Search of Another Country: Mississippi and the Conservative Counterrevolution* (Princeton: Princeton University Press, 2009).

CHAPTER 1

1. Robert M. Collins, *More: The Politics of Economic Growth in Postwar America* (Oxford: Oxford University Press, 2000), 41; David Farber, *The Age of Great Dreams: America in the 1960s* (New York: Hill & Wang, 1994), 7–24; William L. O'Neil, *American High: The Years of Confidence, 1945–1960* (New York: Macmillan, 1986); James T. Patterson, *America in the Twentieth Century: A History* (Fort Worth: Harcourt College Publishers, 2000), 347–48; Bureau of the Census, *Statistical Abstract of the United States* (U.S. Department of Commerce, 1940, 1956, 1965). The South is defined as the eleven former states of the Confederacy. The border states of Delaware, Kentucky, Maryland, Missouri, Oklahoma, and West Virginia are sometimes included for analysis, comparison, evidence, and reference. In 1945, 1.212 million American births occurred, which increased every year, so the number reached 1.837 million in 1957. As a whole, the U.S. population grew 19 percent, from approximately 151 million to 180 million. The southern and western sections each gained over 8 million new citizens

during this same period (O'Neil, 25–26). The U.S. gross national product (GNP)—measured in constant 1954 dollars—rose from $282.3 billion in 1947 to $439.9 billion in 1960, an increase of 56 percent. Measured in per capita (accounting population growth), the increase between 1947 and 1960 remains 24 percent. Moreover, personal consumption spending—measured in constant 1954 dollars—increased from $195.6 billion to $298.1 billion in 1960 (Collins, 41). Southern manufacturing output increased 51 percent from 1947 to 1953. The Southeast led industrial expansion in the decade after World War II, with 569 large manufacturing plants, each employing at least 100 workers, built there by 1956. Southern industrial expansion overall rose from $3.681 billion in 1947 to $5.549 billion in 1953. The plants were located as follows: Alabama, 57; Florida, 74; Georgia, 117; Mississippi, 54; North Carolina, 113; South Carolina, 72; and Tennessee 82. In comparison, New England built 19 new plants, while there were 208 in the mid-Atlantic states, 334 in the east-north central region, 136 in the west-north central, 293 in the west-south central, 79 in the mountain region, 562 in the Pacific Coast, and 169 elsewhere. In 1956, the southeastern region reported 1,658,078 in manufacturing employment. The Federal Reserve Board's Index of Manufacturing Production as a whole rose from 100 in 1947 to 163 in 1960. In addition, defense industries increasingly located in the South with the rapid expansion of the Cold War's military-industrial complex, growing state and local revenues. The defense industry accounted for from 10 to 20 percent of income growth in Alabama, Florida, Georgia, Mississippi, North Carolina, Texas, Alabama, and Virginia. The South's economic and population growth was seen foremost in Florida. The Sunshine State's population grew from 1,613,500 in 1935 to 3,452,000 in 1955. In 1956, Florida received approximately 3,000 migrants per week, which produced approximately 120,000 registered black voters in the state. From 1940 to 1960, furthermore, the South's total farm population and the number of farms decreased by nearly one-half due to unit consolidation. Farm tenancy, once the typical form of labor organization, largely disappeared. In the eleven former Confederate states, plus West Virginia and Oklahoma, the number of tenant farmers decreased from approximately 1,800,000 in 1936 to 750,000 in 1950 and 300,000 in 1959. Farm population declined from 10,390,000 in 1945 to 5,932,000 in 1960. From 1940 to 1960, the total number of farms decreased by nearly one-half, from 2,424,138 to 1,322,946. {*Newsweek*, May 7, 1956, 30–31; *U.S. News & World Report*, January 27, 1956, 48–55, March 2, 1956, 45, and April 13, 1956, 69; *New Republic*, February 13, 1956, 3; *The South*, November 12, 1956, 5; Richard Brevard Russell (RBR) Papers, Series VI, Sub-series A1, Box 12, Folder 5, Russell Memorial Library, University of Georgia, Athens; Bruce J. Schulman, *From Cotton Belt to Sunbelt: Federal Policy, Economic Development, and the Transformation of the South, 1938–1980* (New York: Oxford University Press, 1991), 140; James C. Cobb, *The Selling of the South: The Southern Crusade For Industrial Development, 1936–1980* (Baton Rouge: Louisiana State University Press, 1982); Kari Frederickson, "Confronting the Garrison State: South Carolina in the Early Cold War Era," *Journal of Southern History (JSH)* 72, No. 2 (May 2006): 349–378; Thomas Becnel, *Senator Allen Ellender of Louisiana: A Biography* (Baton Rouge: Louisiana State University Press, 1995), 176; Pete Daniel, *Lost Revolutions: The South in the 1950s* (Chapel Hill: University of North Carolina Press, 2000), 7–21; Gilbert C. Fite, *Cotton Fields No More: Southern Agriculture, 1865–1980* (Lexington: University Press of Kentucky, 1984), 233–235; Donald Holley, *The Second Great Emancipation: The Mechanical Cotton Picker, Black Migration, and How They Shaped the Modern South* (Fayetteville: University of Arkansas Press, 2000).}

2. During the first half of the twentieth century, African Americans constituted roughly 10 percent of the U.S. population. In 1900, there were approximately 9 million African Americans in a total population of 76 million. By 1956, there were approximately 16 million in a total population of 168 million. In 1900, approximately 85 percent lived in the South, three-quarters in rural areas, making up at least 40 percent of the population of six southern states. In the 1950s, however, blacks exceeded that percentage only in Mississippi. The largest percentages were in Mississippi (45.3 percent), South Carolina (38.8 percent), Louisiana (32.9 percent), Alabama (32 percent), and Georgia (30.9 percent). Black men's annual median income rose from $460 in 1939 to $2,436 in 1957. Black women's income increased from $246 to $1,019. Black men's annual median income was, however, just 67 percent of white men's. Black women fared just slightly better, earning 70 percent of white women's income. By mid-century, of the approximately 6 million African Americans living in the North, 2.8 million were born in the South. During the 1950s, nearly 3,000 relocated to Chicago every month, so that the city's black population increased from 239,345 in 1930 to some 700,000 in 1955. During the period, however, 17.7 percent of black men completed only one to four years of formal matriculation. Of those in the 20-to-24-year age group, only 17.7 percent completed high school. Of those aged 30 to 34 years, only 2.2 percent graduated from college. In the South, functional illiterates (those adults with less than a fifth-grade education) were three times more prevalent among young blacks than young whites. {Dwight David Eisenhower (DDE) Papers, Papers as President of the United States, 1953–61 (Ann Whitman File), Cabinet Series, Box 6, File, "Cabinet Meeting of 3/9/56," 3, 7, Dwight D. Eisenhower Library, Abilene, Kansas; *Life*, September 27, 1956, 111; *U.S. News & World Report*, April 13, 1956, 29–35; *Atlantic*, January 1956, 59; *Ebony*, Tenth Anniversary Issue: November 1945–November 1955; *New Republic*, April 2, 1956, 2; *Crisis*, August–September 1955, 405–421; Robert E. Weems, Jr., *Desegregating the Dollar: African American Consumerism in the Twentieth Century* (New York: New York University Press, 1998), 72; Collins, 42; Michael B. Katz, Mark J. Stern, and Janine J. Fader, "The New African American Inequality," *Journal of American History (JAH)* 91, No. 1, (June 2005): 75–108; *Time*, June 4, 1956, 56, 58.}

3. Patricia Sullivan, *Lift Every Voice: The NAACP and the Making of the Civil Rights Movement* (New York: Free Press, 2009); Robert L. Carter, *A Matter of Law: A Memoir of Struggle in the Cause of Equal Rights* (New York: Free Press, 2005); Oliver Allen, "Chief Counsel for Equality," RBR Papers, Series III, Sub-series A, Box 27, Folder 9.

4. *Time*, February 20, 1956, 40; Waldo E. Martin, Jr., ed., *Brown v. Board of Education: A Brief History with Documents* (Boston: Bedford/St. Martin's, 1998), 110; Anthony W. James, "The College Social Fraternity Antidiscrimination Debate, 1945–1949," *The Historian* 62, No. 2 (Winter 2000): 303–324; Clarence Walker, "The Effects of *Brown*: Personal and Historical Reflections on American Racial Atavism," *JSH* 70, No. 2 (May 2004): 298; Sidney S. McMath, *Promises Kept: A Memoir* (Fayetteville, University of Arkansas Press, 2003), 206–209, 332–333; Robert A. Leflar, "One Life in the Law: Black Law Students," *Arkansas, Arkansas: Writers and Writings from the Delta to the Ozarks, 1541–1969*, ed. John Caldwell Guilds, Vol. 1 (Fayetteville: University of Arkansas Press, 1999, 569–572); *U.S. News & World Report*, February 24, 1956, 142); DDE Papers, Papers as President of the United States, 1953–61 (Ann Whitman File), Cabinet Series, Box 6, File, "Cabinet Meeting of 3/9/56," 2; Darlene Clark Hine, *Black Victory: The Rise and Fall of the White Primary in Texas* (Columbia: University of Missouri Press, 2003); V. O. Key, *Southern Politics in State and Nation* (New York: A. A. Knopf, 1949), 619–643; Steven F. Lawson, *Running for Freedom: Civil Rights and Black Politics in America since 1941*, 2nd ed. (New York: McGraw-Hill, 1997), 81.

5. The District of Columbia's public schools were simultaneously desegregated in *Bolling v. Sharpe* (1954). Federal Circuit Court Judge John B. Parker outlined *Brown*'s parameters in *Briggs v. Elliot* (1955), the South Carolina case included in *Brown*. In his subsequent ruling on implementation, Parker stressed that the scope of the decision upheld the constitutional tenet of freedom of association. Long known as the *Briggs* dictum, Parker declared: "[All] that [*Brown*] has decided, is that a state may not deny to any person on account of race the right to attend any school that it maintains. . . . If the schools which it maintains are open to children of all races, no violation of the Constitution is involved even though the children of different races voluntarily attend different schools, as they attend different churches. Nothing in the Constitution or in the decision of the Supreme Court takes away from the people freedom to choose the schools they attend. The Constitution, in other words, does not require integration. It merely forbids discrimination." {"Segregation in the Public Schools: Opinion of the Supreme Court of the United States, *Brown v. Board of Topeka, Kansas*," Senate, 83rd Congress, 2nd Session (Washington: United States Government Printing Office, 1954), 11, and *Bolling v. Sharpe*, Senate, 83rd Congress, 2nd Session (Washington: United States Government Printing Office, 1954), 11, John L. McClellan Papers, Riley Hickingbotham Library, File 25, Drawer 3 (25-E), "Segregation Material 1954–56," Ouachita Baptist University, Arkadelphia, Arkansas; Martin, 168–175, 194–198; James T. Patterson, *Brown v. Board of Education: A Civil Rights Milestone and Its Troubled*

Legacy (New York: Oxford University Press, 2001); Mark Whitman, ed., *Removing a Badge of Slavery: The Record of Brown v. Board of Education* (Princeton: Mark Wiener Publishing, 1993); *Briggs v. Elliot*, 132 F. Supp. 776 (1955), at 777, Raymond Wolters, "From *Brown* to *Green* and Back: The Changing Meaning of Desegregation," *JSH 70*, No. 2 (May 2004): 319.}

6. At the end of the 1955–56 school year, in the seventeen states and the District of Columbia affected by *Brown*, 537 of 4,791 school districts were desegregated, with approximately 256,000, or 10 percent, of black children in the region attending desegregated classrooms. By 1956, 50 percent of the 208 public colleges and universities of the South admitted African Americans. It is unknown, however, whether this latter statistic includes only undergraduate education or also graduate school admissions as well as students matriculating at historically black colleges. Of the approximately 2,000 blacks enrolled in both public and private southern institutions of higher education, over one-quarter were enrolled in formerly all-white public colleges and universities. Many of these students lived in desegregated facilities, without major instances of confrontation or violence. Only Alabama, Georgia, Mississippi, and South Carolina openly refused to admit African Americans into their public institutions of higher education. {*Southern School News*, January–February 1956, 6, April 1956, 1–2; C. Vann Woodward, "The 'New Reconstruction' in the South: Desegregation in Historical Perspective," *Commentary* 21, No. 6 (June 1956): 507; *Newsweek*, February 6, 1956, 26; Adam Fairclough, "The Costs of Brown: Black Teachers and School Integration," *JAH* 91, No. 1 (June 2004): 43–55; David L. Chappell, *Inside Agitators: White Southerners in the Civil Rights Movement* (Baltimore: The Johns Hopkins University Press, 1994), 18–24; *Ebony*, February 1956, 18–19, May 1956, 78, and June 1956, 115; *Time*, March 26, 1956, 27; *New Republic*, February 20, 1956, 6–7, February 27, 1956, 11–13, and March 19, 1956, 5; *Nation*, September 29, 1956, 268; Daniel, 30–32; DDE Papers, Papers as President of the United States, 1953–61 (Ann Whitman File), Cabinet Series, Box 6, File, "Cabinet Meeting of 3/9/56," 21; Congress, Senate, 83rd Congress, 1st sess., *Congressional Record* (January 19, 1955): A538–542,Thomas Hennings Papers, F. 2988, Western Historical Manuscripts Collection (WHMC), Ellis Library, University of Missouri–Columbia. For statistics that are substantially smaller for the same period, see Congress, Senate, Arthur G. Klein (NY), American Jewish Committee, "The People Take the Lead," *Congressional Record* 102, pt. 4 (January 19, 1956): A538–544, F. 2988.}

7. *Pine Bluff Commercial*, November 8, 1955, n.p., McClellan Papers, "L. G. Baker to McClellan," March 21, 1956, [File 19-B "Segregation"]; *Nation*, January 7, 1956, 1, February 11, 1956, 101, 128, and May 19, 1956, 426–428; *Southern School News*, January 1956, n.p., April 1956, 1–2; *Time*, February 27, 1956, 26–27 and March 26, 1956, 25; *Newsweek*, March 5, 1956, 51; *Arkansas Gazette*, February 9, 1956, 1-2A, James William Fulbright (JWF) Papers, BCN 19, F45, 14-A, Special Collections, Mullins Library,

University of Arkansas at Fayetteville; *Amsterdam News* (New York), May 22, 1954, quoted in Clive Webb, "A Continuity of Conservatism: The Limitations of *Brown v. Board of Education*," *JSH* 70, No. 2 (May 2004): 327.

8. *Ebony*, July 1956, 70; *Nation*, July 7, 1956, 14.

9.David Chappell, *A Stone of Hope: Prophetic Religion and the Death of Jim Crow* (Chapel Hill: University of North Carolina Press, 2004); *Newsweek*, April 2, 1956, 86; "Leslie E. and Elizabeth S. Carpenter to Lyndon Baines Johnson," January 1956, Lyndon Baines Johnson (LBJ) Papers, File, "Mr. And Mrs. Leslie [1945–63], LBJA (Subject File), Lyndon Baines Johnson Presidential Library, University of Texas, Austin; Darlene Clark Hine, William C. Hine, and Stanley Harrold, *The African American Odyssey* (Upper Saddle River, 2000), 503; *New Republic*, January 16, 1956, 4–5; Clenora Hudson Weems, with an introduction by Robert E. Weems, Jr., *Emmett Till: The Sacrificial Lamb of the Civil Rights Movement* (Troy: Bedford, 1994); and Stephen J. Whitfield, *A Death in the Delta: The Story of Emmett Till* (Baltimore: The Johns Hopkins University Press, 1988); *Newsweek*, April 2, 1956, 86; Chappell, *Inside Agitators*, 45–83; David Garrow, *Bearing the Cross: Martin Luther King, Jr., and the Southern Christian Leadership Conference* (New York: William Morrow and Company, 1986), 11–82; Alonzo Hamby, *Liberalism and Its Challengers: From F.D.R. to Bush* (New York: Oxford University Press, 1991), chap. 4; *Ebony*, May 1956, 78, July 1956, 65–68; *Telegram*, March 18, 1956, 6, RBR Papers, Series X, Box 171, Folder "Civil Rights #9"; Martin Luther King, Jr., with an introduction by Coretta Scott King, *I Have a Dream: Writings and Speeches That Changed the World*, ed. James M. Washington (New York: HarperCollins, 1992), 3–13; *Time*, January 30, 1956, 20; *Newsweek*, March 5, 1956, 24–26. For coverage of the Montgomery Bus Boycott, see *Time, Newsweek*, and *Nation*, January–June, 1956; *Ebony*, June 1956, 86, July 1956, 66.

10. *Ebony*, May 1956, 78; *Nation*, July 7, 1956, 13 and September 29, 1956, 268; Martin, 110–120; *U.S. News & World Report*, February 24, 1956, 142; *New Republic*, February 27, 1956, 11–13 and March 19, 1956, 5; Daniel, 30–32; *Nation*, May 19, 1956, 426–428; Chappell, *A Stone of Hope*, 5, 140–144; *Newsweek*, March 5, 1956, 51 and March 12, 1956, 64; DDE Papers, Papers as President of the United States, 1953–61 (Ann Whitman File), Cabinet Series, Box 6, File, "Cabinet Meeting of 3/9/56," 2; John Kyle Day, "The Fall of Southern Moderation: The Defeat of Brooks Hays in the 1958 Congressional Election for the Fifth District of Arkansas" (M.A. thesis, University of Arkansas, 1999), 73–74, 105–106; RBR Papers, Series X, Box 163, Folder 6; "Resolution," Oklahoma Baptist General Assembly of Missionary Baptists, September 11–12, 1955, Robert S. Kerr Collection, Legislative Series, Box 5, Folder 9, The Carl Albert Center, University of Oklahoma, Norman; Eugene Genovese, *A Consuming Fire: The Fall of the Confederacy in the Mind of the White Christian South* (Athens: University of Georgia Press, 1998) and *The Southern Front: History and Politics in the Culture War* (Columbia: University of Missouri Press, 1994); "Williams to Ervin," March

15, 1956, Sam J. Ervin Papers, Subgroup A, Senate Records, 1954–1975, Folder 1120, Southern Historical Collection (SHC), Wilson Library, University of North Carolina, Chapel Hill; Daniel, 180–85; "Mrs. James M. Dabbs to Gov. James F. Byrnes," May 19, 1954, "McCall to Gore," March 22, 1956, William D. Workman Papers, Modern Political Collections (MPC), South Caroliniana Library, University of South Carolina, Columbia; *Catholic Action of the South*, February 1956, 1, *New Orleans States*, February 24, 1956, 1, Earl K. Long "Scrapbook," Vol. 7, 1955–1957, 1–44, Long (Earl K.) Collection, 3700, Hill Memorial Library, Louisiana State University, Baton Rouge; Albert Gore, Sr., Papers, Issue Mail Series 4, 1956 Segregation, File 57 "Southern Manifesto–Nashville," Albert Gore Congressional Research Center, Middle Tennessee State University, Murfreesboro; *Time*, December 12, 1955, 88 and February 27, 1956, 70; "Resolution of the Louisiana School Board Association," February 7, 1956, Hale Boggs Papers, File "Segregation," 1956 Subject Files, Volume II, MC 1000, Middleton Library, Tulane University, New Orleans, Louisiana; Memphis *Commercial Appeal*, February 27, 1956, n.p., McClellan Papers, "L. G. Baker to McClellan," March 21, 1956 [File 19-B "Segregation"].

11. The Federal Bureau of Investigation (FBI) believed there were 116,000 members in the United States by the spring of 1956. {DDE Papers, Papers as President of the United States, 1953–61 (Ann Whitman File), Cabinet Series, Box 6, File "Cabinet Meeting of 3/9/56," 16, 20; McMillen, *The Citizens' Council: Organized Resistance to the Second Reconstruction, 1954–64* (Urbana: University of Illinois Press, 1971), 19, 153; Key, 329; *New Republic*, January 16, 1955, 4–5; *Time*, December 12, 1955, 24–25; Daniel, 196; "Michigan Citizens Councils to Olin Johnston," November 11, 1956, Olin D. Johnston Papers, MPC; "Robertson to Carleton," February 7, 1956, A. Willis Robertson Papers, Drawer 40, Folder 27, Earl Gregg Swem Library, College of William and Mary, Williamsburg, Virginia.}

12. *Time*, December 12, 1955, 24; *Life*, February 6, 1956, 22, 24; James Oliver Eastland Papers, File Series 2, Subseries 6, Box 1, Folder "Dec 1955," J. D. Williams Library, Department of Archives and Special Collections, University of Mississippi; Workman Papers, Box 34, Folder "Integration/Civil Rights, Reference Material, Judiciary 1955–1969"; Tom P. Brady, *Black Monday* (Jackson: Citizens Councils of America, 1955).

13. Hennings Papers, "Resolution," F. 2988; "Sam Fore to LBJ," April 16, 1956, LBJ Papers, LBJA (Subject File), Box 106, Folder "Floresville Chronicle Journal, Sam Fore, Jr. [1955–56]; "Workman–S. E. Rogers correspondence," May 1956 and "Kershaw Citizens Council Statement of Principle," Workman Papers, Box 32, Folders "Integration/Civil Rights, Citizens Councils, South Carolina, 1955–56," "1957–1959," "1960–1961," "1962–1963," "1964–1968," and "N. D."; "Gordon Hines to John Stennis," December 6, 1956, John Stennis Papers, Series 29, Sub-series "Organizations," File 6, John C.

Stennis Congressional Research Center, Mitchell Memorial Library, Mississippi State University, Starkville, Mississippi; McMillen, 159–204.

14. *U.S. News & World Report*, February 26, 1954, 138; *Nation*, April 28, 1956, 360; Robert Penn Warren, *Segregation: The Inner Conflict in the South* (New York: Random House, 1956), 13–14.

15. According to the U.S. Justice Department, from 1882 to 1955 there were 4,730 lynchings in the continental United States, with 4,038 of these occurring below Mason and Dixon's Line. From 1939 to 1955, a total of 39 lynchings occurred, contrasted with 317 during the previous seventeen-year period. The FBI investigated cases involving federal voting questions, but did not investigate murders such as Till's, which fell under state jurisdiction. {DDE, Papers as President of the United States, 1953–61 (Ann Whitman File), Cabinet Series, Box 6, File "Cabinet Meeting of 3/9/56," 22; Graeme Cope, "'Honest White People of the Middle and Lower Classes'? A Profile of the Capital Citizens Council during the Little Rock Crisis of 1957," *Arkansas Historical Quarterly (AHQ)* 61, No. 1 (Spring 2002): 37–58; *New Republic*, January 16, 1956, 4–5 and May 7, 1956, 13; McMillen, 217–18; *Time*, December 12, 1955, 25.}

16. *Nation*, April 28, 1956, 360–61; Robert A. Caro, *Master of the Senate*, Vol. 3 of *The Years of Lyndon Johnson* (New York: Alfred A. Knopf, 2002), 698; David Halberstam, "The White Citizens Councils: Respectable Means for Unrespectable Ends," *Commentary* 22, No. 4 (October 1956): 300; *New Republic*, January 16, 1956, 4–5; Daniel, 211, 221; DDE, Papers as President of the United States, 1953–61 (Ann Whitman File), Cabinet Series, Box 6, File "Cabinet Meeting of 3/9/56," 17–18.

17. Numan Bartley and Hugh D. Graham, *Southern Politics and the Second Reconstruction* (Baltimore: The Johns Hopkins University Press, 1975), 53; *Southern School News*, January 1956, Vol. II, No. 7, n. p., "Shoemaker to Russell," March 1, 1956, RBR Papers, Series X, Box 177, Folder 9; Elizabeth Jacoway, "*Brown* and the Road to Reunion," *JSH* 70, No. 2 (May 2004): 304–305.

18. James W. Ely, Jr., *The Crisis of Conservative Virginia: The Byrd Organization and the Politics of Massive Resistance* (Knoxville: University of Tennessee Press, 1976), 39; *Life*, February 6, 1956, 24; Bartley, 127, 126–149; Joseph J. Thorndike, "'The Sometimes Sordid Level of Race and Segregation': James J. Kilpatrick and the Virginia Campaign against *Brown*," in Matthew D. Lassiter and Andrew B. Lewis, eds., *The Moderates' Dilemma: Massive Resistance to School Desegregation in Virginia* (Charlottesville: University Press of Virginia, 1998), 51–71; "Interposition: What Is It?" by Judge Leander Perez of Louisiana before the American Bar Association, Dallas, Texas, August 27, 1956, Ervin Papers, Subgroup A: Senate Records, Folder 13948; *Shreveport Journal*, February 11, 1956, 2A, Wright Patman Papers, Box 94 (a), File "Integration–general 1955," 7, LBJ Library; *Texarkana Gazette*, February 29, 1956, 4, JWF Papers, Box 10:1; William Old, *The Segregation Issue: Suggestions Regarding the Maintenance of State Autonomy* (Chesterfield, VA: 1955).

19. *Newsweek*, January 23, 1956, 24; *Nation*, July 7, 1956, 13; *Christian Science Monitor*, March 12, 1956, n.p., LBJ Papers, LBJ Senate, Box 423, File "Southern Manifesto"); Ronald L. Heinemann, *Harry Byrd of Virginia* (Charlottesville: University Press of Virginia, 1996), 325–354; *Nation*, January 21, 1956, 45–47; Ely; Robbins L. Gates, *The Making of Massive Resistance: Virginia's Politics of Public School Desegregation, 1954–1956* (Chapel Hill: University of North Carolina Press, 1964); Benjamin Muse, *Virginia's Massive Resistance* (Bloomington: Indiana University Press, 1961); Lassiter and Lewis.

20. Mississippi Governor, 1956–1960 (Coleman), Inaugural Address, January 17, 1956, Mississippi Department of Archives and History, Jackson; *Southern School News*, February 1956, 1; *Life*, February 6, 1956, 22–23; *Time*, February 6, 1956, 20.

21. *Time*, February 6, 1956, 20; *U.S. News & World Report*, February 24, 1956, 142; "Stennis to Hodges," November 18, 1955, Stennis Papers, Series 29, Box 5, Folder 10; Daniel, 205; J. Michael McElreath, "The Cost of Opportunity: School Desegregation's Complicated Calculus in North Carolina," in *With All Deliberate Speed: Implementing Brown v. Board of Education*, ed. Brian J. Daughterity and Charles C. Bolton (Fayetteville: University of Arkansas Press, 2008), 21–40; Anders Walker, *The Ghost of Jim Crow: How Southern Moderates Used Brown v. Board of Education to Stall Civil Rights* (New York: Oxford University Press, 2009), 49–84.

22. JWF Papers, Series 71, Tom Dearmore, "The Ozark Outlook," *Baxter Bulletin* (Mountain Home, AR), March 22, 1956, 2, and *Northwest Arkansas Times*, February 25, 1956, n.p., Box 10:1, and Andrew Howard, "Interposition, Not Integration, May Rule Arkansas," March 28, 1956, Box 10:2; Roy Reed, *Faubus: The Life and Times of an American Prodigal* (Fayetteville: University of Arkansas Press, 1997); *Southern School News*, February 1956, 1; *Life*, February 6, 1956, 22–23; *Newsweek*, February 6, 1956, 26, May 21, 1956, 38;

23. *Southern School News*, March 1956, 14; *Time*, January 30, 1956, 14 and March 5, 1956, 2; Heinemann, 333–334; Ely, 40; Gates, 108–116; Muse, 20–25; Lassiter and Lewis, 62; Reinhold Niebuhr, "Nullification," March 5, 1956, *The New Leader*, 3–4, RBR Papers, Series X, Box 177, Folder "civil rights #9."

24. On May 30, 1955, Florida adopted a resolution urging the U.S. Congress to adopt a constitutional amendment maintaining segregation. In December 1956, Louisiana became the sixth state to adopt an interposition resolution, which was written by the state's leading Citizens' Councilor, Democratic state Senator W. M. "Willie" Rainach of Homer. {"Daniel to Gray," July 26, 1955, Price Daniel Papers, Box 144, Sam Houston Regional Library and Research Center, Liberty, Texas; *Southern School News*, February 1956, 6; *Newsweek*, January 30, 1956, 33; *Time*, January 30, 1956, 15; "RBR-McDonald Correspondence," RBR Papers, Series X, Box 163, Folder 5, "School Segregation"; Workman Papers, Box 34, Folder "Integration/Civil Rights, Reference Material, School Desegregation, General, 1956"; ODJ Papers, Box 53, Folder "Civil

Rights, Gen," Folders 1956–25 and 1956–26; Strom Thurmond Collection (STC), Speeches, B: Originals, Box 4, Folder 60, J. Strom Thurmond Institute, Clemson University Libraries, Special Collections, South Carolina; Boggs Papers, Vol. II, MC 1000, Box 21, Folder "Segregation"; Stennis Papers, Series 61, Box 5, Folder 7; "Rainach to Gore," November 25, 1956, Gore Papers, Series 20, File, "1956–1958 Segregation," 4.}

25. Griffin referred to Article III, Section 2 of the federal Constitution. {*The Declaration of Independence and the Constitution of the United States* (Williamsburg: The Colonial Williamsburg Foundation, n.d.), 26–27; Bartley, *The Rise of Massive Resistance*, 127; "RBR–McDonald Correspondence," RBR Papers, Series X, Box 163, Folder 5, "School Segregation," "Gubernatorial Address," 3–8; William G. McLoughlin, *Cherokees and Missionaries, 1789–1839* (Norman: University of Oklahoma Press, 1995), 239–265; James C. Davis Papers, Folder "Marvin Griffin," Series 5, Correspondence, Box 89; Manuscript, Archive, and Rare Book Library (MARBL), Emory University, Georgia.}

26. RBR Papers, "RBR-McDonald Correspondence," Series X, Box 163, Folder 5, "School Segregation," "Gubernatorial Address," 3–8; "Resolution," 1–4; Congress, House, "'Hon. Hugh G. Grant Warns University of Georgia Students of Race War in United States,' 'Extension of Remarks of Hon. James C. Davis of Georgia in the House of Representatives,'" *Congressional Record*, 84th Cong., 2nd Sess. (February 27, 1956), 5–6, Vertical File, Folder "Civil Rights General."

27. *Southern School News*, April 1956, 7; *New Republic*, March 26, 1956, 3–4; RBR Papers, Series X, *Tampa Sunday Tribune*, February 26, 1956, 10A, and "Richard Russell to Iney Watzon," March 2, 1956, Box 149, Folder 4, and *The South*, June 11, 1956, 12, Box 177, Folder 4; Gore Papers, Issue Mail Series 4, "Issue Mail 1956, Segregation—Southern Manifesto—Murfreesboro, File 56," Cabinet A18; *Southern School News*, February 1956, 6 and April 1956, 2; *Pine Bluff Commercial*, March 4, 1956, "L. G. Baker to McClellan," March 21, 1956, McClellan Papers [File 19-B "Segregation"]; *Nation*, July 7, 1956, 12; Boggs Papers, Subject Files, Vol. II, MC1000, Folder "Segregation 1956"; ODJ Papers, Box 53, Folder "Civil Rights, Gen." Folders 1956–25 and 1956–26; STC, Speeches, B: Originals, Box 4, Folder 60; *Washington Star*, March 18, 1956, Workman Papers; Jeff Woods, *Black Struggle, Red Scare: Segregation and Anti-Communism in the South, 1948–1968* (Baton Rouge: Louisiana State University Press, 2004), 66.

28. "Excerpts of remarks by U.S. Senator John Stennis—Television Interview Station WTOK–TV—Meridian, Mississippi," December 27, 1955, 2, Stennis Papers, Series 61, Box 15, Folder 7 and Box 5, Folder 7; DDE Papers, Papers as President of the United States, 1953–61 (Ann Whitman File), Cabinet Series, Box 6, File "Cabinet Meeting of 3/9/56," 20; Gore Papers, Issue Mail Series 4, "Issue Mail 1956, Segregation—Southern Manifesto—Murfreesboro, File 56," Cabinet A18; *Southern School News*, April 1956, 1; *Pine Bluff Commercial*, March 4, 1956, "L. G. Baker to McClellan,"

March 21, 1956, McClellan Papers [File 19-B "Segregation"]; *Nation*, July 7, 1956, 11; Daniel, 209.

29. DDE Papers, Papers as President of the United States, 1953–61 (Ann Whitman File), Cabinet Series, Box 6, File "Cabinet Meeting of 3/9/56," 20, 23.

30. Thorndike, 51–71; Tom Brady, *Black Monday* (Jackson: Citizens Councils of America, 1955); William D. Workman, *The Case for the South* (New York: Devin-Adair Company, 1960); Eastland Collection, Series 2, Subseries 6, Box 1, Folder 23 "January 1956"; Kilpatrick, "Not to be Solved by a Slide Rule: A Southerner Looks at the Problem of Integrated Schools," *Human Events* 12, No. 20 (May 14, 1955), RBR Papers, Series X, Box 177, Folder 6, and *The Sovereign States: Notes of a Citizen of Virginia* (Chicago: H. Regnery Co., 1957), 281; *Harper's*, January 3, 1956, 44.

31. Kilpatrick, "Not to be Solved by a Slide Rule," and *The Sovereign States*, 259–262, 264, 281, 282–283.

32. *Harper's*, January 3, 1956, 39–45 and March 1956, 6, 9–10, 12, 14.

33. Kilpatrick, "Not to be Solved by a Slide Rule," and *The Sovereign States*, 259–262, 264, 281, 282–283; *Harper's*, January 3, 1956, 39–45 and March 1956, 6, 9–10, 12, 14.

34. Kilpatrick, "Not to be Solved by a Slide Rule," and *The Sovereign States*, 259–262, 264, 281, 282–283; Jane Dailey, "Sex, Segregation, and the Sacred after *Brown*," *The Journal of American History (JAH)* 91, No. 1 (June 2004): 119–144; RBR Papers, Herbert Ravenell Sass, "Mixed Schools and Mixed Blood," *Atlantic*, November 1956, Series X, Box 163, Folder 6, "School Segregation Material," and Congress, House, "Remarks of U.S. Rep. James C. Davis," *Congressional Record*, 84th Cong., 2nd Sess. (February 27, 1956), 1–4, Vertical File, Folder "Civil Rights General"; *Harper's*, January 3, 1956, 39–45 and March 1956, 6, 9–10, 12, 14; LBJ Papers, "Knowles to LBJ," December 29, 1955, "1956 General Files," "Segregation," Box 568, U.S. Senate, 1949–1961; *U.S. News & World Report*, February 24, 1956, 48; *Nation*, n.d., 84; "Where Is the Reign of Terror?," March 27, 1956 84th Congress, 2nd Session, *Congressional Record*, John Bell Williams Collection, Mississippi Department of Archives and History, Jackson; and Brady, 1–18.

35. Brooks Hays, *A Southern Moderate Speaks* (Chapel Hill: University of North Carolina Press, 1959).

36. *U.S. News & World Report*, February 3, 1956, 16.

37. Life, February 6, 1956, 22; *Southern School News*, February 1956, 8; *Time*, February 6, 1956, 20–21; *Newsweek*, February 6, 1956, 25.

38. *Memphis Press*, March 7, 1956, n.p., Estes Kefauver Collection, Series 5G, Box 2, File "Clement," 2 of 3, Special Collections Division, James D. Hoskins Special Collections Library, University of Tennessee–Knoxville.

39. Gilbert Fite, *Richard B. Russell, Jr.: Senator From Georgia* (Chapel Hill: University of North Carolina Press, 1991), 147; *Atlantic*, April 1956, 34; Mary Dudziak, *Cold*

War Civil Rights: Race and the Image of American Democracy (Princeton: Princeton University Press, 2000); Carol Anderson, *Eyes Off the Prize: The United Nations and the African American Struggle for Human Rights, 1944–1955* (Cambridge: Cambridge University Press, 2003); Warren, 55.

40. *Atlantic*, April 1956, 31; *New Republic*, May 7, 1956, 16, May 28, 1956, 14–15, April 2, 1956, 8–9; C. A. McKnight, "Troubled South: Search for a Middle Ground," *Collier's*, June 22, 1956, 25–31. For an alternative perspective of Muse's philosophy, see Matthew D. Lassiter, "A 'Fighting Moderate': Benjamin Muse's Search for the Submerged South," in Lassiter and Lewis, 168–201.

41. James W. Silver, "The Twenty-First Annual Meeting," *JSH* 22 (February–November 1956): 60–61; *Harper's Magazine*, June 1956, 32–34; *New Republic*, May 28, 1956, 14–15; Warren, 55–56; Fite, *Richard B. Russell*, 147; *Atlantic*, April 1956, 34; *Life*, March 5, 1956, 51–52; *Arkansas Gazette*, JWF Papers, BCN 19, F45, 14-A; William Faulkner, *Essays, Speeches, and Public Letters*, ed. James B. Meriwether (New York: Random House, 1965); *Ebony*, September 1956, 70–73; *Harper's*, 29, 32–34; *Nation*, March 31, 1956, 259; *Time*, March 26, 1956, n.p., April 23, 1956, 12; *Newsweek*, March 26, 1956, 90, April 9, 1956, 58; James B. Meriwether and Michael Millgate, eds., *Lion in the Garden: Interviews with William Faulkner, 1926–1962* (New York: Random House, 1968), 257–266.

42. *Life*, March 12, 1956, 37; *Harper's*, June 1956, 1; *New York Herald Tribune*, March 14, 1956, n.p., *Washington Post*, March 8, 1956, n.p., Kefauver Collection, Series 5G, Box 9, File "Civil Rights," 2 of 2; *Ebony*, June 1956, 86; *Nation*, July 7, 1956, 9–17; RBR Papers, "A Southerner Looks at Moderation," *The Christian Century*, May 30, 1956, reprinted by the National Association for the Advancement of Colored People, New York, New York, Series X, Box 177, Folder 6 and Oliver Allen, "Chief Counsel for Equality," Series III, Sub-series A, Box 27, Folder 9; *New Republic*, April 2, 1956, 8–10.

CHAPTER 2

1. "RBR to Barry R. Weaver," March 22, 1956, Richard B. Russell (RBR) Papers, Series X, Box 163, Folder 3, "School Segregation," and "RBR to Grady Knight," March 6, 1956, Series I, Folder 16, "Civil Rights," Richard B. Russell Memorial Library, University of Georgia, Athens; *Time*, March 26, 1956, 26; *U.S. News & World Report*, March 16, 1956, 85; Thomas Hennings Papers, F. 7254, Western Historical Manuscripts Collection (WHMC), University of Missouri–Columbia; Numan Bartley, *The Rise of Massive Resistance: Race and Politics in the South During the 1950's* (Baton Rouge: Louisiana State University Press, 1969), 119; *Nation*, February 18, 1956, 129; *Charleston News & Courier*, December 15, 1955, William Workman Papers, Modern Political Collections (MPC), South Caroliniana Library, University of South Carolina, Columbia; "Thurmond Statement," January 26, 1956, State Citizens' Councils, J. Strom

Thurmond Collection (STC), "Speeches, B: Originals," Folder 59, J. Strom Thurmond Institute, Clemson University Libraries, Special Collections, South Carolina.

2. "Newsletter," May 25, 1956, Long Family Papers (Russell M. and Earl K.), Special Issue Files, Folder "Segregation," Civil Rights, 556–50, 1949–1963, Hill Memorial Library, Louisiana State University, Baton Rouge, Louisiana; "Excerpts of remarks by U.S. Senator John Stennis–Television Interview Station WTOK-TV–Meridian, Mississippi," December 27, 1955, John Stennis Papers, 1–3, Series 61, Box 15, Folder 7, Stennis Congressional Research Center, Mitchell Memorial Library, Mississippi State University, Starkville.

3. "Thurmond Statement," January 26, 1956, State Citizens' Councils, STC, "Speeches, B: Originals," Folder 59; "Thurmond to Carr," December 26, 1959, Stuart Symington Papers, Box 37, "Education File," WHMC; Joseph Crespino, *Strom Thurmond's America* (New York: Hill and Wang, 2012), 107–110; *U.S. News & World Report* Interview, Nov. 1955," 2–3, Stennis Papers, Series 29, Box 5, Folder 10, 6–7; *Time*, March 26, 1956, 26; *Memphis Press-Scimitar*, August 13, 1955, n.p., "NAACP appeal to remove Senator Eastland from Judiciary Committee," 3, Hennings Papers, F. 3334 "1934–1960"; "Senator Eastland's remarks," January 23, 1956, James Oliver Eastland Collection, Series 2, Sub-series 6, Box 1, Folder 23 "January 1956," and File Series 2, Sub-series 6, Box 1, Folder 55-56," J. D. Williams Library, Department of Archives and Special Collections, University of Mississippi, Oxford; *Jackson Daily News*, December 1, 1955, n.p., J. William Fulbright (JWF) Papers, Series 71, Box 10, Folder 2, Special Collections Division, Mullins Library, University of Arkansas at Fayetteville; Workman Papers, Box 34, Folder "Integration/Civil Rights, Reference Material, January 1955–1969; "Ellender to Voelker," February 18, 1956, 2, Allen J. Ellender Papers, University Archives, Nicholls State University, Thibodaux, Louisiana.

4. "RBR to A. C. Mann," March 14, 1956, Series X, Box 195, Folder 11, "Supreme Court," and "RBR to Weaver," March 22, 1956, Series X, Box 163, Folder 3, "School Segregation," RBR Papers; *Charleston News & Courier*, December 15, 1955, Workman Papers.

5. "RBR to R.M. Harris," February 24, 1956, RBR Papers, Series I, Box 17, Folder 6, "Civil Rights"; *Charleston News & Courier*, December 15, 1955, Workman Papers; 84th Cong., 1st Sess. *Congressional Record* 102 (May 25, 1955), 6963–64, Bartley, 120; "Johnston to Eastland," March 15, 1956 and "Press Release," Olin D. Johnston (ODJ) Papers, Box 63, Folder "Civil Rights, Gen 1956– 25," MPC; *Congressional Record*, 84th Congress, 2nd Sess., March 1, 1956. Myrdal's *The American Dilemma* is cited in *Brown*'s famous footnote eleven, where the court refers to other prominent works of sociology. {Waldo E. Martin, Jr., ed., *Brown v. Board of Education: A Brief History With Documents* (Boston: Bedford/St. Martin's, 1998), 168–75, 194–98; "Civil Rights in the 84th Congress" by the Washington D.C. office, Anti-Defamation League of B'nai B'rith, Lyndon Baines Johnson (LBJ) Papers, File, "Reedy: Civil Rights," Series

"LBJ-Senate," Box 418, Lyndon Baines Johnson Presidential Library, University of Texas at Austin; *Newsweek*, January 23, 1956, 24.}

6. "RBR to Herman T. Mobley," April 6, 1956, RBR Papers, Series X, Box 163, Folder 12, "School Segregation Material"; "*U.S. News & World Report* Interview, Nov. 1955," 2–3, Stennis Papers, Series 29, Box 5, Folder 10, 21–22; *Congressional Record*, 83rd Cong., 2nd Sess. (May 27, 1954): 7257, in Bartley, 118–119; *Time*, March 26, 1956, 26; Dwight David Eisenhower (DDE) Papers, Papers as President of the United States, 1953–61 (Ann Whitman File), Cabinet Series, Box 6, File, "Cabinet Meeting of 3/9/56," 2, Dwight D. Eisenhower Library, Abilene, Kansas.

7. "Radio Address," Text, 3, New Orleans, Louisiana, 8:30 p.m. C.S.T., Saturday, March 17, 1956, Ellender Papers; *Jackson Daily News*, December 1, 1955, n.p., JWF Papers, series 71, Box 10, Folder 2; Workman Papers, Box 34, Folder "Integration/Civil Rights, Reference Material, January 1955–1969 and News Flash," October 1955, Box 32, Folder "Integration/Civil Rights, Citizens' Councils, South Carolina 1955–1956"; Stephen J. Whitfield, *A Death in the Delta: The Story of Emmett Till* (Baltimore: The Johns Hopkins University Press, 1988), 117.

8. "Thurmond to Carr," December 26, 1959, Symington Papers, Box 37, "Education File"; "*U.S. News & World Report* Interview, Nov. 1955," 2–3, Stennis Papers, Series 29, Box 5, Folder 10, 6–7; *Shreveport Journal*, November 8, 1957, in Robert Mann, *Legacy to Power: Senator Russell Long of Louisiana* (New York: Paragon House, 1992), 186; "Radio Address," Text, p. 3, New Orleans, Louisiana, 8:30 p.m. C.S.T., Saturday, March 17, 1956, Ellender Papers.

9. Stennis Papers, "*U.S. News & World Report* Interview, Nov. 1955," 2–3, Series 29, Box 5, Folder 10, 4, 21–22, "Excerpts of Speech Made by U.S. Senator John Stennis in 1955 County Courthouse Tour," Series 61, Box 5, Folder 7; "Memorandum," May 1, 1954, Series 46, Box 1, Folder 1; "Ellender to Voelker," February 18, 1956, 2, Ellender Papers.

10. Workman Papers, *Charleston News & Courier*, December 15, 1955, and January 27, 1956, *Aynor Daily*, October 26, 1955, *Greenville News*, October 25, 1955, *State*, January 27, 1956, Box 34, Folder "Integration/Civil Rights, Reference Material, January 1955–1969"; "RBR to Herman T. Mobley," April 6, 1956, RBR Papers, Series X, Box 163, Folder 12, "School Segregation Material"; Stennis Papers, "Stennis-Day Correspondence," January 1956, Series 29, Box 7, Folder 6, and "Stennis-East correspondence," January 1956, "Stennis to McCully," April 28, 1956, Folder 10; Eastland Collection, File Series 1, Sub-series 18, Box 9, Folder 9–39, and "Eastland-Day correspondence," File Series 1, Sub-series 7, Box 1, Folder 1–19 and Series 3, Sub-series 1, Box 36, Folder "1956 Civil Rights (3 of 3), File Series 2, Sub-series 6, Box 1, Folder "December 1955," "Patterson to Lipscomb," February 16, 1956, and "Englehardt to Eastland," Series 3, Sub-series 1, Box 35, Folder "1956 Civil Rights (1 of 3), and "Eastland to Graham," February 15, 1956, Folder "1956 Civil Rights (2 of 3), Series 2, Sub-series 6, Box 1, Folders

"10 February 1956," "55–56"; *U.S. News & World Report*, March 16, 1956, 85; *Jackson Daily News*, December 1, 1955, n.p., JWF Papers, Series 71, Box 10:2; DDE Papers, Papers as President of the United States, 1953–61 (Ann Whitman File), Cabinet Series, Box 6, File, "Cabinet Meeting of 3/9/56," 15; *Life*, February 6, 1956, 22–23; Nadine Cohodas, *Strom Thurmond and the Politics of Southern Change* (New York: Simon & Schuster, 1993), 282; *Time*, February 6, 1956, 20 and March 26, 1956, 26; John Bell Williams Collection, Constituent Correspondence, Box 10382, Series 2416 and Box 10251, Series 2430, Mississippi Department of Archives and History, Jackson.

11. Gilbert Fite, *Richard B. Russell, Jr.: Senator from Georgia* (Chapel Hill: University of North Carolina Press, 1991), 332; RBR Papers, "Russell to Daniel B. Maher," March 10, 1956, "Russell to Gen. Eugene Cook," March 10, 1956, Series I, Box 17, Folder 6, "Civil Rights," Series X, Boxes 177–78; Stennis Papers, Series 61, Box 5, Folders 7–8, "Stennis to Walter Sillers," February 11, 1956, Folder 7, "Stennis to Coleman, January 21, 1956, Series 50, Box 1, Folder 59, "Preparatory Material for U.S. News Interview," Series 29, Box 5, Folder 4, "Excerpts of remarks by U.S. Senator John Stennis–Television Interview Station WTOK-TV–Meridian, Mississippi," December 27, 1955, Series 61, Box 15, Folder 7, 1–3.

12. "McClellan-Poynter Correspondence," February 22, 1956, John L. McClellan Papers, File 19-B, "Segregation," Riley-Hickingbotham Memorial Library, Ouachita Baptist University, Arkadelphia, Arkansas;"Ellender to Voelker," February 18, 1956, 2–3, Ellender Papers; A. Willis Robertson (AWR) Papers, "Robertson to Judge Leander Perez," October 19, 1956, Folder 29, "Robertson to Harrison," February 7, 1956, Folder 27, Drawer 40, Earl Gregg Swem Library, College of William and Mary, Williamsburg, Virginia; *Washington Post*, April 8, 1956, n.p., JWF Papers, Series 71, Box 10:1.

13. Thomas A. Becnel, *Senator Allen Ellender of Louisiana: A Biography* (Baton Rouge: Louisiana State University Press, 1995), 198; "Ellender to Voelker," February 28, 1956, Ellender Papers, 3; DDE Papers, Papers as President of the United States, 1953–61 (Ann Whitman File), Cabinet Series, Box 6, File "Cabinet Meeting of 3/9/56," 15; *Life*, February 6, 1956, 22–23; Cohodas, 282; *Charleston News & Courier* and *The State*, January 27, 1956, Workman Papers; David L. Chappell, *A Stone of Hope: Prophetic Religion and the Death of Jim Crow* (Chapel Hill: University of North Carolina Press, 2004), 153–178.

14. Key, 355; Samuel P. Huntington, *American Politics: The Promise of Disharmony* (Cambridge: Harvard University Press, 1981), 227; Joseph A. Schlesinger, *Political Parties and the Winning of Office* (Ann Arbor: University of Michigan Press, 1991), 179; Robert Caro, *Master of the Senate: The Years of Lyndon Johnson* (New York: Alfred Knopf, 2002), 31–32.

15. In the 1954 midterm elections, the Democrats attained a 48 to 47 majority, but improved to 49 to 47 after Senator Wayne Morse of Oregon abandoned the Re-

publican Party to caucus with the Democrats. {*U.S. News & World Report*, March 9, 1956, 30; LBJ Papers, LBJA Congressional File, Box 50, Folder "Morse, Wayne"; Donald R. Matthews, *U.S. Senators and Their World* (Chapel Hill: University of North Carolina Press, 1960), 147–175, 151–152, 234–235}. According to Matthews, the most powerful committees, and hence the most difficult in which to attain a seat, were, in descending order, Foreign Relations, Appropriations, Finance, Armed Services, Agriculture and Forestry, Judiciary, Interstate and Foreign Commerce, Banking and Currency, Interior, Public Works, Labor and Public Welfare, Government Operations, Rules and Administration, Post Office and Civil Service, and District of Columbia. The Senate's southern chairs were Harry F. Byrd (VA)—Finance; James O. Eastland (MS)—Judiciary; Allen J. Ellender (LA)—Agriculture and Forestry; J. William Fulbright (AR)—Banking and Currency; Walter F. George (GA)—Foreign Relations; Lister Hill (AL)—Labor and Public Welfare; Olin D. Johnston (SC)—Post Office and Civil Service; John McClellan (AR)—Government Operations; and Richard B. Russell (GA)—Armed Services. In the House, the southern Democratic chairs were Graham H. Barden (NC)—Education and Labor; Herbert C. Bonner (NC)—Merchant Marine and Fisheries; Omar Burleson (TX)—House Administration; Clarence Cannon (MO)—Appropriations; Harold D. Cooley (NC)—Agriculture; Jere Cooper (TN)—Ways and Means; John L. McMillan (SC)—District of Columbia; Tom Murray (TN)—Post Office and Civil Service; J. Percy Priest (TN)—Interstate and Forestry Commission; James P. Richards (SC)—Foreign Affairs; Howard W. Smith (VA)—Rules; Brent Spense (KY)—Banking and Currency; Olin E. Teague (TX)—Veterans' Affairs; and Carl Vinson (GA)—Armed Services. This list includes the border states of Kentucky and Missouri. Both had segregated school systems. All of these states were Democratic bastions, save the aforementioned border states and Tennessee, even though GOP state parties were steadily gaining strength through Eisenhower's popularity. {Paul T. David, *Party Strength in the United States, 1872–1970* (Charlottesville: University Press of Virginia, 1972), 44–48; File "Minority Groups 1956," Hall, Leonard W., Chairman of Republican National Committee: Papers 1953–57, Box 114, Eisenhower Library; *Nation*, July 7, 1956, 13; William S. White, *The Citadel: The Story of the U.S. Senate* (New York: Harper & Brothers, 1956), 70–71; David W. Rhode, "Parties and Committees in the House: Member Motivations, Issues, and Institutional Arrangements," *Legislative Studies Quarterly* 19 (3 August 1994): 341–359.}

16. John Kyle Day, "Filibuster," in James Ciment, ed., *Postwar America: An Encyclopedia of History and Politics* (San Juan Capistrano: M. E. Sharpe, 2006), 542–543; Hennings Papers, "NAACP appeal to remove Senator Eastland from Judiciary Committee," 6, F. 3334 "1934–1960," and "Joseph L. Rauh to Hennings," January 7, 1957, F. 3334, "1934–1960," *New York Times*, July 18, 1952, n.p., F. 5829, "1934–1960"; Folders "Rule Twenty Two, Parts I & II," Senate Historical Office (SHO), Hart Senate Office

Building, Washington D.C.; White, 62; "George Reedy, Interview 8," 46–47, 97–105, August 16, 1983, Oral History Manuscripts, AC 84–50, LBJ Library; Fite, 246.

17. Fite, 125; Reedy Interview 3, AC 76–23, LBJ Library, 8–14, 18–21; David Daniel Potenziani, "Look to the Past: Richard B. Russell and the Defense of White Supremacy" (dissertation, University of Georgia: Athens, 1981), 8; Matthews, 151; *Richard B. Russell: Georgia Giant* (Russell Memorial Library, UGA Libraries, Athens, GA 30602), television transcripts, 27–29; William E. Leuchtenberg, *Franklin D. Roosevelt and the New Deal, 1933–1940* (New York: Harper-Torch, 1963), 41–62; Bartley, 153–56; Caro, 164–202.

18. Fite, 499 and "RBR notes"; transcript, Harry McPherson Oral History Interview I, 12/5/68, by T.H. Baker, Electronic Copy, Reedy 3, AC 76–23 (8–14, 18–21), 9, Humphrey, 2, LBJ Library, 23; *Georgia Giant*, 39–40; "Eulogy to Richard B. Russell," Eastland Collection, Series 1, Sub-series 18, Box 10, Folder 10-10.

19. The lone senator that did not join the group was Democratic Senator Claude Pepper of Florida, who supported the Truman Commission.

20. Fite, 182, 202, 228, 231–233, 241; "Russell to Eastland," June 8, 1949, Eastland Collection, Series 1, Sub-series 18, Box 9, Folder 9-9; Reedy, "Interview 8," 98, LBJ Library.

21. Fite, 225, 241, 500; Robert Mann, *The Walls of Jericho: Lyndon Johnson, Hubert Humphrey, Richard Russell, and the Struggle for Civil Rights* (New York: Harcourt Brace & Co., 1996), 43–45; D. B. Hardeman and Donald C. Bacon, *Rayburn: A Biography* (Austin: Texas Monthly Press, 1987), 336–337.

22. Fite, 225, 241, 500; Reedy no. 3, 8–14, 18–21, LBJ Library; Mann, 122–128; John A. Goldsmith, *Colleagues: Richard B. Russell and His Apprentice, Lyndon B. Johnson* (Washington D.C.: Seven Locks Press, 1993), 27–30; David Robertson, *Sly and Able: A Political Biography of James F. Byrnes* (New York: W. W. Norton & Company, 1994), 528; Fite, 225, 266–270, 277, 500; Caro, 471–473; Potenziani, 112–118; *Georgia Giant*, 39–40; *U.S. News & World Report*, April 20, 1956, 42–52; "The South Likes Russell," *Freeman*, May 5, 1952, 491–494, John Temple Graves II Papers, 830.1.17, Birmingham Public Library, Department of Archives and Manuscripts, Alabama.

23. Numan Bartley and Hugh D. Graham, *Southern Politics and the Second Reconstruction* (Baltimore: The Johns Hopkins University Press, 1975), 81; Key, 58–81, 277–297; Hugh Davis Graham, "Tennessee Editorial Response to Changes in the Bi-Racial System, 1954–1960" (dissertation, Stanford University, 1964), in Tara Mitchell Mielnik, "Resisting Massive Resistance: Tennessee's Senators and the Southern Manifesto," March 27, 1997, Albert Gore, Sr. Congressional Research Center, Middle Tennessee State University, Murfreesboro; Charles L. Fontenay, *Estes Kefauver: A Biography* (Knoxville: University of Tennessee Press, 1980), 137–163; Joseph Bruce Gorman, *Kefauver: A Political Biography* (New York: Oxford University Press, 1971), 35–73, 237; Fite, 24; Estes Kefauver Collection, Series 5G, Box 12, Folder "Congressmen support-

ing Kefauver, May 24, 1956," "Kefauver to Powell," June 2, 1952, Series 1, Box 11, Folder 16, "Kefauver to White," December 18, 1954, Series 1, Box 11, Folders 16-17, Special Collections Division, Hoskins Memorial Library, University of Tennessee–Knoxville; Matthews, 109, 113; White, 78; Kari Frederickson, *The Dixiecrat Revolt and the End of the Solid South* (Chapel Hill: University of North Carolina Press, 2001), 227–228.

24. Kyle Longley, "White Knight for Civil Rights?: The Civil Rights Record of Senator Albert A. Gore, Sr.," *Tennessee Historical Quarterly (THQ)* 57, No. 2–3 (1998): 116–117, 120, 128; Albert A. Gore, Sr., *Let the Glory Out: My South and Its Politics* (New York, 1972), 9, 13, 66, 118, 130; Fite, 241; Albert Gore Papers, "Gore to Falls," September 11, 1954, Legislative–Judiciary–Civil Rights–Segregation, "Gore to Dr. Joseph Robertson," January 9, 1956, Series 20, "1956–58, Segregation," Folder 1, Special Civil Rights Issue Mail 1956, Located in D32, Folder "Special Civil Rights General 1956," Albert Gore Center, Middle Tennessee State University, Murfreesboro.

25. Tony Badger, "Southerners Who Refused to Sign the Southern Manifesto," *Historical Journal* 42, No. 2 (1999): 517–534; Reedy, "Interview 8," 46–47, 97–105; "Mexican-Americans Favor Negro School Integration," *News Bulletin (American G.I. Forum)*, September–October 1955, 1, 8–9, Kefauver Papers, Series 5G, Box 10, Folder "School Segregation"; Howard E. Shuman, interview by Donald A. Ritchie, Senate Historical Office (SHO), Hart Senate Office Building, Washington D.C. (July 22–October 22, 1987); Fite, 225, 500; *Georgia Giant*, 21; Mann, *The Walls of Jericho*, 117–120, 128–130; Floyd M. Riddick, interview by Donald Ritchie, SHO (June 26, 1978–February 15, 1979); White, *The Professional: Lyndon B. Johnson* (Boston: Houghton Mifflin, 1964), 169–174.

26. In addition to Johnson and Russell, DPC membership in the Eighty–Fourth Congress was composed of senators Earle C. Clements of Kentucky, Theodore Francis Green of Rhode Island, Carl Hayden of Arizona, Thomas Hennings of Missouri, Lister Hill of Alabama, Robert S. Kerr of Oklahoma, and James E. Murray of Montana. Green, Hill, and Russell had served perpetually on the DPC since its inception in 1947. The South and the border states thus composed two-thirds of the DPC membership, with Hayden and Murray representing western states. Hennings, Hill, and Murray supported organized labor, but only the Missourian was an outspoken civil rights advocate. The sole New Englander was Green, who was nearly ninety years old and well past his prime. Green, Hayden, and Murray were immune from electoral pressure on civil rights because of their states' diminutive black populations and one-party political systems. Johnson, moreover, ensured that any potential dissenters were excluded from the DPC. When Kefauver asked to serve on the DPC, Johnson rejected him, explaining, "I never had the particular feeling that when I called up my first team and the chips were down that Kefauver felt he ought to be on that team." (William S. White, "Democrats' Board of Directors," *New York Times Magazine*, July 10, 1955, Sec. 6, Hennings Papers, F. 3000, F. 181; "Memorandum," January 16, 1956;

Committee Assignments," LBJ Papers, United States Senate, 1949–1961, Papers of the Democratic Leader, Box 364; unpublished manuscript, August 1998, chap. 2, 4, Folder "Democratic Policy Committee History Project," SHO); Scott I. Peek, interview by Donald A. Ritchie, SHO (January 13, 1992): 31–36; Caro, 482, 658, chap. 21; "LBJ to Symington," March 14, 1956, and "Paul Butler to Symington," April 2, 1956, Symington Papers, DSCC-1955-June 1956, F. 2030; Donald A. Ritchie, ed., *Minutes of the Senate Democratic Conference: Fifty-eighth Congress through Eighty-eighth Congress, 1903–1964* (Washington: U.S. Government Printing Office, 1998), 497–98; Shuman, SHO, 105, 143; John Kyle Day, "The Southern Manifesto: Making Opposition to the Civil Rights Movement" (dissertation, University of Missouri–Columbia, 2006), 136–181; McPherson Interview I, 8–9; transcript, Gerald Siegel Oral History Interview III, February 11, 1977, by Michael Gillette, 18–20, in Folder "DPC," Part II, SHO; Dorothy G. Scott, *When the Senate Halls Were Hallowed* (Los Angeles: Corillon Press, 2000); Donald A. Ritchie, Dorothy G. Scott, oral interview, June 3–June 24, 1992, 39, SHO; Ritchie and Craig, 3–58; Hugh Bone, "An Introduction to the Senate Policy Committees," *American Political Science Review* (June 1956), 339– 344, 352; *Congressional Quarterly Almanac*, 84th Congress, 1st Sess., 1955, Vol. XI, Folder "84th Congress," SHO; Matthews, chap. 6; Folders "Democratic Policy Committee," parts I–II, "Democratic Policy Committee Minutes," SHO.

27. Hennings Papers, "NAACP appeal to remove Senator Eastland from Judiciary Committee," 6, F. 3334 "1934–1960," and "Joseph L. Rauh to Hennings," January 7, 1957, F. 3334, "1934–1960," *New York Times*, July 18, 1952, n.p., F. 5829, "1934–1960."

28. The Civil Rights Caucus included Democratic U.S. senators Humphrey, Herbert Lehman of New York, Douglas, Morse and Richard I. Neuberger of Oregon, and Hennings. {William S. White, *The Citadel: A Story of the U.S. Senate* (New York: 1956), 83; Shuman, SHO; Hennings Papers, "We're Tellin'" by "Mel and Thel" (editorial), October 8, 1936, "Hennings to Mr. William H. Parker, Sr.," n.d., F. 7, "General Correspondence" 1934–1940, "J. E. Mitchell to Thomas Hennings," December 11, 1934, October 1, 1935, and March 1, 1936, F. 8, "Correspondence of St. Louis Argus, 1934–36," "Memorandum to subcommittee No. 1," F. 30, "Correspondence, members of Congress, 1947," "Press release," March 17, 1956, F. 444, "Raymond to Langdon West and Dick Brown," June 16, 1956, F. 201, "Hennings Campaign 1956," "J.E. Mitchell to Thomas Hennings," December 11, 1934, October 1, 1935, and March 1, 1936, F. 8, "Correspondence, members of Congress, 1947," *Cleveland Plain Dealer*, August 2, 1950, n.p., F. 31, "Newspaper clippings from the 1940's," "The Cooperative Citizen," November 3, 1950, F. 2987, 2989, "1934–1960," "Press release," March 17, 1956 and "Friendly Sons of Saint Patrick, Philadelphia, PA," March 17, 1956, F. 444, "Speeches and Press Releases, 1956," "Mitchell to Hennings," June 8, 1954, F. 2355, "1934–1960," F.2024, "Civil Rights," *Congressional Record* 100, pt. 1 (n.d.): 352, F. 5829, "1934–1960," "The Fight For Majority Rule In The United States Senate," 25, and "Foreign Policy Speech,"

7, 10, and "Missouri Association For Social Welfare (Pamphlet)," November 25, 1953, "L. F. Martin to Hennings," May 19, 1954, F. 2355, "Segregation," "1934–1960," F. 195, "Papers, campaign speeches, and source material for speeches," "DNC to Hennings," October 4, 1954, F. 175, "1954 campaign, Election Material," "Speeches and Press Releases," January 11–14, 1956, F. 440A, *Congressional Record*, September 4, 1940, 11486, F. 175, "1954 campaign, Election material," "Memorandum," January 16, 1959?, F. 5835, "1934–1960," F. 5836, "Richard H. Brown to Langdon West," September 28, 1955, F. 178, "Political Correspondence, 1955" G4, Murrey Marder, "Democrats Map Strategy to Win Passage of Own Civil Rights Bills," n.d., n.p., F. 2988, "Report No. 2, April 13, 1953, Status of Legislation," F. 5831, 2987–89, "1934–1960," "Press Release," March 4, 1956, F. 444, "Speeches and Press Releases, March 1956," "John Block to Hennings," February 4, 1956, F. 2984, "1934–1960," "Press Release," March 28, 1956, F. 444, and F. 2984, 2986, 2990–91, "1934–1960," "Speeches and Press Releases, 1956"; "Memorandum," January 16, 1956, "Committee Assignments," LBJ Papers, United States Senate, 1949–61, Papers of the Democratic Leader, Box 364; Transcript, Harry McPherson Oral History Interview I, December 5, 1968, by T.H. Electronic Copy, LBJ Library, 24; Dick Dabney, *A Good Man: The Life of Sam J. Ervin* (Boston: Houghton Mifflin, 1976), 182; *Southern School News*, August 1956, 8; Fite, 309; George Lipsitz, *A Life in the Struggle: Ivory Perry and the Culture of Opposition* (Philadelphia: Temple University Press, 1988), chap. 3; *Nation*, July 7, 1956}, 13; Kefauver Collection, Series III: Committee Files, Box 25, Folder "Jud. Civil Rights File, 84th Congress"; *Nation*, January 14, 1956, 21–22; Caro, 783; Folder "DPC minutes," February 15, 1956, 62 (84th–2d), SHO.}

29. Wil Haygood, *King of the Cats: The Life and Times of Adam Clayton Powell, Jr.* (Boston: Houghton-Mifflin, 1993), chap. 4, 186, 205–206; Caro, 600–601; Bartley, 283; *Newsweek*, May 21, 1956, 43; Adam Clayton Powell, Jr., *Adam by Adam: The Autobiography of Adam Clayton Powell, Jr.* (New York: The Dial Press, 1971), 124–125; *Washington Post*, January 12, 1956, 31; "NAACP circular letter," January 14, 1955, Hennings Papers, F. 2543; *New Republic*, January 16, 1956, 4–5; *Nation*, January 28, 1956, 64; *Southern School News*, January 1956, 16; Charles V. Hamilton, *Adam Clayton Powell, Jr.: The Political Biography of an American Dilemma* (New York: Athenaeum, 1991), 118–236; "Powell to Boggs," February 14, 1956, Hale Boggs Papers, File, "Segregation." Quotation appears on attached copy of the *Congressional Record*, Special Collections Division, Howard Tilton Memorial Library, Tulane University, New Orleans, Louisiana.

30. Robert M. Collins, *More: The Politics of Economic Growth* (New York: Oxford University Press, 2001); Eastland Collection, File Series 1, Sub-series 18, Box 7, Folder 7–14; "Lehman to McClellan," January 7, 1955; "Statement of Senator John L. McClellan, Press Release," McClellan Papers, File 19-E, "Federal Aid to School Construction"; Brooks Hays, *A Southern Moderate Speaks* (Chapel Hill: University of North Caro-

lina Press, 1959), 88; C. Vann Woodward, *Origins of the New South, 1877–1913* (Baton Rouge: Louisiana State University Press, 1951).}

31. "Timmerman to Thurmond," February 11, 1956, STC, Speeches, B: Originals, Box 4, Folder 61; ODJ Papers, Box 53, Folder 1956-40, "Timmerman-Johnston correspondence," February 1956, "Rogers-Johnston correspondence," June 1956; "News Release," Robertson Papers, Drawer 140, Folder 54"; Wilbur Mills Collection, "Final draft—Address to the State Democratic Convention, Little Rock, AR," October 14, 1955, "Caldwell to Mills," January 30, 1956, Box 259, Folder 56/3, "HR 7535, Committee on Educ & Labor Providing Fd Aid to School Constr," "Ford to Mills," January 26, 1956, Box 783, File 16, 10–11, Wilbur D. Mills Center Building, Hendrix College, Conway, Arkansas; Sam J. Ervin Papers: Subgroup A, Senate Records, 1954–1975, Folder 763, Folders 1115-1118, Wilson Library, Southern Historical Collection, University of North Carolina at Chapel Hill; *Newsweek*, January 23, 1956, 94; Carl Albert Collection, Legislative Series, Box 22, Folder 47, Carl Albert Center, University of Oklahoma, Norman. Some southern congressmen like Thurmond and U.S. Representative James C. Davis of Georgia opposed the Kelly Bill because it would result in "too much Federal control," in the latter's words. {"Davis to Archer," January 30, 1956, James C. Davis Papers, Folder "School Construction–1956," Series Additions, Box 216, Manuscript, Archive, and Rare Book Library (MARBL), Emory University, Georgia.}

32. *Nation*, July 7, 1956, 5; *Nashville Tennessean*, February 26, 1956, n.p., "Gore–Mrs. J. Harvill Hite correspondence," Gore Papers, Series 20, "Special, 1953–1970, Folder "1956–1958 Segregation," 3; *Pine Bluff Commercial*, n.d., n.p., "L. G. Baker to McClellan," March 21, 1956, McClellan Papers, File 19-B, "Segregation"; RBR Papers, *Los Angeles Times*, March 11, 1956, n.p., "Jones to Russell," March 14, 1956, Series X, Box 195, Folder 11 "Supreme Court," and George Gallup, "U.S. School Aid Favored Despite Segregation," March 20, 1956, Series X, Box 177, Segregation File 8; 84th Congress, 2nd Sess., *Congressional Record* 102, pt. 3 (February 21, 1956): 3058–3061; *New Republic*, February 6, 1956, 3; *Washington Post*, February 19, 1956, A12; *Newsweek*, February 20, 1956, 25; Kefauver Collection, Series 58, Box 10, Folder "School Segregation," and "Frank Reeves to Kefauver," Series 5G, Box 52, Folder "Powell Amendment," Box 39, Folder "Civil rights," 1 of 2; *Newsweek*, February 6, 1956, 25–26; Hennings Papers, "Memorandum," March 21, 1956, F. 3227, "Hennings to Carl R. Johnson," June 17, 1955, F. 2825, "1934–1960," "Hennings to Mrs. William J. McMillan," July 27, 1955, F. 2825, "1934–1960," "Hennings to Hubert L. Brown," June 14, 1955, F. 3227, "1934–1960"; "Harry McPherson Oral History Interview with Michael Gillette, VI, LBJ Library, May 16, 1985, 8–9; Alan Brinkley, *The End of Reform: New Deal Liberalism in Recession and War* (New York: Alfred A. Knopf, 1995), 269–270.

33. Stephen E. Ambrose, *Nixon: The Education of a Politician* (New York: Simon and Schuster, 1987), 409, 413, 436, and *Eisenhower: Volume Two, The President* (New York: Simon and Schuster, 1984), 189–192; Cohodas, 275; Democratic Senatorial

Campaign Committee, 1953–54, "Latest Republican Propaganda," 3, Symington Papers, F. 2029; Martin, 165–168; *New York Times*, August 2, 1956, 1, 14; *Ebony*, March 1956, 40.

34. DDE Papers, Diary 1956, 3/21, File: "Mar '56," Diary, Ann Whitman Diary Series, Box 8, File "Graham, Billy [Race Relations, Politics]," Name Series, Box 16, Papers as President of the United States, 1953–61 (Ann Whitman File); Brooks Hays, *A Southern Moderate Speaks* (Chapel Hill, University of North Carolina Press, 1959), 90–91; Day, "The Fall of Southern Moderation: The Defeat of Brooks Hays in the 1958 Congressional Election for the Fifth District of Arkansas" (M.A. thesis, University of Arkansas, 1999); LBJ Papers, LBJ Oral History Manuscripts, Brooks Hays, AC 79-10, Interview 1 (24-29), October 5, 1971.

35. Steven Lawson, "Oral History Interview with Maxwell Rabb," October 6, 1970, Columbia University Oral History Project, DDE Library, 2–3.

36. E. Frederic Morrow, *Black Man in the White House: A Diary of the Eisenhower Years by the Administrative Officer for Special Projects, the White House, 1955–1961* (New York: Coward-McCann, Inc., 1963).

37. Ed Edwin, "Interview with Frederic Morrow," 1, 2, January 31, 1968, and April 15, 1968, Columbia University Oral History Project, DDE Library; Morrow, *Black Man in the White House*, *Way Down South Up North* (Philadelphia: United Church Press, 1973), and *Forty Years a Guinea Pig* (New York: Pilgrim Press, 1980).

38. DDE Library, "Morrow to Rabb," November 19, 1955; "Wilkins to Morrow," December 2, 1955; "Morrow to Adams," December 16, 1955, Morrow, E. Frederic: Records, 1950–61, Box 10, File "Civil Rights–Official Memoranda 1955–1956," File "138-A-6 Negro Voting," Central Files: Official File, OF 138-A-5-B, Box 704, "State of the Union Jan 1956" (3), Papers as President of the United States, 1953–61 (Ann Whitman File) Speech Series, Box 14.

39. DDE Papers, "State of the Union Message," Draft of November 30, 1955, File "Cabinet Meeting of 12/2/55," and "Cabinet Meeting of 12/16/55," "Cabinet Meeting of 12/2/55," State of the Union Message draft," 12/29/55, "State of the Union Remarks, 1/5/56," "State of the Union Address," 1/5/56, Official Text, File "State of the Union, Jan. 195 (1)," Cabinet Series, Box 6, Speech Series, Box 14, Papers as President of the United States, 1953–61 (Ann Whitman File); Day, "The Southern Manifesto," chap. 6; "Thurmond Statement on the State of the Union," January 5, 1956, STC, Speeches, B: Originals, Box 4, Folder 60; *New York Times*, March 28, 1956, 1, 24, Hennings Papers, F. 2988; *The Pittsburgh Courier*, January 19, 1956, n.p., Morrow Records, 1950–61, Box 10, File "Civil Rights–Official Memoranda 1955–1956."

40. Morrow, *Black Man in the White House*, 34–37; DDE Papers, Morrow Records, "Morrow to Gov. Sherman Adams," February 27, 1956, Box 1, File "Civil Rights," Ed Edwin, "Interview with Frederic Morrow," 1 and 2, January 31, 1968, and April 15, 1968, Columbia University Oral History Manuscripts, 61, *Washington Post*, January

12, 1956, 31, Box 10, File "Civil Rights–Official Memoranda 1955–1956," Private Diary Entry, File "Jan '56 Diary," "Summary of Congressional Mail Addressed to the President," March 15, 1956, File "Mar '56 Miscellaneous" (3), DDE Diary Series, Boxes 12 and 14, "Memorandum to Hon. Rowland R. Hughes, Director, Bureau of the Budget," January 10, 1956, "Legislative Leaders' Meetings 1956" (1) [January–February], Legislative Meeting Series, Box 2 Papers as President of the United States, 1953–61 (Ann Whitman File); *Tupelo Journal*, "Lumpkin to Eastland," January 28, 1956, Eastland Collection, Series 3, Sub-series 1, Box 35, Folder "1956 Civil Rights (2 of 3)"; *New York Times*, March 28, 1956, 1, 24, Hennings Papers, F. 2988.

41. "Morrow to Adams," February 27, 1956, Morrow Papers, File "Civil Rights"; Morrow, *Black Man in the White House*, 45–48, 52; Ed Edwin, DDE Library, "Interview with Frederic Morrow," 1 and 2, January 31, 1968, and April 15, 1968, Columbia University Oral History Project, DDE Library, 33, "Rabb Interview," DDE Diary Series, Box 13, File "Feb '56 Miscellaneous (1)," "Press Conference Transcript," March 21, 1956, 21, Box 4, Papers as President of the United States, 1953–61 (Ann Whitman File); Elmo Richardson, *The Presidency of Dwight D. Eisenhower* (Lawrence: University Press of Kansas, 1979), 110–111.

42. Ambrose, *Eisenhower: Vol. Two*; *U.S. News & World Report*, March 2, 1956, 16, 44; *Newsweek*, February 27, 1956, 21–22 and March 12, 1956, 27–29; *Time*, March 12, 1956, 19–27; "Press Release," February 29, 1956, DDE Papers, Papers as President of the United States (Ann Whitman File), Speech Series, Box 15, File "1956 Campaign Decision 2/29/56 (1)"; *Life*, March 12, 1956, 18.

43. *Jet* IX, No. 16 (February 23, 1956): 3.

44. Elizabeth Carpenter, "Shivers Lunches With Ike But Sidesteps Questions On Either's Political Intent," January 25, 1956, LBJ Papers, LBJA (Subject File), Box 100, File "Public Information–Press, National"; *U.S. News & World Report*, March 9, 1956, 102; Folder "DPC minutes," May 15, 1956, 66 (84th–2d), SHO), *Time*, February 27, 1956, 24–25; U.S. Congress, House, Remarks of Hon. James C. Davis. 84th Cong., 2nd sess., *Congressional Record* 102 (February 27, 1956): 2, RBR Papers, Vertical File, Folder "Civil Rights General"; *Crisis*, August–September 1955, 389.

45. "Diary," 2/9/56, 2–3 and 3/19/56, File "Mar. '56 Diary-acw (2)," DDE Papers, Papers as President of the United States, 1953–61 (Ann Whitman File), Ann Whitman Diary Series, Box 8; Tyler Abell, ed., *Drew Pearson: Diaries, 1949–1959* (New York: Holt, Rinehart & Winston, 1974), 360.

46. *Time*, February 27, 1956, 25 and March 12, 1956, 19–27; *Life*, March 12, 1956, 37.

47. Bartley, 64, 140, 146–147.

48. *U.S. News & World Report*, March 9, 1956, 30–32.

49. LBJ Senate Political Files, 1949–61, Box 58, File "Senatorial Candidates, 1956"; *U.S. News & World Report*, January 16, 1956, 36; *Harper's*, June 1956, 11.

50. "Booth Mooney to LBJ," November 28, 1955, LBJ Papers, LBJA Congressional

File, Box 53, "Russell, Richard B.," File 2 of 2; *Newsweek*, May 21, 1956, 35–36, and April 2, 1956, 29; Fite, 312; *Nation*, November 17, 1956, 425–426; *U.S. News & World Report*, March 9, 1956, 30–31.

51. Herbert J. Muller, *Adlai Stevenson: A Study in Values* (New York: Harper & Row, 1967); *Newsweek*, April 2, 1956, 28, and June 22, 1956, 78–80; *Time*, February 20, 1956, n.p., August 27, 1956, 17, and September 10, 1956, 3; *Norfolk Virginian Pilot*, December 14, 1955, n.p., LBJ Papers, Senate Political Files, 1949–61, Box 2021; "Smathers to LBJ," November 1, 1955, LBJ Papers, 2, LBJA Congressional File, Box 54, File "Smathers, George," 1 of 2; "Stevenson to Thurmond," January 23, 1956, STC, Box 11 (political folder).

52. *Saint Louis Globe-Democrat*, October 18, 1955, n.p., Hennings Papers, F. 184; *Washington Daily News*, October 18, 1955, n.p., Kefauver Collection, Series 1, Subject, Box 44, Folder "Elections 1956: General Correspondence, 1 of 3; Ervin Papers, *Dunn Daily Record*, October 13, 1955, Subgroup A, Scrapbook, Series XII, Vol. 2, 3847, and "Sam Ervin Says," February 23, 1956 (Col. No. 59), Subgroup A, Box 396.

53. *Southern School News*, March 1956, 13; *Time*, December 12, 1955, 23; October 15, 1956, 35.

54. J. N. Rushing, D.D.S., "Scrapbook," Albert Sidney Farms, Jerome, Arkansas; JWF Papers, BCN 116, F49, Box A636, "Fulbright to Dr. Shelton Rushing, El Dorado, AR," September 27, 1955, "Erickson to Oren Harris and Nolen Rushing," November 22, 1955, "Rushing to Erickson," November 23, 1955, BCN 116, F49, Box A636. "Memorandum," n.d., "Fulbright to Long, n.d., "Rub-A-Dub-Dub," December 26, 1955; "Fulbright to Russell," October 19, 1955, BCN 96, F11, in Gilbert Fite, "RBR notes"; "Hennings to Stevenson," November 16, 1955, Hennings Papers, "political correspondence, 1955 G-4," F 178; F 182, "Eugene McCarthy Press Releases referring to H. Humphrey as Vice-Pres.," RBR Papers, I.C. Box 2, dictations political, in Fite, "RBR notes"; "Booth Mooney to Johnson," November 28, 1955, LBJ Papers, LBJA Congressional File, Box 53, Folder "Russell, Richard B." 2 of 2; Kefauver Collection, Box 3, Audiovisual Series 14.

55. Kefauver Collection, "Kefauver to Weary," January 10, 1956, Series 1, Box 11, Folder 16; "constituent reply letter," February 2, 1956, Series III, Box 25, Folder "Jud. Civil Rights File 84th Congress."

56. *Newsweek*, April 2, 1956, 25, 29–30; Kefauver Collection, *New York Times*, December 23, 1955, n. p., Series 5G, Box 52, Folder "Powell Amendment," *Chattanooga Free Press*, September 30, 1955, n.p., Series 5G, Box 2. Folder "Williams"; "Kefauver-Williams correspondence," Series 1, Box 44, "Elections 1956: General Correspondence," Folder 2 of 3, Series 5G, Box 12, Folder "Congressmen supporting Kefauver, May 24, 1956"; and Series 6, Box 10–12, "Trip Files"; *Time*, September 17, 1956, 23–28 and December 12, 1955, 23–24; Fontenay; "Kefauver to Truman," December 15, 1955, Truman Presidential Papers, Post-Presidential Files, Box 88, Folder "Estes Kefauver,"

Harry S. Truman Presidential Library, Independence, Missouri; *Atlanta Constitution*, February 24, 1956, 6, RBR Papers, Series 6, Sub-series A1, Box 12, Folder 5; *Nation*, April 21, 1956, 336; *Christian Science Monitor*, February 16, 1956, LBJ Papers, LBJA Famous Names, Box 3, File, "Corcoran, Thomas G., 1938–1961."

57. Kefauver Collection, Civil Rights, Segregation, Memphis *Commercial Appeal*, February 5, 1956, p. 5, Series 5G, Box 9, File "Civil Rights," 2 of 2, and "Waring to Kefauver," January 7, 1956, Series 1: Subject, Box 11, Folder 16; James B. Gardner, "Political Leadership in a Period of Transition: Frank G. Clement, Albert Gore, Estes Kefauver, and Tennessee Politics, 1948–56" (dissertation, Vanderbilt University, 1978); Tara Mitchell Mielnik, "Resisting Massive Resistance: Tennessee's Senators and the Southern Manifesto," March 27, 1997, unpublished seminar paper in Gore Papers; Martin, Jr., 126–137; Key, 627–632.

58. *Newsweek*, April 2, 1956, 28; Memphis *Commercial Appeal*, February 5, 1956, 5, Kefauver Collection, Series 5G, Box 9, Folder "Civil Rights," 2 of 2; *Christian Science Monitor*, February 16, 1956, LBJ Papers, LBJA Famous Names, Box 3, Folder "Corcoran, Thomas G., 1938–1961;" *Life*, June 11, 1956, 92; *Time*, December 12, 1955, 23, February 13, 1956, 15–16.

59. *Time*, December 12, 1955, 23; "Memorandum from U.S. Reps. James J. Delaney, Victor L. Anfuso, and Eugene J. Keogh (D–NY)," June 6, 1956, JWF Papers, Series 71, Box 10:2.

60. Symington Papers, "Saint John AME Church to Symington," November 21, 1956; "Theodore W. Keel, President of the National Urban League to Symington," November 10, 1956; "Ruth M. Wheeler to Symington," January 19, 1956, Box 119, "NAACP Correspondence"; Box 119, "NAACP"; Box 28, "Contributions, 1956," "Loeb to Symington," March 23, 1956; March 5, 1956 (telephone dictation), "Loeb to Symington," March 26, 1956, "McClellan to Symington," March 21, 1956; "Symington to Loeb," March 7, 1956, Box 106, Folder "Loeb, William 1956"; *Newsweek*, April 2, 1956, 28.

61. Bartley, 146, 233, 285, 310; Richard K. Scher, *Politics of the New South: Republicanism, Race and Leadership in the Twentieth Century* (Armonk: M. E. Sharpe, 1997), 180, 216; Francis Wilhoit, *The Politics of Massive Resistance* (New York: George Braziler, 1972), 46–47, 112, 197; *U.S. News & World Report*, February 17, 1956, 18; *Life*, n.d., 28; *Time*, February 20, 1956, 40.

62. *New Republic*, February 20, 1956, 5; *Newsweek*, February 20, 1956, 30, and February 27, 1956, 86; *Life*, n.d., 28; *Time*, February 20, 1956, 40.

63. *Life*, n.d., 28; *New Republic*, February 27, 1956, 11; *Newsweek*, February 20, 1956, 30; *Time*, February 13, 1956, 53, and February 20, 1956, 40; *Southern School News*, March 1956, 6.

64. *Life*, n.d., 31; *Time*, February 20, 1956, 40; *New Republic*, February 20, 1956, 6; *U.S. News & World Report*, February 17, 1956, 18; *Newsweek*, February 27, 1956, 86.

65. *Life*, n.d., 32; *Time*, February 20, 1956, 40.

66. *Time*, February 20, 1956, 40, March 12, 1956, 97; *The South*, March 19, 1956, 10, RBR Papers, Series VI, Sub-series A1, Box 12, Folder 5 "Personal-Political"; *Newsweek*, March 22, 1956, 38–39, February 27, 1956, 86, March 26, 1956, 25; *Montgomery Advertiser*, March 2, 1956, 1A, 6A.

67. *Newsweek*, February 20, 1956, 30–31, May 21, 1956, 43; *Time*, February 20, 1956, 40; *Life*, n.d., 28, 31; Buford Boone Papers, Series: Correspondence, Box 254, Folders 1–13, Hoole Library, University of Alabama, Tuscaloosa; *U.S. News & World Report*, February 24, 1956, 44–45, 47–48, 137; *St. Petersburg Times*, February 9, 1956, 6, Spessard Holland Papers, Box 336, folder 5-D "Segregation," Special and Regional Studies Collections, University of Florida Smathers Libraries, Gainesville; Bartley, 281–286.

68. *Atlanta Journal*, February 27, 1956, 1, RBR Papers, Series X, Box 149, Folder 4, "Civil Rights Racial"; Tony Badger, "Fatalism, Not Gradualism: The Crisis of Southern Liberalism, 1945–65," in Brian Ward and Badger, eds., *The Making of Martin Luther King and the Civil Rights Movement* (New York: New York University Press, 1996), 88; *Newsweek*, March 26, 1956, 25; *Atlanta Journal*, March 13, 1956, 16.

69. *U.S. News & World Report*, February 24, 1956, 144; *Nation*, September 29, 1956, 269; *New Republic*, February 27, 1956, 11–13; *Life*, March 12, 1956, 37.

70. *Life*, March 12, 1956, 37; *Telegram*, March 18, 1956, 6, RBR Papers, Series X, Box 177, Folder "Civil Rights 9"; Chappell, 175, 289–290; "Memorandum," March 6, 1956, Stennis Papers, Series 29, Sub-series: "Organizations, Box 7, Folder 5; *New Republic*, February 20, 1956, 6; *Nation*, April 21, 1956, 334; *Washington Post*, March 8, 1956, n.p., Kefauver Collection, Series 5G, Box 9, File "Civil Rights," 2 of 2.

71. "Kefauver to Williams," February 10, 1956, Kefauver Collection, Series X, Box 7, File, "Feb 10, 1956 Senate Floor, Powell Amendment re Segregation in public schools"; *U.S. News & World Report*, February 17, 1956, 46–47; *New Republic*, February 20, 1956, 3; *U.S. News & World Report*, February 24, 1956, 43; Johnson, *Stevenson Papers*, 51–53, 65–67; *Time*, February 6, 1956, 21, February 20, 1956, 18–19; *Newsweek*, February 20, 1956, 30–31; Kenneth S. Davis, *The Politics of Honor: A Biography of Adlai E. Stevenson* (New York: G. P. Putnam's Sons, 1967), 326; Stuart Gerry Brown, *Adlai E. Stevenson: A Short Biography, The Conscience of a Country* (Woodbury: Barron's, 1965), 135–136; *Jet* IX, No. 16 (February 23, 1956): 4–5; Walter Johnson, ed., *Toward a New America*, Vol. VI of *The Papers of Adlai E. Stevenson* (Boston: Little, Brown, & Co., 1976), 45–68.

72. *Newsweek*, February 20, 1956, 25, 30–31; *Time*, 13, 1956, 16–17, February 20, 1956, 18–19; *Washington Star*, February 6, 1956, n.p., RBR Papers, Series VI, Sub-series 12, Box 28, Folder 4, "Democratic Party"; *The State*, February 4, 1956, STC "Originals," Box 4, Folder 37; *New Republic*, February 13, 1956, 3 and February 20, 1956, 3; *U.S. News & World Report*, February 17, 1956, 46–47 and February 24, 1956, 43.

73. Reinhold Niebuhr, "Nullification," *The New Leader*, March 5, 1956, 3–4, RBR Papers, Series X, Box 177, Folder "civil rights #9"; *U.S. News & World Report*, Febru-

ary 24, 1956, 43; *Christian Science Monitor*, February 16, 1956, n.p., LBJ Papers, Series LBJA, Box 3, Folder "Famous Names (Thomas Corcoran: 1938–61)"; *Nation*, February 18, 1956, 129–131; Johnson, *Stevenson Papers*, 65.

74. "Russell to Maudins," January 30, 1956, RBR Papers, Series X, Box 163, Folder 5, and January 23, 1956, EG 1133A, Series VI, Sub-series A1, Box 12, Folder 5; *New Republic*, February 13, 1956, 3; *Newsweek*, May 7, 1956, 30–31; *Southern School News*, March 1956, 13.

75. *Newsweek*, February 27, 1956, 25.

76. *Charlotte Times*, February 15, 1956, n.p., Kefauver Collection, Series 5G, Box 9, Folder "Civil Rights," 2 of 2; *Southern School News*, March 1956, 13.

77. *Pine Bluff Commercial*, n.p., n.d., "L. G. Baker to McClellan," March 4, 1956, McClellan Papers, File 19-B "Segregation"; *New Republic*, February 27, 1956, 4–5; Morrow, *Black Man in the White House*, 53.

CHAPTER 3

1. C. Vann Woodward, *Origins of the New South, 1877–1913* (Baton Rouge: Louisiana State University Press, 1951), 23–50.

2. Numan V. Bartley, *The Rise of Massive Resistance: Race and Politics in the South During the 1950's* (Baton Rouge: Louisiana State University Press, 1969), 116–117; Anthony J. Badger, "The Southern Manifesto: White Southerners and Civil Rights, 1956," in Rob Kroes and Eduard Van de Bilt, eds., *The U.S. Constitution after 200 Years* (Amsterdam: Free University Press, 1988), 82, and "Fatalism, Not Gradualism: The Crisis of Southern Liberalism, 1945–65," in *The Making of Martin Luther King and the Civil Rights Movement*, Badger and Brian Ward, eds. (New York: New York University Press, 1996), 67–95, and "*Brown* and Backlash," in *Massive Resistance: Southern Opposition to the Second Reconstruction*, ed. Clive Webb (New York: Oxford University Press, 2005), 46, and "The South Confronts the Court: The Southern Manifesto of 1956," *Journal of Policy History* (JPH) 20, No. 1 (2008), 126–142; Karl E. Campbell, *Senator Sam Ervin: Last of the Founding Fathers* (Chapel Hill: University of North Carolina Press, 2007), 105; Francis M. Wilhoit, *The Politics of Massive Resistance* (New York: George Braziller, 1973), 51, 53; Nadine Cohodas, *Strom Thurmond and the Politics of Southern Change* (New York: Simon & Schuster, 1993) 283, 285; Richard K. Scher, *Politics in the New South: Republicanism, Race and Leadership in the Twentieth Century* (Armonk: M. E. Sharpe, 1997), 203; George Lewis, *Massive Resistance: The White Response to the Civil Rights Movement* (London: Hodder, 2006), 65–69; Brent J. Aucoin, "The Southern Manifesto and Southern Opposition to Desegregation," *Arkansas Historical Quarterly (AHQ)* 55, No. 2 (Summer 1996): 174–189; Jack Bass and Walter DeVries, *The Transformation of Southern Politics: Social Change and Political Consequence Since 1945* (New York: Basic Books, 1976), 346; Bruce J. Dieren-

field, *Keeper of the Rules: Congressman Howard W. Smith of Virginia* (Charlottesville: University Press of Virginia, 1987), 148–149; Dewey W. Grantham, *The Life & Death of the Solid South: A Political History* (Lexington: University Press of Kentucky, 1988), 138; Ronald L. Heinemann, *Harry Byrd of Virginia* (Charlottesville: University Press of Virginia, 1996); Timothy S. Huebner, "Looking Backward: The Southern Manifesto of 1956," *Historically Speaking* VII, No. 5 (May/June 2006): 36–39; Kyle Longley, "White Knight for Civil Rights?: The Civil Rights Record of Senator Albert A. Gore, Sr.," *Tennessee Historical Quarterly (THQ)* 57, No. 2–3 (1998): 114–131 and *Senator Albert Gore, Sr.: Tennessee Maverick* (Baton Rouge: Louisiana State University Press, 2004), 123–124; Robert Mann, *The Walls of Jericho: Lyndon Johnson, Hubert Humphrey, Richard Russell, and the Struggle for Civil Rights* (New York: Harcourt, Brace & Company, 1996), 161–162; Tara Mitchell Mielnik, "Resisting Massive Resistance: Tennessee's Senators and the Southern Manifesto," March 27, 1997, seminar paper, Albert Gore Sr. Congressional Research Center, Middle Tennessee State University, Murfreesboro; James T. Patterson, *Brown v. Board of Education: A Civil Rights Milestone and Its Troubled Legacy* (New York: Oxford University Press, 2001), 98; Roy Reed, *Faubus: The Life and Times of an American Prodigal* (Fayetteville: University of Arkansas Press, 1997), 356; Jason Morgan Ward, *Defending White Democracy: The Making of a Segregationist Movement and the Remaking of Racial Politics, 1936–1965* (Chapel Hill: University of North Carolina Press, 2011), 144–146; Betty Bean Fielder, "Price Daniel, Texas and Segregation" (M.A. thesis, Lamar University), 94; Joseph Crespino, *Strom Thurmond's America* (New York: Hill and Wang, 2012), 105–107.

3. Badger, "Southerners Who Refused to Sign the Southern Manifesto," *Historical Journal*, 42, No. 2 (1999): 517–518 and "'The Forerunner of Our Opposition:' Arkansas and the Southern Manifesto of 1956," *AHQ* LVI, No. 3 (Autumn 1997) and "The South Confronts the Court: The Southern Manifesto of 1956," *JPH* 20, No. 1 (2008), 126–142; Robert Caro, *Master of the Senate* (New York: Alfred A. Knopf, 2002), 785, Vol. III of *The Years of Lyndon Johnson;* Keith M. Finley, *Delaying the Dream: Southern Senators and the Fight against Civil Rights, 1938–1965* (Baton Rouge: Louisiana State University Press, 2008), 138–154; Dick Dabney, *A Good Man: The Life of Sam J. Ervin* (Boston: Houghton Mifflin Company, 1976), 178–179; Gilbert C. Fite, *Richard B. Russell: Senator from Georgia* (Chapel Hill: University of North Carolina Press, 1991), 331–336; Potenziani, 132–137; Randall Woods, *Fulbright: A Biography* (New York: Cambridge University Press, 1995), 207–211 and *LBJ: Architect of American Ambition* (New York: Free Press, 2006), 303–304; Herman Talmadge, *Talmadge: A Political Legacy, A Politician's Life* (Atlanta: Peachtree Publishing, 1987), 178; John A. Goldsmith, *Colleagues: Richard Russell and His Apprentice, Lyndon B. Johnson* (Washington, D.C.,: Seven Locks Press, 1993), 50–51, 192; Dan Murph, *The Life of Price Daniel: Texas Giant* (Austin: Eakin Press, 2002), 136–139.

4. Bartley, 116–117, and *The New South, 1945–1980* (Baton Rouge: Louisiana State

University Press, 1995), 187–222; Grantham, 138, 216; Matthew D. Lassiter and Andrew B. Lewis, *The Moderates' Dilemma: Massive Resistance to School Desegregation in Virginia* (Charlottesville: University Press of Virginia, 1998), 7, 205; Waldo E. Martin, Jr., ed., *Brown v. Board of Education: A Brief History with Documents* (Bedford/ St. Martin's: Boston, 1998), 219; Scher, 203, 383; Heinemann, 335, 467; Wilhoit, 53, 295; *Time*, March 26, 1956, 25; *The South*, March 19, 1956, 9–10, Richard B. Russell (RBR) Papers, Series VI, Sub-series A1, Box 12, Folder 5 "Personal Political," Richard B. Russell Memorial Library, University of Georgia, Athens; "Drew Pearson's Washington Merry-Go-Round," Jackson *Clarion-Ledger*, March 18, 1956, p. 3, sec. 4; Harry Ashmore, *An Epitaph for Dixie* (New York: W. W. Norton, 1958), 33; Drew Pearson, "Byrd Masterminded the Manifesto," *Washington Post*, March 19, 1956, Spessard Holland Papers, Box 336, Folder 5-d "Segregation," Special and Regional Studies Collections, Smathers Memorial Libraries, University of Florida, Gainesville; Lee Riley Powell, *J. William Fulbright and His Time: A Political Biography* (Memphis: Guild Bindery Press, 1996), 108–112; *Arkansas Gazette*, March 18, 1956, 5f; Cohodas, 284; Aucoin, 174. Bartley used the *Washington Evening Star*, March 12, 1956, *Atlanta Journal*, March 18, 1956, *Charleston Gazette*, March 16, 1956, *Arkansas Gazette*, March 18, 1956, and the notes of Hayes Mizell, later a graduate student at the University of South Carolina.

5. "Howard Crouse to Wright Patman," February 7, 1956, Wright Patman Papers, Box 94 (A): Defense Plant Files; misc. Banking Files, Folder 6, "Segregation," Lyndon Baines Johnson Presidential Library, University of Texas at Austin.

6. David Garrow, *Bearing the Cross: Martin Luther King, Jr., and the Southern Christian Leadership Conference* (New York: William Morrow and Company, Inc., 1986), 60; *Time*, February 6, 1956, 21.

7. Garrow, 60–66; David L. Chappell, *Inside Agitators: White Southerners in the Civil Rights Movement* (Baltimore: The Johns Hopkins University Press, 1994), 75–83; *Time*, March 5, 1956, 21; Joseph Kip Kosek, "Richard Gregg, Mohandas Gandhi and the Strategy of Nonviolence," *Journal of American History (JAH)* 91, No. 4 (March 2005): 1344; *New Republic*, March 5, 1956, 6.

8. *New Republic*, March 5, 1956, 6; *Tampa Tribune*, February 26, 1956, n.p., RBR Papers, Series X, Box 149, Folder 4; *Chattanooga News–Free Press*, February 29, 1956, James Oliver Eastland Collection, Series 3, Sub-series 1, Box 35, Folder "1956 Civil Rights (1 of 3)," J. D. Williams Library, the Department of Archives and Special Collections, University of Mississippi, Oxford.

9. *Pine Bluff Commercial*, n.d., n.p., "L. G. Baker to McClellan," March 21, 1956, John L. McClellan Papers, File 19-B "Segregation," Riley-Hickingbotham Memorial Library, Ouachita Baptist University, Arkadelphia, Arkansas; *Southern School News*, April 1956, 2; *Atlanta Journal*, February 27, 1956, 1, RBR Papers, Series X, Box 149, Folder 4, "Civil Rights Racial"; Thomas Hennings Papers, "Press Release," March 5,

1956, F. 2990, "1934–1960," and "Press releases," March 4 and 17, 1956, F. 444; Ellis Library, Western Historical Manuscripts Collection (WHMC), University of Missouri–Columbia; Estes Kefauver Collection, *Washington Post*, March 6, 1956, Series 5G, Box 9, Folder "Civil Rights," 2 of 2, and Series III, Committee Files, Box 25, Folder "Jud. Civil Rights File, 84th Congress," Special Collections Division, Hoskins Memorial Library, University of Tennessee–Knoxville.

10. "Adlai Stevenson Address," Hartford, Connecticut, February 26, 1956, and *New York Times*, February 26, 1956, James William Fulbright (JWF) Papers, Series 71, Box 10: 1, Special Collections Division, Mullins Library, University of Arkansas at Fayetteville; Walter Johnson, ed., *Toward a New America*, Vol. VI of *The Papers of Adlai E. Stevenson* (Boston: Little, Brown, & Co., 1976), 77–78; *Tampa Tribune*, February 26, 1956, n.p., RBR Papers, Series X, Box 149, Folder 4; Stuart Gerry Brown, *Adlai E. Stevenson: A Short Biography, The Conscience of the Country* (Woodbury: Barron's, 1965), 136–137; *Newsweek*, March 5, 1956, 22.

11. "Dabney to Graves," March 5, 1956, John Temple Graves II Papers, 830.1.18, Birmingham Public Library, Department of Archives and Manuscripts, Alabama; "Memorandum," Citizens' Councils of Mississippi, Winona, MS, December 14, 1955, William Workman Papers, Box 32, Folder "Integration/Civil Rights, Citizens' Councils, South Carolina, 1955–1956," and Olin D. Johnston (ODJ) Papers, Box 53, Folder "Citizens' Councils" 1956-24, Modern Political Collections (MPC), South Caroliniana Library, University of South Carolina, Columbia; "McCarter to Fulbright," January 30, 1956, JWF Papers, BCN 19, F45 (14a); "Gamble to Russell," February 24, 1956, RBR Papers, Series X, Box 163, Folder 4 and *Atlanta Journal*, February 27, 1956, 1 and 6, Series X, Box 149, Folder 4, "Civil Rights Racial"; Brooks Hays, *A Southern Moderate Speaks* (Chapel Hill: University of North Carolina Press, 1959), 88.

12. Hale Boggs Papers, Volume II, MC 1000, Subject Series, Box 21, File "Segregation, 1956," Special Collections Division, Jones Hall, Tulane University, New Orleans, Louisiana; Jane Dailey, "Sex, Segregation, and the Sacred after *Brown*," *JAH*, 91, No.1 (June 2004): 119–144; "Foster to JWF," February 7, 1956, JWF Papers, BCN 19, F45 (14a) and *Arkansas Faith*, Series 71, Box 10:2 and *Arkansas Recorder*, March 2, 1956, Series 71, Box 10:1; *Pine Bluff Commercial*, n.d., n.p., "L. G. Baker to McClellan," March 4, 1956, McClellan Papers, File 19–B "Segregation"; James T. Patterson, *Congressional Conservatism and the New Deal: The Growth of the Conservative Coalition in Congress* (Lexington: University of Kentucky Press, 1967).

13. "Richard B. Russell: Georgia Giant," Television transcripts, Russell Memorial Library, University of Georgia Libraries, Athens, Georgia, 30602; Chappell, *Inside Agitators*, 43–44;Talmadge, *Talmadge*, 38–39; V. O. Key, Jr., *Southern Politics in State and Nation* (New York: Alfred A. Knopf, 1949), 468, 472, 605; Ashmore, 99–103; Donald R. Mathews, *U.S. Senators and Their World* (Chapel Hill: University of North Carolina Press, 1960), 251–253.

14. Key, 106–129; 570, 635–637; Talmadge, 40, 79–96; Steven Weisenburger, "The Columbians, Inc.: A Chapter of Racial Hatred from the Post–World War II South," *Journal of Southern History (JSH)* 69, No. 4 (November 2003): 821–860; David Potenziani, "Look to the Past: Richard Russell and the Southern Defense of White Supremacy" (dissertation, University of Georgia, Athens, 1981), 63–64; *U.S. News & World Report*, February 17, 1956, 32, 34.

15. Talmadge, 78, 169 and *You and Segregation* (Birmingham: Vulcan Press, 1955); *Harper's*, January 1956, 22.

16. "Press Release," February 11, 1956, ODJ Papers, Box 102, Folder 12; Workman Papers, Box 38, Topical File Series, Folder "Persons, Talmadge, Herman E., 1954–1960"; Talmadge, *Talmadge*, 236.

17. *U.S. News & World Report*, February 17, 1956, 32–33; *Arkansas Gazette*, March 18, 1956, 1A; Woods, *Fulbright*, 208; Talmadge, *Talmadge*, 169; Badger, "The Southern Manifesto: White Southerners and Civil Rights, 1956," 82; Key, 467.

18. Cohodas, 194–216, 239–267; LBJ Oral History Manuscripts AC 89–64, J. Strom Thurmond, "Interview 1, May 7, 1979, 1–2, LBJ Presidential Library; *Charlotte Observer*, October 6, 1955, *Charleston News & Courier*, December 15, 1955, Workman Papers.

19. Cohodas, 273, 283; Donald A. Ritchie, ed., *Minutes of the Senate Democratic Conference: Fifty-eighth Congress through Eighty-eighth Congress* (Washington: U.S. Government Printing Office, 1999), 498; "Press Releases," September 27, 1955, and March 3, 1956, Strom Thurmond Collection (STC), "Originals," Box 4, Speeches, B: Originals, Folders 44 and 56, Clemson University Libraries, Special Collections; Thurmond, "Interview 1," 3, LBJ Library; Harry Flood Byrd, Sr., Papers, Box 409, Folder "Remarks–March 7, 1956 on the resignation of Senator Strom Thurmond from the Senate," Albert and Shirley Small Special Collections Library, University of Virginia, Charlottesville.

20. ODJ Papers, Box 158, Folder 219, and "Byrnes-Johnston correspondence, 1956," Box 112, Folder "General, 1956"; *Atlanta Journal*, March 11, 1956, 9E; "Radio and Television Report," February 15, 1956, STC Originals, Box 4, Folder 59.

21. *Charlotte Observer*, October 6, 1955, Workman Papers; LBJ Oral History Manuscripts AC 84-50, George Reedy, Interview 8, August 16, 1983, 99.

22. *State*, February 26, 1956, Workman Papers.

23. Chappell, *A Stone of Hope: Prophetic Religion and the Death of Jim Crow* (Chapel Hill: University of North Carolina Press, 2004), 172; Cohodas, 213; Reedy, "Interview 8," 99–100 and "Interview 3," June 7, 1975, 19–20; Gilbert Fite, interview with author, summer 2002; Thurmond, "Interview 1," May 7, 1979, 8–10.

24. Benjamin Muse, *Virginia's Massive Resistance* (Bloomington: Indiana University Press, 1961), 25; J. Harvie Wilkinson III, *Harry Byrd and the Changing Face of Virginia Politics, 1945–1966* (Charlottesville: University Press of Virginia, 1968), 153;

Key, 34, 19–35, 336–337; James Ely, Jr., *The Crisis of Conservative Virginia: The Byrd Organization and the Politics of Massive Resistance* (Knoxville: University of Tennessee Press, 1976), 106; transcript, Harry McPherson Oral History Interview I, December 5, 1968, by T. H. Baker, Electronic Copy, LBJ Library, 28.

25. Heinemann, 329, 332–333; Wilkinson, 152.

26. "Origin of the Southern Manifesto," STC "Originals," Box 4, Folder 39.

27. "Russell to Mizell," April 30, 1962, RBR Papers, Series I, Box 18, Folder 6: "1958 Manifesto." After South Carolina's interim senator resigned, Thurmond was appointed on December 24, 1954, before the opening session, so that he would have seniority over other incoming senators (Cohodas, 272).

28. RBR Papers, "Russell to Manders," January 30, 1956, Series X, Box 163, Folder 5 and 1/23, EG 1133A, Series VI, Sub-series A1, Box 12, Folder 5 and "Russell to Mizell," April 30, 1962, Series I, Box 18, Folder 6: "1958 Manifesto"; "Dorothy to LBJ," Memorandum, February 6, 1956, LBJ Papers, LBJA Series, Box 44, Sub-series Congressional File, Folder "George, Walter F."; "Skeeter Johnston," 12:30 p.m., February 9, 1956, Long (Russell B.) Collection 3700, U.S. Senate Series: Senate Office Files, Special Issue Files: Civil Rights, 1941–1962, Hill Memorial Library, Louisiana State University, Baton Rouge; "Memorandum," February 6, 1956, John Stennis Papers, Series 46, Box 1, File 21, Stennis Congressional Research Center, Mitchell Memorial Library, Mississippi State University, Starkville; Reedy, "Interview 8," 102; "Gore to M. I. Jones," March 6, 1956, Series 20, Special 1953–1970, File "1956–1958 Segregation #3," Albert Gore, Sr., Congressional Research Center, Middle Tennessee State University, Murfreesboro.

29. Thurmond's biographer Nadine Cohodas has mistaken these two separate drafts. She is likely referring to his address to the Virginia State Bar Association the previous year, where he first articulated some of the ideas that would later appear in his first draft (Cohodas, 284); "Origin of the Southern Manifesto," "first draft of Manifesto for study," February 6, 1956, and "Thurmond's second draft," STC, "Originals," Box 4, Folder 37; "Thurmond's suggestions?," Stennis Papers, Series 29, Box 5, Folder 5; *Arkansas Gazette*, March 18, 1956, 5f; Thurmond, "Interview 1," 8–10; Eastland Collection, "Johnston to Eastland," March 15, 1956, File Series 1, Sub-series 18, Boxes 4,5, and 9, Folders 4-20, 5-46, and 9-9 and "Strom Thurmond Address," August 6, 1955, Box 10, Folder 10-10; RBR Papers, "Russell to Mizell," April 30, 1962, Series I, Box 18, Folder 6, "1958 Manifesto," and *The South*, March 19, 1956, 9, Series VI, Sub-series A1, Folder 5 "Personal-Political," and "Russell to Mizell," April 30, 1962, Series X, Box 232, Folder "Manifesto Correspondence," and "Ervin to Mizell," April 13, 1962, Series X, Box 186, Folder 10, "Southern Caucus, 182," and "George to RBR," February 9, 1956, Series III, Sub-series A, Box 27, Folder 9, "Southern Manifesto"; "Ervin to George," February 10, 1956, Sam Ervin Papers, Subgroup A: Senate Records, 1954–1975, Box 15, Folder 1119, Southern Historical Collection, Wilson Library, University of North Carolina, Chapel Hill; Congress, Senate, Politics in the Supreme Court, *Congressional*

Record 102 (March 1, 1956), ODJ Papers, Box 53, Folders 1956–27 through 29; Lister Hill Collection, Series "Political, 1946–47, Racial, 1939–1967, Boxes 367–377, and John Sparkman Papers, Boxes 1–3, W. S. Hoole Special Collections Library, University of Alabama, Tuscaloosa.

30. Congress, Senate, 83rd Cong. 2nd sess., *Congressional Record* 101, pt. 5 (May 18, 1954): 6749; Stennis Papers, Series 61, Box 5, Folders 7–8.

31. Dabney, 179; Badger, "The Southern Manifesto: White Southerners and Civil Rights, 1956," 85; *U.S. News & World Report*, November 18, 1955; "Alexander Hamilton's Phantom," 4, in RBR Papers, Series III, Sub-series A, Box 27, Folder 9.

32. Ervin Papers, Subgroup A, Senate Records, 1954–1975, Folders 783–87, 13453–13477, 13556, 13458, 13460; Francis J. Attig, Reporter of Senate Debates, interview by Donald A. Ritchie, Senate Historical Office (SHO), Hart Senate Office Building, Washington, D.C. (April 5, 1978), 40.

33. *Greenville News*, February 9, 1956, STC "Originals," Box 4, Folder 37; *Richmond Times-Dispatch*, February 9, 1956; "Walter Sillers to Stennis," February 9, 1956, Stennis Papers, Series 61, Box 5, Folder 7; "Walter R. McDonald to RBR," February 9, 1956, RBR Papers, Series X, Box 163, Folder 5, "School Segregation"; Ervin Papers, Subgroup A, Senate Records, 1954–1975, "Feb. 12, 1956 Radio Program," Box 406, Folders 17233, 17238; "Robertson to Harrison," February 7, 1956, A. Willis Robertson Papers, drawer 40, Folder 27, Earl Gregg Swem Library, College of William and Mary, Williamsburg, Virginia.

34. Gore Collection, "Gore–H. A. Skelton correspondence," "Gore to Mr. M. I. James," March 6, 1956, Series 20, Special 1953–1970, File 3 "1956–1958 Segregation"; *The South*, March 12, 1956, n.p.; RBR Papers, Series VI, Box 12, Sub-series A1, Folder 5, "Personal Political"; *Charleston News & Courier*, January 22, 1956; *Spartanburg Herald*, February 9, 1956; Frank Van Der Linden, "Strom Pushing For Dixie Racial Bloc," January 22, 1956, "Move to Revise Southern Bloc," January 26, 1956, "Thurmond, Byrd Were 'Behind Scenes' Men At Strategy Meet," February 12, 1956; *State*, "Thurmond and Byrd Lead Senate Strategy Meeting," February 14, 1956, STC "Originals," Box 4, Folder 37; *Baltimore Sun*, March 12, 1956, LBJ Papers, Senate, Box 423, File "The Southern Manifesto."

35. Muse, 27; Robbins L. Gates, *The Making of Massive Resistance: Virginia's Politics of Public School Desegregation, 1954–1956* (Chapel Hill: University of North Carolina Press, 1964), 118; Heinemann, 334; *New Republic*, March 5, 1956, 6; *Tampa Sunday Tribune*, February 26, 1956, RBR Papers, Series X, Box 149, Folder 4.

36. For Byrd's role, scholars have generally relied upon contemporary accounts such as *Southern School News*, April 1956, 1–2; *Washington Star*, March 133, 1956, LBJ Senate, Box 243, Folder "Southern Manifesto"; Ely, 42; Gates, 118; Heinemann, 334–335; Lassiter and Lewis, 6–7; Muse, 27; J. Douglas Smith, "'When Reason Collides with Prejudice': Armistead Lloyd Boothe and the Politics of Moderation," in Las-

siter and Lewis, 42–43; Wilkinson, 140–141, 152–153; *Anderson Independent*, April 6, 1956, 2, ODJ Papers, Series "Clippings," Box 153, Folder 48; Byrd Papers, Appointment Book 1956, Boxes 291, 356, 409.

37. RBR Papers, "RBR to Mrs. C. A. Lauthner," October 11, 1962, Civil Rights X, Box 175, Folder "Racial Miss. 1962 October 10–11," found in Gilbert Fite, "RBR notes," Series I, Box 17, Folder 6, and Series III, Sub-series A, Box 27, Folder 9; Thurmond, "Interview 1," 11.

CHAPTER 4

1. John Stennis Papers, Series 29, Box 5, Folder 5 and Series 61, Box 5, Folder 7, Stennis Congressional Research Center, Mitchell Memorial Library, Mississippi State University, Starkville; Richard B. Russell (RBR) Papers, Series III, Sub-series A, Box 27, Folder 9, Russell Memorial Library, University of Georgia, Athens; C. Vann Woodward, *Origins of the New South, 1877–1913* (Baton Rouge: Louisiana State University Press, 195), 462–469; "Robertson to Russell," February 8, 1956, A. Willis Robertson Papers, Drawer 140, Folder 56, Earl Gregg Swem Library, College of William and Mary, Williamsburg; Mark Whitman, ed., *Removing a Badge of Slavery: The Record of Brown v. Board of Education* (Princeton: Markus Wiener Publishing, Inc., 1993), 27–36; *Congressional Record–Senate* 100, pt. 3, 83rd Congress, 2nd sess. (May 18, 1954): 6742–6750; Clare Cushman and Melvin I. Urofsky, eds., *Black, White, and Brown: The Landmark School Desegregation Case in Retrospect* (Washington D.C.: CQ Press, 2004), 242–245; J. Strom Thurmond Collection (STC), "Thurmond statement," January 26, 1956, State Citizens' Councils, "Speeches, B: Originals," Folder 59, J. Strom Thurmond Institute, Clemson University Libraries, Special Collections, South Carolina; Thurmond's "Address to the Virginia State Bar Association," White Sulphur Springs, West Virginia, August 8, 1955, William Workman Papers, Box 182, Folder "Education, School Desegregation, Speeches, 1955–1958," Modern Political Collections (MPC), South Caroliniana Library, University of South Carolina, Columbia; Price Daniel Papers, Box 144, Sam Houston Regional Library & Research Center, Liberty, Texas; Betty Bean Fielder, "Price Daniel, Texas and Segregation" (M.A. thesis, Lamar University, Texas, 1997), 83.

2. Whitman, 48–72; *The Congressional Record* 101, pt. 5 (May 18, 1954): 6746–48; "Eugene Cook to RBR," February 20, 1956, RBR Papers, Series X, Box 163, Folder 5; Daniel Papers, Box 74.

3. RBR Papers, Series III, Sub-series A, Box 27, Folder 9, "Southern Manifesto"; Congress, Senate, 83rd Cong. 2nd sess., *Congressional Record* 101, pt. 5 (May 18, 1954): 6749.

4. RBR Papers, Series X, "RBR to Mizell," April 30, 1962, Box 232, Folder "Manifesto Correspondence"; "Sam J. Ervin, Jr., to M. Hayes Mizell," April 13, 1962, Box 186, Folder 10, "Southern Caucus, 182."

5. *Congressional Record* 101, pt. 5 (May 18, 1954): 6750; Stennis Papers, Series 29,

Box 5, Folder 5; John L. McClellan Papers, File 19-B, "Segregation," Riley-Hickingbotham Memorial Library, Ouachita Baptist University, Arkadelphia, Arkansas.

6. Colonial Williamsburg Foundation, *The Declaration of Independence and Constitution of the United States*, 29, 21; Stennis Papers, Series 61, Box 5, Folder 7 and Series 29, Box 5, Folder 5.

7. Whitman, 133–148; William H. Harbaugh, *Lawyer's Lawyer: The Life of John W. Davis* (New York: Oxford University Press, 1973), 483–519; Workman Papers, Box 27, Folder "Education, School Desegregation, *Briggs v. Elliot* (1951); Stennis Papers, "Thurmond draft," "Whose draft is this?," Series 29, Box 5, Folder 5 and Series 61, Box 5, Folder 7; RBR Papers, "RBR draft," "Senator A. Willis Robertson to RBR," February 8, 1956, "Stennis notes," 2/17/56, Series III, Sub-series A, Box 27, Folder 9 "Southern Manifesto" and "Walter R. McDonald–RBR correspondence," February 1956, Series X, Box 63, Folder 5, "School Segregation."

8. *Gong Lum v. Rice* (1927) entailed a Chinese American who unsuccessfully sued the state of Mississippi because he wanted his child to attend a white school rather than a school designated for African Americans. {Whitman, 27–36; *Congressional Record* 101, pt. 5 (May 18, 1954): 6742–6750; Clarence Walker, "The Effects of *Brown:* Personal and Historical Reflections on American Racial Atavism," *Journal of Southern History (JSH)* LXX, No. 2 (May 2004): 298; Sam J. Ervin Papers, Subgroup A, Senate Records, 1954–1975, Folder 13455, Wilson Library, Southern Historical Collection (SHC), University of North Carolina, Chapel Hill; Stennis Papers, "Thurmond draft," "Whose draft is this?," "Stennis to RBR," February 24, 1956, and "Committee draft," Series 29, Box 5, Folder 5; "Thurmond's second draft," STC, "Originals," Box 4, Folder 37; "RBR draft" and "Robertson to RBR," February 8, 1956, RBR Papers, Series III, Sub-series A, Box 27, Folder 9 "Southern Manifesto."}

9. Stennis Papers, "Stennis to RBR," February 24, 1956, "Thurmond draft," and "Committee draft," Series 29, Box 5, Folder 5; RBR Papers, Series III, Sub-series A, Box 27, Folder 9 "Southern Manifesto."

10. RBR Papers, "RBR draft," "Robertson to RBR," February 8, 1956, Series III, Sub-series A, Box 27, Folder 9 "Southern Manifesto"; Fite, *Richard B. Russell*, 207; "Committee draft," "Thurmond draft," Stennis Papers, Series 29, Box 5, Folder 5; Arthur Schlesinger, Jr., *The Age of Roosevelt*, 3 vols. (Boston: Houghton-Mifflin, 1959).

11. RBR Papers, "Robertson to RBR," "RBR draft," February 8, 1956, Series III, Sub-series A, Box 7, Folder 9 "Southern Manifesto"; Stennis Papers, "Thurmond draft," "Committee draft," "Stennis suggestions," Series 29, Box 5, Folder 5; "Robertson to Meredith," February 24, 1956, "Robertson to Broyhill," March 7, 1956, and "Robertson to Elebash," March 10, 1956, "Robertson to RBR," February 8, 1956, Robertson Papers, Drawer 40, Folder 29.

12. A few years later, Russell told a constituent, Mrs. C. A. Lauthner of Augusta: "I drew upon suggestions of the other members of the Committee and members of

the Senate, but I am altogether responsible for the last two paragraphs" ("RBR to Mrs. C. A. Lauthner," October 11, 1962, RBR Papers, Series X, Box 175, Folder "Racial Miss. 1962," Oct 10–11, found in Fite "RBR notes"); Stennis Papers, "Stennis suggestions," "Committee draft," "Thurmond draft," Series 29, Box 5, Folder 5; "Thurmond to Johnston," March 2, 1956, Olin D. Johnston (ODJ) Papers, Modern Political Collections (MPC), South Caroliniana Library, University of South Carolina, Columbia; "Thurmond to McClellan," March 2, 1956, McClellan Papers, File 19-B "Segregation"; "Thurmond to Eastland," March 2, 1956, James Oliver Eastland Collection, Series 1, Sub-series 18, Box 10, Folder 10-10, J. D. Williams Library, Department of Archives and Special Collections, University of Mississippi, Oxford; "Eastland to Robertson," March 2, 1956, Robertson Papers, Drawer 140, Folder 56.

13. "Stennis to Senator Spessard L. Holland," and "Stennis to Senator Price Daniel," March 1, 1956, Stennis Papers, Series 29, Box 5, Folder 5.

14. "Thurmond to McClellan," March 2, 1956, McClellan Papers, File 19-B "Segregation"; "Thurmond memos," March 2, 1956, STC, Subject Correspondence, Segregation, Folder II, Box 12; *Greenville News*, March 2, 1956, "Thurmond to Johnston," March 2, 1956, ODJ Papers.

15. RBR Papers, Series X, "RBR to Mizell," April 30, 1962, Box 232, Folder "Southern Manifesto," "Ervin to Mizell," April 13, 1962, Box 186, Folder 10 "Southern Caucus, 182"; "RBR to McDonald," February 15, 1956, Box 163, Folder 5 "School Segregation"; Stennis Papers, "Special Memorandum," March 1956, Series 29, Box 5, Folder 6 and "Stennis to Walter Sillers," February 11, 1956, Series 61, Box 5, Folder 7.

16. David Daniel Potenziani, "Look to the Past: Richard B. Russell and the Defense of White Supremacy" (dissertation, University of Georgia, Athens, 1981), 135; Brent J. Aucoin, "The Southern Manifesto and Southern Opposition to Desegregation." *Arkansas Historical Quarterly* 55, No. 2 (1996): 175–184; Elizabeth Carpenter, "Three from State Sign 'Manifesto" After 'Softening,'" *Arkansas Gazette*, March 18, 1956, 5F; *Time*, March 26, 1956, 25; "Drew Pearson's Washington Merry-Go-Round," Jackson *Clarion-Ledger*, March 18, 1956, p. 3, sec. 4, and "Byrd Masterminded the Manifesto," *Washington Post*, March 19, 1956, Spessard Holland Papers, Box 336, Folder 5-d "Segregation," Special and Regional Studies Collections, Smathers Memorial Libraries, University of Florida, Gainesville; "Mizell to Ervin," April 10, 1962, RBR Papers, Series X, Box 186, Folder 10, "Southern Caucus, 182; Anthony J. Badger, "The Southern Manifesto: White Southerners and Civil Rights, 1956," in Rob Kros and Eduard van de Bilt, eds., *The US Constitution After 200 Years* (Amsterdam: Free University Press, 1988), 80; Timothy S. Huebner, "Looking Backward: The Southern Manifesto of 1956," *Historically Speaking* VII, No. 5 (May/June 2006): 36–37.

17. RBR Papers, Series X, "Ervin to Mizell," April 13, 1962, Box 186, Folder 10, "Southern Caucus, 182," and "RBR to Mizell," Box 232, Folder "Manifesto Correspon-

dence," *The South*, March 19, 1956, 9, Series VI, Sub-series A1, Box 12, Folder 5 "Personal Political"); STC "Originals," Box 4, Folder 39; *Baltimore Sun*, March 12, 1956, Lyndon Baines Johnson (LBJ) Papers, Senate, Box 423, Folder "The Southern Manifesto," LBJ Library; *State*, March 10, 1956, Workman Papers; *Washington Evening Star*, March 12, 1956.

18. Haynes Bonner Johnson and Bernard Gwertzman, *Fulbright: The Dissenter* (Garden City: Doubleday, 1968), 175; Randall Woods, *Fulbright: A Biography* (New York: Cambridge University Press, 1995), 208–211. According to Woods, Thurmond's initial draft, which he describes as an "uncompromising diatribe" that "called for resistance inside or outside the law, whatever the price," was "too much even for the other fire-breathers," so the Southern Caucus asked Ervin to rewrite the statement. Woods does not acknowledge the drafting committee in which, according to the historical evidence, Ervin actually played a tertiary role. Furthermore, Woods mistakes Ervin's suggestions for an actual draft, describing it as a separate and distinct "version" of the statement altogether. Woods incorrectly attributes the last principle of Russell's dictated draft, which is misquoted, as part and parcel of Ervin's suggestions, implying that these two completely separate documents are one and the same. Woods states: "The Brown decision of 1954 was based on neither law nor precedent, Ervin argued, but solely on 'psychology and sociology.' Given the fact the Warren Court had 'usurped and exercised a power denied it by the very instrument it was professing to interpret,' its decision was inoperative. 'We pledge ourselves,' Ervin concluded, 'to do all within our power to reverse and set aside this illegal and unconstitutional decision.'" Woods's citation for this quotation is "#41 Ervin draft, 1956, Southern Manifesto, Papers of Richard Russell, University of Georgia, Athens, Ga." See Woods, 208. I have looked through every file related to the Southern Manifesto in Russell's papers and, to my knowledge, these two excerpts do not exist in the same document. Russell's dictated version actually states in conclusion: "We solemnly pledge ourselves to support any and all lawful means and measures calculated to bring about a reversal of this illegal and unconstitutional decision of the Supreme Court." See RBR Papers, Series III, Sub-series A, Box 27, Folder 9 "Southern Manifesto." A very similar quote appears in Stennis's following suggestions. Thus, Stennis simply agreed with Russell's initial phrase and let it stand. See "Stennis to RBR," February 24, 1956, Stennis Papers, Series 29, Box 5, Folder 5. Kyle Longley accepts Woods's interpretation. See Longley, "White Knight for Civil Rights?: The Civil Rights Record of Senator Albert A. Gore Sr.," *Tennessee Historical Quarterly* 1998 57, Nos. 2,3 (1998): 118, and *Senator Albert Gore, Sr.: Tennessee Maverick*, with an introduction by Al Gore, Jr. (Baton Rouge: Louisiana State Press, 2004), 123.

19. Badger, "The Southern Manifesto," 79 and "'The Forerunner of Our Opposition': Arkansas and the Southern Manifesto of 1956," *AHQ* 56, No. 3 (1997): 358;

Woods, 208–209, and *LBJ: Architect of American Ambition* (New York: Free Press, 2006), 303–304.

20. "John to JWF," n.d., J. William Fulbright (JWF) Papers, Series 71, Box 10:1, Special Collections Division, Mullins Library, University of Arkansas at Fayetteville; Charles B. Seib & Alan L. Otten, "Arkansas Paradox," *Harper's*, June 1956, 65.

21. Woods, 209–210; Aucoin, 180–181; Johnson and Gwertzman, 175; Badger, "Southerners Who Refused to Sign the Southern Manifesto," *Historical Journal* 42, No. 2 (1999): 517–534 and "Closet Moderates: Why White Liberals Failed, 1940–1970" in Ted Ownby, ed., *The Role of Ideas in the Civil Rights South* (Jackson: University Press of Mississippi, 2002), 100–112, and "Fatalism, Not Gradualism: The Crisis of Southern Liberalism, 1945–65," in *The Making of Martin Luther King and the Civil Rights Movement* (New York: New York University Press, 1996), 81, and "The Forerunner of Our Opposition," 357; Keith M. Finley, *Delaying the Dream: Southern Senators and the Fight Against Civil Rights, 1938–1965* (Baton Rouge: Louisiana State University Press, 2008), 142–151.

22. "Remarks of JWF," JWF Papers, Series 71, Box 10:2; Woods, 229; Julianne Lewis Adams and Tom DeBlack, *Civil Obedience: An Oral History of School Desegregation in Fayetteville, Arkansas, 1954–1965*, with an introduction by Willard Gatewood (Fayetteville: University of Arkansas Press, 1994); Roy Reed, *Faubus: The Life and Times of an American Prodigal* (Fayetteville: University of Arkansas Press, 1997), 172–174; David Appleby, *Hoxie: The First Stand* DVD (Memphis: University of Memphis, 2002).

23. "Remarks of JWF," JWF Papers, Series 71, Box 10:2.

24. "JWF to Mrs. Robert A. Caldwell, Jr.," March 9, 1956, JWF Papers, Series 71, Box 10:1; "Holland to G. G. Ware," March 5, 1956, Holland Papers, Box 336, folder 5-d "Segregation."

25. Badger, "The Forerunner of Our Opposition," 358; JWF Papers, Series 71, Box 10:1, "James Hale to JWF," "John to JWF," n.d.; C. Vann Woodward, "The 'New Reconstruction' in the South: Desegregation in Historical Perspective," *Commentary* 21, No. 6 (June 1956): 501–509.

26. RBR Papers, Series III, Sub-series A, Box 27, Folder 9. Long's logbook records that on March 6, 1956, at 11:30 a.m., the Louisianan met with a "Civil Rights Group" which, considering that the Southern Caucus had virtually no communication with civil rights workers, was likely this group of senators. Long (Russell B.) Collection, #3700, U.S. Senate Series: Senate Office Files, Special Issue Files: Civil Rights, 1941–1962, Hill Memorial Library, Louisiana State University, Baton Rouge, Louisiana; *Arkansas Gazette*, March 18, 1956, 5F; Holland Papers, Box 336, "Thurmond to Holland," March 2, 1956, Box 336, Folder "segregation April 1," and "Holland to Ware," March 5, 1956, Folder 5-d "Segregation," and Box 341, Folder 41 "Diary of Events, 1956"; Daniel Papers, Box 65, Folder "Southern Manifesto, March 12, 1956–Senate," and Box 118, Folder "Southern Manifesto."

27. Fulbright's, Holland's, and Daniel's personally edited copies of the committee draft, as well as Daniel's specific suggestions, appear in their papers. Thurmond's records are problematic, for the copies in his files mistakenly label Russell's committee draft and a supposed "Draft of the Southern Manifesto Prepared by Senators Holland, Daniel, and Fulbright" as one and the same. The latter is simply another copy of the committee draft. STC "Originals," Box 4, Folder 37; "Manifesto Draft," JWF Papers, Series 71, Box 10:1; Holland Papers, Box 336, "Thurmond to Holland," March 2, 1956, Folder "Segregation April 1," and "Holland to Littlejohn," March 29, 1956, Folder 5-d "Segregation"; Daniel Papers, Box 65, Folder "Southern Manifesto, March 12, 1956–Senate," and Box 118, Folder "Southern Manifesto"; Badger, "The Southern Manifesto," 88 and "Southerners Who Refused to Sign the Southern Manifesto," 527; Aucoin, 181.

28. *Congressional Record* 101, pt. 5 (May 18, 1954): 6742, 6749; "Price Daniel," March 9, 1956, RBR Papers, Series III, Sub-series A, Box 27, Folder "Southern Manifesto"; Carl Becker, *The Declaration of Independence: A Study in the History of Political Ideas* (New York: Alfred A. Knopf, 1964), 121.

29. *Arkansas Gazette*, March 18, 1956, 5F; *Southern School News*, April 1956, 1; "Manifesto Draft," JWF Papers, Series 71, Box 10:1; "Holland's drafts," Holland Papers, Box 336, Folder 5-d "Segregation April 1"; "Robertson to Whitehead," March 23, 1956, Robertson Papers, Drawer 140, Folder 56; Daniel Papers, Box 65, Folder "Southern Manifesto, March 12, 1956–Senate," and Box 118, Folder "Southern Manifesto."

30. The full text of the final draft of the Southern Manifesto can be found in numerous sources, such as "Manifesto Draft," JWF Papers, Series 71, Box 10:1; "Holland's drafts," Holland Papers, Box 336, Folder 5-d "Segregation April 1"; "Stennis notes," RBR Papers, Series III, Sub-series A, Box 27, Folder 9 "Southern Manifesto"; Stennis Papers, Series 29, Box 5, Folder 5; Robertson Papers, Drawer 140, Folder 56; Eastland Collection, File Series 1, Sub-series 18, Box 9, Folder 9-29; Daniel Papers, Box 65, Folder "Southern Manifesto, March 12, 1956—Senate," and Box 118, Folder "Southern Manifesto." The text was also printed at the time in numerous periodicals such as *Southern School News*, April 1956, 2; *Washington Evening Star*, March 12, 1956; *State*, March 10, 1956, Workman Papers, MPC; *Atlanta Journal*, March 12, 1956, 1–2.

CHAPTER 5

1. Long (Russell B.) Collection, 3700, U.S. Senate Series: Senate Office Files, Special Issue Files: Civil Rights, 1941–1962, Long Family Papers (Russell B. and Earl K.), Hill Memorial Library, Louisiana State University, Baton Rouge, Louisiana; *Atlanta Journal*, Richard B. Russell (RBR) Papers, Series III, Sub-series A, Box 27, Folder 9, "Southern Manifesto," Russell Memorial Library, University of Georgia, Athens; *Washington Star*, March 9, 1956.

2. *New York Times*, March 11, 1956; Estes Kefauver Collection, Series 5G, Box 56,

James D. Hoskins Special Collections Library, University of Tennessee–Knoxville; Harry Ashmore, *An Epitaph for Dixie* (New York: W. W. Norton, 1958), 33– 34.

3. *Atlanta Journal and Constitution*, March 18, 1956, 13E; *Daily Oklahoman*, March 13, 1956, 1; Anthony J. Badger, "The Southern Manifesto: White Southerners and Civil Rights, 1956," in Rob Kros and Eduard van de Bilt, eds., *The US Constitution After 200 Years* (Amsterdam: Free University Press, 1988), 82–83.

4. Randall Woods, *Fulbright: A Biography* (New York: Cambridge University Press, 1995), 211; Badger, "Southerners Who Refused to Sign the Southern Manifesto," *Historical Journal* 42, No. 2 (1999): 517–534; ANB, 794, Folder "Joseph L. Hill," Senate Historical Office (SHO), Hart Senate Office Building, Washington, D.C.

5. Brent J. Aucoin, "The Southern Manifesto and Southern Opposition to Desegregation," *Arkansas Historical Quarterly* (AHC) 55, No. 2 (1996): 173–193.

6. James T. Baker, *Brooks Hays* (Macon: Mercer University Press, 1989), 113, 122, 126, 156–157; Brooks Hays, *A Southern Moderate Speaks* (Chapel Hill: University of North Carolina Press, 1959), 89.

7. Long Family (Russell B.) Collection, 3700, U.S. Senate Series: Senate Office Files, Special Issue Files: Civil Rights, 1941–1962; Baker, 156; "Interview with Brooks Hays," LBJ Oral History Manuscripts, AC 79-10, Interview 1, October 5, 1971, 24–27, Lyndon Baines Johnson Presidential Library, University of Texas at Austin; Orval Faubus, *Down from the Hills* (Little Rock: Democrat Printing & Lithographing Co., 1980), 119; Roy Reed, *Faubus: The Life and Times of an American Prodigal* (Fayetteville: University of Arkansas Press, 1997), 357.

8. Hays, 89; Orval Faubus and Brooks Hays, interview by John L. Ward, September 20, 1976, "Little Rock School Desegregation Crisis of 1957 Revisited," 17, Brooks Hays Collection, Series 3, Sub-series 1, Box 45, Folder 26, Special Collections Division, Mullins Library, University of Arkansas, Fayetteville; John Kyle Day, "The Fall of a Southern Moderate: Brooks Hays and the 1958 General Election of Arkansas," *AHC* 59, No. 3 (Autumn 2000): 241–264.

9. Badger, "The Southern Manifesto," 88–89, and "Fatalism, Not Gradualism: The Crisis of Southern Liberalism, 1945–65," in *The Making of Martin Luther King and the Civil Rights Movement* (New York: New York University Press, 1996), 81.

10. William Jennings Bryan Dorn Papers, Modern Political Collections (MPC), South Caroliniana Library, University of South Carolina, Columbia; LBJ Papers, LBJA Congressional File, Box 51, "Patman, Wright," Folders 1–2; Congress, House, Deviation from Fundamentals of the Constitution, 84th Congress, 2nd sess., *Congressional Record* 102, vol. 4 (March 12, 1956): 4515–16; Harold Cooley Papers, Box 53, Folder 2309, Southern Historical Collection (SHC), Wilson Library, University of North Carolina, Chapel Hill; *U.S. News & Report*, March 23, 1956, 101; *Washington Star*, March 12, 1956; *State*, March 12, 1956, William D. Workman Papers, MPC; *Baltimore Sun*, March 12, 1956, LBJ Senate, Box 423, Folder "The Southern Manifesto";

The South, March 19, 1956, 9, RBR Papers, Series VI, Sub-series A1, Box 12, Folder 5 "Personal Political."

11. Tara Mitchell Mielnik, "Resisting Massive Resistance: Tennessee's Senators and the Southern Manifesto," March 27, 1997, Albert Gore Sr. Congressional Research Center, Middle Tennessee State University, Murfreesboro; "News from College Press Conference," Kefauver Collection, Series 5G, Box 9, File "Civil Rights," 1 of 2; *Washington Star*, March 12, 1956, n.p.; *The South*, March 19, 1956, 9.

12. *Time*, April 9, 1956, 34; Kefauver Collection, *Washington Post*, March 31, 1956, Series 5G, Box 9, Folder "Civil Rights," 1 of 2 and "Constituent form letter," April 4, 1956, Series III, Box 25, Folder "Judi Civil Rights File 84th Congress."

13. Albert A. Gore, Sr., *The Eye of the Storm: A People's Politics for the Seventies* (New York: Herder and Herder, 1970), 132; *Let The Glory Out: My South and Its Politics* (New York: Viking, 1972), 102; Kyle Longley, "White Knight for Civil Rights? The Civil Rights Record of Senator Albert A. Gore Sr.," *Tennessee Historical Quarterly* (THQ) 1998, Vol. 57, Nos. 2, 3 (1998): 114–131, and *Senator Albert Gore, Sr.: Tennessee Maverick*, with an introduction by Al Gore, Jr. (Baton Rouge: Louisiana State Press, 2004), 123–124.

14. "Gore–Mr. H. A. Skelton correspondence," "Gore to Mr. M. I. James," March 6, 1956, Albert Gore, Sr., Papers, Series 20, Special 1953–1970, Folder 3 "1956–1958 Segregation," Gore Center; *Baltimore Sun*, March 12, 1956, LBJ Papers, Senate, Box 423, Folder "The Southern Manifesto"; *Washington Star*, March 12, 1956, n.p.; *The South*, March 19, 1956, 9; *Atlanta Journal and Constitution*, March 18, 1956, 13E; Gore, *Let the Glory Out*, 104; Longley, *Tennessee Maverick*, 124.

15. *Atlanta Journal and Constitution*, March 18, 1956, 13E; Gore Papers, Series 20, Special, 1953–1970, "Gore to Tomlin," March 28, 1956, and "Gore to Perry," March 17, 1956, Folder "1956–1958 Segregation," 1 and 13; "Gore to Eastland," August 22, 1956, James Oliver Eastland Papers, Series 1, Sub-series 18, Box 4, Folder 4-28, J. D. Williams Library, Department of Archives and Special Collections, University of Mississippi, Oxford; Longley, "White Knight For Civil Rights?," 120–124.

16. *Christian Science Monitor*, March 13, 1956, LBJ Senate, Box 423, Folder "Southern Manifesto"; *Southern School News*, April 1956, 1; *Arkansas Gazette*, March 18, 1956, 5F.

17. Cooley Papers, Box 53, Folder 2309; "Cooley to Foster," March 22, 1956, RBR Papers, Series X, Box 177, Segregation Folder, 8.

18. Badger, "Southerners Who Refused to Sign the Southern Manifesto," *Historical Journal* 42, No. 2 (1999): 517–534; Robert Dallek, *Lone Star Rising: Lyndon Johnson and His Times, 1908–1960* (New York: Oxford University Press, 1991), 496–497; Stanford Phillips Dyer, "Lyndon B. Johnson and the Politics of Civil Rights, 1935–1960: The Art of 'Moderate Leadership'" (dissertation, Texas A&M University, 1978), 107; Robert Mann, *The Walls of Jericho: Lyndon Johnson, Hubert Humphrey, Richard Rus-*

sell, and the Struggle for Civil Rights (New York: Harcourt Brace, 1996), 161–166; Bruce J. Schulman, *Lyndon B. Johnson and American Liberalism: A Brief History with Documents* (Boston: Bedford/St. Martin's, 1995), 51; Irwin and Debi Unger, *LBJ: A Life* (New York: John Wiley & Sons, 1999), 194; William S. White, *The Professional: Lyndon B. Johnson* (Boston: Houghton Mifflin, 1964), 211–213; Robert Caro, *Master of the Senate: The Years of Lyndon Johnson* ,Vol. 3 (New York: Alfred Knopf, 2002), 785–788; David Chappell, *Inside Agitators: White Southerners and Civil Rights* (Baltimore: The Johns Hopkins University Press, 1994), 153–154; Keith M. Finley, *Delaying the Dream: Southern Senators and the Fight against Civil Rights, 1938–1965* (Baton Rouge: Louisiana State University Press, 2008), 150–151; John A. Goldsmith, *Colleagues: Richard B. Russell and His Apprentice, Lyndon B.* Johnson (Washington, D.C.: Seven Locks Press, 1993), 51–52; Merle Miller, *Lyndon: An Oral Biography* (New York: G. P. Putnam's Sons, 1980), 187–188; George E. Reedy, *The U.S. Senate: Paralysis or a Search for Consensus?* (New York: Crown Publishers, 1986), 107; Woods, *LBJ: Architect of American Ambition* (New York: Free Press, 2006), 303–305; John Bullion, *Lyndon B. Johnson and the Transformation of American Politics* (New York: Pearson Longman, 2008); *New York Times*, March 12, 1956, LBJ Papers, Senate, Box 423, Folder "The Southern Manifesto"; Howard E. Shuman, interview by Donald A. Ritchie (July 22–October 22, 1987), SHO.

19. Kefauver Collection, Series 5G, *Baltimore Sun*, March 14, 1956, Box 9, Folder "Civil Rights," 2 of 2 and "News Bulletin," September–October 1955, Box 10, Folder "School Segregation"; *Houston Informer*, June 16, 1956, 12.

20. LBJ Papers, George Reedy, AC 76-23, Interview 3, June 7, 1975, 20–21 and Thurmond, Interview 1, 11 and James H. Rowe, Jr., AC-15, Interview 6, December 9, 1983, 1–2 and Senate, "Press Release," Box 423, Folder "Southern Manifesto," and "LBJ to Dr. Charles L. Hatcher," May 18, 1956, Box 568, "1956 General File."

21. *Newsweek*, February 20, 1956, 25; *Washington Star*, March 12, 1956, n.p.; *Fort Wayne Journal Gazette*, March 12, 1956, 1; *Dallas Morning News*, March 12, 1956, 1–2, Patman Papers, Box 94 (A), Folder "Segregation," 6 and *Washington Star*, March 13, 1956, LBJ Senate, Box 243, Folder "Southern Manifesto."

22. LBJ Oral History Manuscripts, Hubert H. Humphrey, AC 79-43, Interview 3, June 21, 1977, 8.

CHAPTER 6

1. "Holland to Littlejohn," March 29, 1956, "O'Connor to Holland," March 12, 1956, and "misc. correspondence," Spessard Holland Papers, Box 336, Folder 5-d "Segregation," Special and Regional Studies Collections, University of Florida Smathers Libraries, Gainesville.

2. *Greenville News*, March 13, 1956, 1, William Workman Papers, Modern Political

Collections (MPC), South Caroliniana Library, University of South Carolina, Columbia; Congress, Senate, *Congressional Record* 102, pt. 4, (March 12, 1956): 4444–4445; "Holland to Littlejohn," March 29, 1956, "O'Connor to Holland," March 12, 1956, and "misc. correspondence," Holland Papers, Box 336, Folder 5-d "Segregation."

3. *New York Herald-Tribune*, March 16, 1956, Lyndon Baines Johnson (LBJ) Papers, Senate, Box 423, Folder "Southern Manifesto," Lyndon Baines Johnson Presidential Library, University of Texas at Austin.

4. Congress, Senate, The Decision of the Supreme Court in the School Cases—Declaration of Constitutional Principles, 84th Cong., 2nd sess., *Congressional Record* 102, pt. 4 (March 12, 1956): 4459–4462; *Atlanta Journal*, March 12, 1956, 1.

5. *Congressional Record* (March 12, 1956): 4461–4462; Strom Thurmond Collection (STC), Series "Originals," Box 4, Folder 37 and Box 7, Folder 44, Photo 1236, *Washington Star*, March 12, 1956, *Fort Wayne Journal-Gazette*, March 12, 1956, 1, and *Montgomery Advertiser*, March 12, 1956, 1, J. Strom Thurmond Institute, Clemson University, South Carolina; *U.S. News & World Report*, March 23, 1956, 100–103; Workman Papers, *Greenville News*, March 13, 1956, 1, and *The State*, March 12, 1956; Wright Patman Papers, *Dallas Morning News*, March 12, 1956, Box 94 (A), File 6 "Segregation," and "Statement," Box 17(A), Folder "Civil Rights," LBJ Library; James Oliver Eastland Collection, Series 2, Sub-series 4, Box 4, Folder "March 1956 Civil Rights," J. D. Williams Library, Department of Archives and Special Collections, University of Mississippi; *Baltimore Sun*, March 12, 1956, LBJ Papers, Senate, Box 423, File "The Southern Manifesto." Some congressmen improved on Thurmond's mendacity. U.S. Representative William M. Colmer of Mississippi, for instance, claimed to be the head of the House delegation that drafted the manifesto, while U.S. Representative Wright Patman of Texas boasted that he had "participated in its preparation," in correspondence with his district newspapermen.

6. *Time*, March 26, 1956, 25; STC, "Thurmond to Time Magazine," March 27, 1956, Originals, Box 13 (Segregation Folder IV), and *Florence Morning News*, March 12, 1956, 1, Box 4, Folder 37; *Charleston News and Courier*, March 12, 1956, 1; David Chappell, *A Stone of Hope: Prophetic Religion and the Death of Jim Crow* (Chapel Hill: University of North Carolina Press, 2004), 106; Joseph Crespino, *Strom Thurmond's America* (New York: Hill and Wang, 2012), 105–107. In graduate school, I met the eminent historian Carl Degler, who, after I informed him that I was studying the Southern Manifesto, immediately replied, "Ah, Strom Thurmond and the boys."

7. *Newsweek*, March 26, 1956, 23–24; *New York Amsterdam News*, March 17, 1956, 1; *Congressional Record* (March 12, 1956): 4462; *Greenville News*, March 13, 1956, 1, Workman Papers.

8. *Congressional Record* (March 12, 1956): 4463–4464; *Las Vegas Review-Journal*, March 13, 1956, 1; *Greenville News*, March 15, 1956, 1, Workman Papers; Senator Pat McNamara (D-MI), "Press Release," March 14, 1956, RBR Papers, Series X, Box 177,

Folder 9 "Civil Rights"; *New York Times*, March 15, 1956; *Chicago Defender*, March 17, 1956, 1. Clearly referring to the Southern Manifesto, on March 14 the Soviet Union introduced a resolution to the United Nations Human Rights Commission proposing an international ban on discrimination in education. (*Washington Post*, March 15, 1956, LBJ Papers, Senate, Box 423, Folder "The Southern Manifesto.")

9. Some congressmen had not signed yet when the Senate record was published later that day. Absent were two Republicans (Florida's William Cramer and North Carolina's Charles Raper Jonas) and three Democrats (Tennessee's Ross Bass and Joe L. Evins and Texas's Martin Dies). Their endorsements came later that morning and appeared on the list inserted into the House's proceedings in the *Congressional Record*. The complete list appeared on the subsequent copies distributed by the Southern Congressional Delegation in their districts and states, as well as those reprinted by segregationist organizations. (Congress, House, Deviation from Fundamentals of Constitution, 84th Congress, 2nd sess. *Congressional Record* 102, vol. 4 [March 12, 1956]: 4515–4516; Long [Russell B.] Collection, 3700, U.S. Senate Series: Senate Office Files, Special Issue Files: Civil Rights, 1941–1962, Hill Memorial Library, Louisiana State University, Baton Rouge.)

10. *Greenville News*, March 13, 1956, 1, Workman Papers; E. Frederic Morrow, *Black Man in the White House: A Diary of the Eisenhower Years by the Administrative Officer for Special Projects, The White House, 1955–1961* (New York: Coward-McCann, Inc., 1963), 53.

11. Transcript, White House News Conference, President Dwight D. Eisenhower (DDE), Box 4, March 14, 1956, File "President's Press and Radio Conference 82," 9–30, Transcript, "President's Press and Radio Conference 83," March 21, 1956, 29–30, "Minutes of Cabinet Meeting," March 23, 1956, Cabinet Series, Box 7, 2–3, Papers as President of the United States, 1953–1961 (Ann Whitman File), Dwight D. Eisenhower Library, Abilene, Kansas.

12. Herbert Brownell, "*Brown v. Board of Education* Revisited," in Clare Cushman and Melvin I. Urofsky, eds., *Black, White, and Brown: The Landmark School Desegregation Case in Retrospect* (Washington, D.C.: CQ Press, 2004), 198.

13. *Pine Bluff Commercial*, "L. G. Baker to McClellan," March 21, 1956, John McClellan Papers, (File 19B–Segregation), Riley-Hickingbotham Memorial Library, Ouachita Baptist University, Arkadelphia, Arkansas.

14. LBJ Senate, Box 423, Folder "The Southern Manifesto"; *New Republic*, 19 March 1956, 5, 7 May 1956, 2; *Newsweek*, 26 March 1956, 23–25, 21 May 1956, 38; Charles O. Gridely, "Fight Seen For Northern Negro's Vote," *Arkansas Democrat*, "L. G. Baker to McClellan," March 21, 1956, McClellan Papers, File "19B–Segregation"; Jackson *Clarion-Ledger*, March 19, 1956, 1; Marquis Childs, "Democratic Party Near State of Bankruptcy," March 20, 1956, Richard Brevard Russell (RBR) Papers, Series X, Box 177, Segregation File 8, Richard B. Russell Memorial Library, University of Georgia,

Athens; *Washington Star*, March 13, 1956, STC, Series "Originals," Box 4, Folder 37; *Portland Press-Herald*, March 24, 1956, Estes Kefauver Collection, Series 5G, Box 10, Folder "Civil Rights," 1 of 7, James D. Hoskins Special Collections Library, University of Tennessee–Knoxville; *Springfield Union*, March 14, 1956, 8; *Arkansas State Press*, March 16, 1956, 4; *Houston Informer*, March 31, 1956, 12.

15. Walter Lippmann, "The Disunited Democrats," March 29, 1956, Kefauver Collection, Series 5G, Box 1, File "Butler"; *Greenville News*, March 13, 1956, Workman Papers; *Washington Star*, March 20, 1956, *New York Post*, March 13, 1956, LBJ Senate, Box 423, Folder "Southern Manifesto"; Harry S. Ashmore, *An Epitaph for Dixie* (New York: W.W. Norton & Co., 1958), 32–33; *New York Times*, March 18, 1956, 10E, Allen J. Ellender Papers, 33-L, Box 628, Folder "Civil Rights Data," University Archives, Nicholls State University, Thibodaux, Louisiana.

16. C. Vann Woodward, "The 'New Reconstruction' in the South: Desegregation in Historical Perspective," *Commentary* 21, No. 6 (June 1956): 501–509; George Lewis, *Massive Resistance: The White Response to the Civil Rights Movement* (London: Hodding, 2006), 66; Stewart Alsop, "Where Reasonableness Fails," *Washington Post*, April 8, 1956, J. William Fulbright (JWF) Papers, Series 71, Box 10:1, Special Collections Division, Mullins Library, University of Arkansas, Fayetteville.

17. *U.S. News & World Report*, March 16, 1956, 38–39, April 6, 1956, 72; JWF Papers, "Political Revolt in the South," April 20, 1956, 42–52, "Virginia Jordan to J.W. Fulbright," n.d., Series 77, Box 10:1, "Outside the Law," April 23, 1956, Box 10:2; LBJ Senate, Box 423, Folder "Southern Manifesto"; *Congressional Record* 102, pt. 4 (March 22, 1956): 4750–4751, Thomas J. Hennings Papers, Folder 2988, Western Historical Manuscripts Collection (WHMC), Ellis Memorial Library, University of Missouri–Columbia; Memphis *Commercial Appeal*, JWF Papers, Series 71, Box 10:2; *Wall Street Journal*, March 14, 1956; *San Antonio News*, March 14, 1956, 2C, Price Daniel Papers, Sam Houston Regional Library & Research Center, Liberty, Texas.

18. *New Republic*, April 2, 1956, 10, April 9, 1956, 8, April 23, 1956, 11; LBJ Senate, Box 423, Folder "The Southern Manifesto"; Kefauver Collection, Series 5G, Box 9, Thurgood Marshall, "Address to the UAW Seventh Int'l Education Conference, Washington D.C.," April 22, 1956, 1 of 2, *Philadelphia Inquirer*, Folder "Civil Rights," 2 of 2; *Richmond Afro-American*, March 31, 1956, 4–9; "Hunter to Fulbright," March 14, 1956, JWF Papers, Series 71, Box 10:1; *Chicago Daily Tribune*, March 14, 1956, 16, Ellender Collection; *Nation*, March 31, 1956, 249; *Houston Informer*, March 17, 1956, 12.

19. Ashmore, 32; LBJ Senate, Washington, D.C., office, Anti-Defamation League of B'nai B'rith, "Civil Rights in the 84th Congress," 3, Box 418, Folder "Reedy: Civil Rights," and *Washington News*, March 16, 1956, Box 423, Folder "Southern Manifesto"; Marshall, "Address," Kefauver Collection, Series 5G, Box 9, Folder "Civil Rights," 1 of 2; *New Republic*, April 9, 1956, 8 and April 23, 1956, 12; Alexander M. Bickel, *The Least*

Dangerous Branch: The Supreme Court at the Bar of Politics, 2nd ed. (New Haven: Yale University Press, 1962); *San Antonio News*, March 14, 1956, 2C.

20. John C. Stennis Papers, Series 29, Box 5, Folder 6, Stennis Congressional Research Center, Mitchell Memorial Library, Mississippi State University, Starkville; Long Collection, "Press Release," March 12, 1956, U.S. Senate Series: Senate Office Files, Special Issue Files: Civil Rights, 1941–1962, Range 27, Box 393, Folder 107,"Louisiana Schools," Folders 556–84, "1955–62," "Press Release," May 13, 1956, "Press Files, 1954–Oct. 21, 1956," Box 593, p. 27, Folder 123, "Press Release," May 18, 1956, Box 351, Folder 351–51, "1955–1956"; *Times and Democrat*, March 17, 1956, *Greenville News*, March 14, 1956, Workman Papers; Eastland Collection, Series 2, Sub-series 4, Box 4, Folder "March 1956 Civil Rights"; "Statement," Patman Papers, Box 17(A), Folder "Civil Rights"; "Radio and TV Broadcast," March 15, 1956, STC "Originals," Box 4, Folder 59; "Text of Radio Address recorded by Senator Allen J. Ellender of Louisiana," 8:30 p.m. C.S.T., March 17, 1956, Ellender Papers; Thomas A. Becnel, *Senator Allen Ellender of Louisiana: A Biography* (Baton Rouge: Louisiana State University Press, 1995), 210–211; *Baltimore Sun*, March 18, 1956, LBJ Senate, Box 423, File "Southern Manifesto"; "Press Release," March 12, 1956, Box 399, Folder 16213, and "Scrapbook," Vol. 3847, S-2, Sam J. Ervin Papers, Southern Historical Collection (SHC), Wilson Library, University of North Carolina, Chapel Hill; *Memphis Press-Scimitar*, May 9, 1956; "RBR to Mann," March 14, 1956, Series X, Box 195, Folder 11 "Supreme Court"; "Davis to Roy W. Abel," March 28, 1956, in "Green Sheets, March 1956, A–K," and Folder "Supreme Court 1956," Series 5: Correspondence, Box 93, James C. Davis Papers, Manuscript, Archive, and Rare Book Library (MARBL), Emory University, Georgia; "Where Is the Reign of Terror?," March 27, 1956, 84th Congress, 2nd sess., *Congressional Record*, John Bell Williams Collection, Mississippi Department of Archives and History, Jackson.

21. Memphis *Commercial Appeal*, March 13, 1956, May 9, 1956; *The South*, March 19, 1956, 9, RBR Papers, Series VI, Sub-series A1, Box 12, Folder 5 "Personal-Political"; *Nashville Banner*, March 13, 1956, 4, March 15, 1956, 6; *Atlanta Journal*, March 13, 1956, 20; *Lumberton Post*, March 22, 1956, *Greensboro Daily News*, March 17, 1956, Ervin Papers, "Scrapbook," Vol. 3847, S–2; *Pine Bluff Commercial*, March 17, 1956, "L. G. Baker to McClellan," McClellan Papers, File 19-B "Segregation"; *St. Petersburg Independent*, March 14, 1956, 6; *Roanoke Times*, March 20, 1956, July 17, 1956, 6, A. Willis Robertson Papers, Drawer 140, Folder 56, Earl Gregg Swem Library, College of William and Mary, Williamsburg, Virginia; *Arkansas Gazette*, March 18, 1956, 4F; *Rocky Mount, N.C., Evening Telegram*, March 14, 1956, 3801, Harold Dunbar Cooley Papers, SHC; *Clarke Courier*, March 15, 1956, 12, Hale Boggs Papers, Vol. II, Box 21, MC 1000, Subject Series, Folder "Segregation, 1956," Howard Tilton Memorial Library, Tulane University, New Orleans, Louisiana; *Montgomery Advertiser*, March 14, 1956, 4A.

22. JWF Papers, Series 71, Box 10:2 (in entirety); Boggs Papers, Vol. II., MC 1000, Subject Series, Box 21, Folder "Segregation 1956" (in entirety); "Littlejohn to Patman," March 26, 1956, and "Patman to Stringfellow," May 7, 1956, Patman Papers, Defense Plant File; Misc. Banking File, Box 94(A), Folder 6 "Segregation"; "Misc. Correspondence," Eastland Collection, Series 3, Sub-series 1, Box 35, Folder "Civil Rights (2 of 3)"; Stennis Papers, Series 29, Box 5, Folders 6 and 12 (in entirety); RBR Papers, Series X, "Mann to Russell," March 12, 1956, and "Coker to Russell," April 17, 1956, Box 195, Folder 11 "Supreme Court," and "Milner to Russell," March 28, 1956, Box 232, Folder 1; "McMillan to McClellan," McClellan Papers, "Manifesto (File 18, Drawer D), "Legislation, 1956"; "Prescott to Ervin," February 14, 1956, Ervin Papers, Subgroup A: Senate Records, Box 15, Folder 1119; Daniel Papers, Box 144, "Segregation," (4 of 4 folders), and Box 143, "Segregation," (2 folders).

23. Ellender Papers, Box 688 A.J.E. 33-L, Folder "Legislation: Civil Rights 1956"; Boggs Papers, MC 1000, Subject Series, Box 21, Folder "Segregation, 1956"; RBR Papers, Series X, Box 10, Folder 195, "Schweppe-Russell correspondence," March–April 1956, Box 163, Folder 12 "School Segregation Material," *The Defender* 30, No. 12 (April 1956): 7–9, Box 177, Folder 7, "Schwab to Russell," March 13, 1956, "Penn to Russell," May 3, 1956, and "Larkin to Russell," March 12, 1956, Box 195, Folder 11; Robertson Papers, Drawer 40, "Miles to Robertson," March 13, 1956, Folder 27, "Misc. correspondence," Folder 56, "Woodridge to Robertson," May 23, 1956, "Lydy to Robertson," July 16, 1956; *Asheville Citizen-Times*, March 25, 1956, "Ervin Scrapbook," Vol. 3847, S–2, Ervin Papers; Stennis Papers, Series 29, Box 5, "Curtis to Stennis," April 4, 1956, Folder 6, "Metcalf to Stennis," March 27, 1956, "Duckworth-Stennis correspondence," March–April, 1956, Folder 12, Sub-series: Correspondence, James Meredith Case, 1955–1981, Box 5, Folder 12, "Hunter to Stennis," March 22, 1956, Series 20, Box 5, Folder 12; James J. Kilpatrick, *The Sovereign States: Notes of a Citizen of Virginia* (Chicago: H. Regnery Co., 1957), 306; JWF Papers, Series 71,"Rood to Fulbright," March 17, 1956, Box 10:2; "Heistand to Fulbright," Box 10:1.

24. "Telegram," March 14, 1956, Box 53, Folder "Citizens' Council" 1956-24, "R. D. Thompson to Johnston," March 15, 1956, Box 53, Folder 1956-27, Olin D. Johnston (ODJ) Papers, MPC; "Rainach to Ellender," March 26, 1956, Ellender Papers, Box 688, Folder "legislation: Civil Rights 1956," A.J.E. 33-L.; "Galbreath to Eastland," April 6, 1956, Eastland Collection, Series 3, Sub-series 1, Box 35, Folder "Civil Rights (1 of 3)"; "Henry to JWF," March 19, 1956, JWF Papers, Series 71, Box 10:2; "Jordan to Holland," March 22, 1956, Holland Papers, Box 336, Folder 5-d "Segregation"; RBR Papers, *Southern Digest* 2, No. 4 (May–June 1956), 16, Series X, Box 177, Folder 6, *Augusta Courier*, March 26, 1956, 1, Series VI, Sub-series A2, Box 14, Folder 6 "Augusta Courier"; Numan Bartley, *The Rise of Massive Resistance: Race and Politics in the South During the 1950's* (Baton Rouge: Louisiana State University Press, 1969); *Arkansas Faith*, March 1956, 12–13, Boggs Papers, Vol. II, MC 1000, Subject Series, Box 21,

Folder "Segregation, 1956"; "Sheldon to Stennis," March 29, 1956, Stennis Papers, Series 29, Sub-series "Correspondence, James Meredith Case, 1955–1981," Box 5, Folder 12 "Southern Manifesto, 1956"; *Southern School News*, June 1956, 3.

25. Albert Gore, Sr., Papers, "Crownover to Gore," March 14, 1956, Series 4 "Issue Mail Series," Folder 57 "1956 Segregation–Southern Manifesto–Nashville," Folder 56 "Segregation–Southern Manifesto–Murfreesboro," Cabinet A18, Series 20 "Special, 1953–1970," Folder 4 "1956–1958 Segregation," Albert Gore Congressional Research Center, Middle Tennessee State University, Murfreesboro; "Wallace to Stennis," March 24, 1956, Stennis Papers, Series 29, Box 5, Folder 12 and "Tubb to Stennis," March 13, 1956, Box 15, Folder 6; "Strom Thurmond Address," June 18, 1956, Nashville War Memorial Auditorium, STC "Speeches, B: Originals," Box 4, Folder 54; *Nashville Banner*, March 13, 1956, 4, Patman Papers, Box 94 (A), Folder 6 "Segregation."

26. "Gore to Crownover," April 23, 1956, and "Gore to Wilson," April 13, 1956, and "Gore to Abernathy," May 1, 1956, and "Gore to Moseley," July 26, 1956, Gore Papers, Series 20 "Special, 1953–1970," Folder 1 "1956–1958 Segregation."

27. William E. Leuchtenburg, *The White House Looks South: Franklin Roosevelt, Harry S. Truman, Lyndon B. Johnson* (Baton Rouge: Louisiana State University Press, 2005), 251; *Augusta Courier* March 26, 1956, 3, RBR Papers, Series VI, Sub-series A2, Box 14, Folder 6, "Augusta Courier"; LBJ Papers, "Shivers Address," March 27, 1956, 12–13, James P. Hart, "Conservatives and Liberals," March 16, 1956, "LBJ Senate Political Files, 1949–1961," Box 55 "1956 Convention, LBJ vs. Shivers"; "Remarks of Governor Allan Shivers," Houston State Democratic Executive Committee Meeting, March 27, 1956, Allan Shivers Papers, Texas State Library, Austin, Texas.

28. RBR Papers, Series VI, Sub-series A2, Box 14, Folder 16 "Augusta Courier," and Series X, "RBR-Mann correspondence," Box 195, Folder 11 "Supreme Court," *The South*, March 26, 1956, 5, Box 177, Folder 9 "Civil Rights," April 9, 1956, Folder 7; *Greenville News*, March 14, 1956, Workman Papers; *Newsweek*, May 21, 1956, 43; "Menger to Stennis," March 26, 1956, Stennis Papers, Series 29, Box 5, Folder 6; *Spartanburg Herald-Journal*, March 4, 1956, ODJ Papers.

29. STC, Subject Correspondence 1956, Box 12 "Segregation," Folder III–IV; *Greenville News*, March 14, 1956, Workman Papers; *The South*, RBR Papers, Series X, Box 177, Folder 9 "Civil Rights."

30. *Greenville News*, March 22, 1956, 1; *The State*, March 22, 1956, 1; "Resolution of the Platform and Rules Committee of the South Carolina Democratic Convention," March 21, 1956, ODJ Papers; George Bell Timmerman, "Address," March 21, 1956, South Carolina Democratic Convention, Columbia, South Carolina, Workman Papers; Congress, Senate, 84th, 2nd sess., *Congressional Record* 102, pt. 6 (March 22, 1956): 4752, Hennings Papers, Folder 2988.

31. "Schnitzer to Hazen," May 12, 1956, and "McFarlane to Robertson," March 13, 1956, Robertson Papers, Drawer 140, Folder 56; "Fair to Boggs," March 20, 1956, Boggs

Papers, Vol. II, MC 1000, Subject Series, Box 21, Folder "Segregation 1956"; "Wylie to Stennis," Series 29, Box 5, Folder 4; JWF Papers, Series 71, "Bill Moore to Editor," *Nashville Banner*, March 15, 1956, and "Comer to JWF," March 12, 1956, Box 10:1, *Baxter Bulletin*, March 22, 1956, 2, Box 10:2; "Newton to Gore," March 15, 1956, "Lillard to Gore," March 20, 1956, "Payne to Gore," March 23, 1956, Gore Papers, Issue Mail Series 4, 1956 Segregation, Folder 57 "Southern Manifesto–Nashville"; *Raleigh Times*, March 12, 1956, Cooley Papers No. 3801; *The South*, March 26, 1956, 7, RBR Papers, Series X, Box 177, Folder 9 "Civil Rights"; Tony Badger, "*Brown* and Backlash," in *Massive Resistance: Southern Opposition to the Second Reconstruction*, Clive Webb, ed. (New York: Oxford University Press, 2005), 49–50.

32. "Manifesto," McClellan Papers (File 18, Drawer D): "Legislation, 1956"; JWF Papers, Series 71, "Campbell to JWF," March 12, 1956, Box 10:1, "Steely to JWF," March 13, 1956, Box 10:2; Daniel Papers, Box 144, "Segregation" (4 of 4 Folders).

33. Holland Papers, "Jennings to Holland," March 15, 1956, "Leonard to Holland," March 8, 1956, Holland Papers, Box 336, Folder 5-d "Segregation"; JWF Papers, Series 71, "Johnson to Fulbright," March 13, 1956, Box 10:2, "Shamblin to Fulbright, March 13, 1956, Box 10:1; LBJ Papers, Senate, *Washington Post*, March 15, 1956, n.p., Box 423, Folder "The Southern Manifesto," and "Kilpatrick-Johnson correspondence," April 13, 1956, Box 568, Folder "1956 General Files"; "Presbyterians Adopt Report on Segregation," RBR Papers, Series X, Box 177, Folder 6; Gore Papers, Issue Mail Series 4, 1956 Segregation, Folder "Southern Manifesto–Nashville" (in entirety); "Holland to Mc-Clellan," March 20, 1956, McClellan Papers (File 18, Drawer D): "Legislation, 1956"; "Rombarts to Boggs," March 15, 1956, Boggs Papers, Vol. II, MC 1000, Subject Series, Box 21, Folder "Segregation 1956"; "Ingle to Ervin," February 13, 1956, Ervin Papers, Subgroup A: Senate Records, Box 15, Folder 1119.

34. JWF Papers, Series 71, Box 10:1–2; "Brown to Holland," March 26, 1956, "Warner to Holland," April 2, 1956, Holland Papers, Box 336, Folder 5-d "Segregation"; "Jones to Robertson," Robertson Papers, Drawer 140, Folder 56.

35. "Weekly Newspaper Column," March 29, 1956, Column No. 64, Ervin Papers, Subgroup A: Senate Records, 1954–1975, Series 6, Box 396, Folders 1119–1126; "McClellan to Steely," March 17, 1956, "Holland-McClellan Correspondence," March 24–April 3,1956, McClellan Papers (File 18, Drawer D): "Legislation, 1956"; JWF Papers, "Fulbright to Marsh," March 17, 1956, "Fulbright to McKinnon," April 3, 1956; "Fulbright to Crabtree," January 7, 1957, Box 10:2; Holland Papers, Box 336, Folder 5–d "Segregation"; "Overton to Daniel," March 13, 1956, Daniel Papers, Box 143.

36. Randall Woods, *Fulbright: A Biography* (New York: Cambridge University Press, 1995), 211; "Fischer to Fulbright," April 16, 1956, JWF Papers, Series 71, Box 10:2; *Houston Informer*, April 14, 1956, 8; James T. Baker, *Brooks Hays* (Macon: Mercer University Press, 1989), 157.

37. *Tri-State Defender*, March 23, 1956, April 7, 1956, 7 (reprinted in *Chicago Defender*, March 24, 1956, 10); *Atlanta Daily World*, March 14, 1956, 6; *Telegram*, March 25, 1956, 9, RBR Papers, Series X, Box 177, Folder 9; *Congressional Quarterly*'s "Fact Sheet," "Harlow to Rabb," May 3, 1956, Bryce N. Harlow Papers, Box 8, Folder "Civil Rights," Eisenhower Library; *New York Amsterdam News*, March 24, 1956, 8; *Chicago Defender*, March 17, 1956, 10; *Houston Informer*, March 24 and 31, 1956, 12, and April 28, 1956, 14.

38. Leuchtenburg, 251–252; *Houston Informer*, April 7, 1956, 12, April 21, 1956, 10, May 5, 1956, 12, May 12, 1956, 12; *Washington Post*, March 15, 1956, LBJ Papers, Senate, Box 423, Folder "The Southern Manifesto."

39. Cooley Papers, *Raleigh Times*, March 13, 1956, Box 53, Folder 2311, and 2309–2312; *Atlanta Daily World*, March 14, 1956, 1; *Winston-Salem Journal*, March 27, 1956, Ervin Papers, "Ervin Scrapbook," Vol. 3847, S-2.

40. "Eastland-Cooley Correspondence," Eastland Collection, Series 1, Sub-series 18, Box 3, Folder 3-17; Cooley Papers, "Cooley to Holliday," March 23, 1956, and "Cooley to Vaiden," May 23, 1956, Folder 2309, 2313; *New Republic*, June 11, 1956, 4; *Richmond News Leader*, May 28, 1956, 10, Boggs Papers, Vol. II, MC 1000, Subject Series, Box 21, Folder "Segregation 1956."

41. *Southern School News*, April 1956, 6; "Clayton to Albert," March 26, 1956, Carl Albert Collection, Series "General," Box 10, Folder 17, Carl Albert Center, University of Oklahoma, Norman; *Baltimore Sun*, March 13, 1956, LBJ Papers, Senate, Box 423, Folder "The Southern Manifesto"; *Daily Oklahoman*, March 18, 1956, 18A; *Madisonville Messenger*, March 13, 1956.

42. JWF Papers, Series 71, Box 10:1, "Heatwole to Fulbright," March 16, 1956, *Saint Louis Post-Dispatch*, March 14, 1956, and March 22, 1956; "Oglesby to Patman," March 14, 1956, Patman Papers, Box 94 (A): Defense Pant Files, Misc. Banking Files, Folder 7 "Integration-general 1955"; Woodward, 507.

43. LBJ Papers, Senate, Box 423, Folder "Southern Manifesto" (in entirety); *New York Herald Tribune*, March 14, 1956, Kefauver Collection, Series 5G, Box 9, Folder "Civil Rights," 2 of 2; *Chicago Daily Tribune*, March 14, 1956, 16, Ellender Collection.

44. *Washington Post*, May 4, 1956, 22, Eastland Collection, Series 2, Sub-series 4, Box 5, Folder "May 1956 Civil Rights."

CONCLUSION

1. The title of the conclusion is derived from Martin Luther King, Jr.'s *Stride Towards Freedom: The Montgomery Story* (New York: Harper, 1958).

2. *Evening Star*, May 4, 1956, James Oliver Eastland Papers, Series 2, Sub-series 4, Box 5, Folder "May 1956 Civil rights," "Byrd to Eastland," September 26, 1956, Series 1,

Sub-series 18, Box 2, Folder 2-17. J. D. Williams Library, Department of Archives and Special Collections, University of Mississippi, Oxford.

3. "1956 Republican Platform," August 21, 1956, 17–18, in "Aug '56 Diary–acw(1)," Dwight D. Eisenhower Papers (DDE), Papers as President of the United States (Ann Whitman File), Ann Whitman Diary Series, Box 8, Dwight David Eisenhower Presidential Library, Abilene, Kansas.

4. Michael Gillette, Transcript, "Louis Martin Oral History Interview II" (Internet copy), June 12, 1986, 17, Lyndon Baines Johnson Presidential Library, University of Texas at Austin; Kyle Longley, "White Knight for Civil Rights?: The Civil Rights Record of Albert A. Gore, Sr.," *Tennessee Historical Quarterly* 57, Nos. 2–3 (1998), 118–119.

5. "LBJ-Thurmond Correspondence," Strom Thurmond Collection (STC), Interim Series, Box 3, Folder "J," "Press Release," October 29, 1956, Speeches, B; "Originals," Box 4, Folder 56, J. Strom Thurmond Institute, Clemson University; U.S. Representative Thomas Abernathy, "In the News," June 21, 1956, Eastland Collection, Series 1, Sub-series 18, Box 1, Folder 1-3; *Time*, August 20, 1956, 9–13; *Seattle Times*, March 16, 1956, LBJ Papers, Senate, Box 423, Folder "The Southern Manifesto"; Randall Woods, *LBJ: Architect of American Ambition* (New York: Basic Books, 2006).

6. A. Willis Robertson Papers, *Washington Post*, September 28, 1956, Drawer 115, Folder 9; *New York Times*, October 20, 1956, Drawer 56, Folder 9, Earl Gregg Swem Library, College of William and Mary, Williamsburg, Virginia.

7. *Louisville Defender*, November 1, 1956, Eastland Collection, Series 3, Sub-series 1, Box 36, Folder "1956 Civil rights (3 of 3)"; David Chappell, *Inside Agitators: White Southerners in the Civil Rights Movement* (Baltimore: The Johns Hopkins University Press, 1994), 155; "1956 Republican Platform," DDE Papers; Harold Flowers Collection, University Museum and Cultural Center, University of Arkansas at Pine Bluff.

8. Isaiah 1:18. "Gregory to Holland," March 24, 1956, Spessard Holland Papers, Box 336, Folder 5-d "Segregation," Special and Regional Studies Collections, University of Florida Smathers Libraries, Gainesville; *New York Amsterdam News*, March 17, 1956, 11; W.E.B. Du Bois, "I Won't Vote," *Nation*, October 20, 1956, 324–325.

9. Martin Luther King, Jr., "Our Struggle," ed. James M. Washington, foreword by Coretta Scott King, *I Have a Dream: Writings and Speeches That Changed the World* (San Francisco: Harper, 1992), 3–13; Martin Luther King, Jr., "When Peace Becomes Obnoxious," March 18, 1956, *The Papers of Martin Luther King, Jr.*, ed. Clayborne Carson, Vol. 6 (Berkeley: University of California Press), 257–259; Martin Luther King, Jr., *Stride Towards Freedom: The Montgomery Story* (New York: Harper, 1958).

10. King, "Letter from Birmingham Jail," April 16, 1963, in David Howard-Pitney, *Martin Luther King, Jr., Malcolm X, and the Civil Rights Struggle of the 1950s and 1960s: A Brief History with Documents* (Boston: Bedford/St. Martin's, 2004), 78, 82, 85.

APPENDIXES

1. Signed by Walter F. George, Richard B. Russell, John Stennis, Sam J. Ervin, Jr., and J. Strom Thurmond. (John Stennis Papers, Series 29, Box 5, Folder 5, Stennis Congressional Research Center, Mitchell Memorial Library, Mississippi State University, Starkville; John McClellan Papers, File 19-B "Segregation," Riley-Hickingbotham Memorial Library, Ouachita Baptist University, Arkadelphia, Arkansas.)

2. The full text of the final draft of the Southern Manifesto can be found in numerous sources, including Stennis Papers, Series 29, Box 5, Folder 5; Richard B. Russell (RBR) Papers, Series III, Sub-series A, Box 27, Folder 9 "Southern Manifesto," Richard Brevard Russell Memorial Library, University of Georgia, Athens; Spessard Holland Papers, Box 336, Folder 5-d "Segregation April 1," Special and Regional Studies Collections, University of Florida Smathers Libraries, Gainesville; A. Willis Robertson Papers, Drawer 140, Folder 56, Earl Gregg Swem Library, College of William and Mary, Williamsburg, Virginia; James Oliver Eastland Collection, File Series 1, Sub-series 18, Box 9, Folder 9-29, J. D. Williams Library, Department of Archives and Special Collections, University of Mississippi, Oxford; Price Daniel Papers, Box 65, Folder "Southern Manifesto, March 12, 1956–Senate," and Box 118, Folder "Southern Manifesto," Sam Houston Regional Library and Archives, Liberty, Texas. The text was also printed in numerous periodicals at the time. (*Southern School News*, April 1956, 2; *Washington Evening Star*, March 12, 1956; *State*, March 10, 1956, William Workman Papers, Modern Political Collections (MPC), South Caroliniana Library, University of South Carolina, Columbia; *Atlanta Journal*, March 12, 1956, 1–2.) The signatories of the Southern Manifesto were as follows. Alabama: Sens. John Sparkman and Lister Hill, U.S. Reps. Frank W. Boykin, George M. Grant, George W. Andrews, Kenneth R. Roberts, Albert Rains, Armistead I. Selden, Jr., Carl Elliot, Robert E. Jones, and George E. Huddleston, Jr.; Arkansas: Sens. John R. McClellan and J. William Fulbright, U.S. Reps. E. C. Gathings, Oren Harris, Brooks Hays, Wilbur D. Mills, F. W. Norrell, and James W. Trimble; Florida: Sens. George A. Smathers and Spessard L. Holland, U.S. Reps. Charles E. Bennett, A. S. Herbert, Jr., James A. Haley, D. R. Matthews, Paul G. Rogers, and Robert L. Sikes; Georgia: Sens. Walter George and Richard B. Russell, Jr., U.S. Reps. Iris F. Blitch, Paul Brown, James C. Davis, John James Flynt, Jr., E. L. Forrester, Phil M. Landrum, Henderson Lanham, John L. Pilcher, Prince H. Preston, and Carl Vinson; Louisiana: Sens. Allen J. Ellender and Russell B. Long, U.S. Reps. Hale Boggs, Overton Brooks, F. Edward Hebert, George S. Long, James H. Morrison, Otto E. Passman, T. Ashton Thompson, and Edwin E. Willis; Mississippi: Sens. James O. Eastland and John Stennis, U.S. Reps. Thomas G. Abernathy, William M. Colmer, Frank E. Smith, John Bell Williams, Arthur Winstead, and Jamie L. Whitten; North Carolina: Sens. Sam J. Ervin, Jr., and W. Kerr Scott, U.S. Reps. Hugh Q. Alexander, Graham A. Barden, Herbert C. Bonner, F. Ertel Carlyle, Carl T. Durham, L. H.

Fountain, Woodrow W. Jones, and George A. Shuford; South Carolina: Sens. J. Strom Thurmond and Olin D. Johnston, U.S. Reps. Robert T. Ashemore, William Jennings Bryan Dorn, John L. McMillan, James P. Richards, John J. Riley, and L. Mendel Rivers; Tennessee: U.S. Reps. Jere Cooper, Clifford Davis, James B. Frazer, Jr., and Tom Murray; Texas: Sen. Price Daniel, U.S. Reps. John Dowdy, O. C. Fisher, Wright Patman, and John Dowdy; Virginia: Sens. Harry Flood Byrd, Sr., and A. Willis Robertson, U.S. Reps. Watkins M. Abbitt, Joel T. Broyhill, J. Vaughn Gary, Porter Hardy, Jr., Burr P. Harrison, W. Pat Jennings, Richard H. Poff, Edward J. Robeson, Jr., Howard W. Smith, and William M. Tuck. Congress, House, Deviation from Fundamentals of the Constitution, 84th Congress, 2nd sess., *Congressional Record* 102, vol. 4 (March 12, 1956): 4515–4516; Harold Cooley Papers, Box 53, Folder 2309, Southern Historical Collection (SHC), Wilson Library, University of North Carolina, Chapel Hill; *U.S. News & World Report*, March 23, 1956, 101; *Washington Star*, March 12, 1956, page unknown; *State*, March 12, 1956, Workman Papers, MPC; *Baltimore Sun*, March 12, 1956, LBJ Senate, Box 423, Folder "The Southern Manifesto"; *The South*, March 19, 1956, 9, RBR Papers, Series VI, Sub-series A1, Box 12, Folder 5, "Personal Political."

Bibliography

UNPUBLISHED RESOURCES

Carl Albert Collection, The Carl Albert Center, University of Oklahoma, Norman.

Harry Byrd, Sr., Papers, Albert and Shirley Small Special Collections Library, University of Virginia, Charlottesville.

James F. Byrnes Papers, Special Collections Libraries, The J. Strom Thurmond Institute, Clemson University, Clemson, South Carolina.

Hale Boggs Papers, Howard Tilton Memorial Library, Tulane University, New Orleans, Louisiana.

Buford Boone Papers, W. S. Hoole Special Collections Library, University of Alabama, Tuscaloosa.

Joel Broyhill Papers, Fenwick Library, George Mason University, Fairfax, Virginia.

Harold Dunbar Cooley Papers, The Southern Historical Collection (SHC), Wilson Library, University of North Carolina, Chapel Hill.

Price Daniel Papers, Sam Houston Regional Library & Research Center, Liberty, Texas.

James C. Davis Papers, Manuscripts, Archive, and Rare Book Library (MARBL), Emory University, Georgia.

William Jennings Bryan Dorn Papers, Modern Political Collections (MPC), South Caroliniana Library, University of South Carolina, Columbia.

James Oliver Eastland Collection, J. D. Williams Library, Department of Archives and Special Collections, University of Mississippi, Oxford.

Dwight D. Eisenhower Papers (Anne Whitman File, etc., including oral history collection), Dwight D. Eisenhower Library, Abilene, Kansas.

Allen J. Ellender Papers, University Archives, Nicholls State University, Thibodaux, Louisiana.

Sam J. Ervin Papers, Wilson Library, Southern Historical Collection, University of North Carolina, Chapel Hill.

Orval E. Faubus Papers, Special Collections Division, Mullins Library, University of Arkansas, Fayetteville.

Gilbert Fite, interview with author, summer 2002, Bella Vista, Arkansas.

Harold Flowers Collection, University Museum and Cultural Center, University of Alabama at Pine Bluff.

J. William Fulbright Papers, Special Collections Division, Mullins Library, University of Arkansas at Fayetteville.

Albert Gore, Sr., Papers, Albert Gore Congressional Research Center, Middle Tennessee State University, Murfreesboro.

John Temple Graves II Papers, Birmingham Public Library, Department of Archives and Manuscripts, Alabama.

Leonard Hall Papers, Dwight D. Eisenhower Library, Abilene, Kansas.

Brooks Hays Papers, Special Collections Division, Mullins Library, University of Arkansas at Fayetteville.

F. Edward Hebert Papers, Howard Tilton Memorial Library, Tulane University, New Orleans, Louisiana.

Thomas Hennings Papers, Western Historical Manuscript Collection (WHMC), Ellis Memorial Library, University of Missouri–Columbia.

Lister Hill Papers, W. S. Hoole Special Collections Library, University of Alabama, Tuscaloosa.

Spessard Holland Papers, Special and Regional Studies Collections, University of Florida Smathers Libraries, Gainesville.

Lyndon Baines Johnson Papers (miscellaneous files, including U.S. Senate and oral history collection), Lyndon Baines Johnson Presidential Library, University of Texas at Austin.

Olin D. Johnston Papers, Modern Political Collections, South Caroliniana Library, University of South Carolina, Columbia.

Estes Kefauver Collection, James D. Hoskins Special Collections Library, University of Tennessee–Knoxville.

Robert S. Kerr Collection, The Carl Albert Center, University of Oklahoma, Norman.

Long Family Papers (Russell B. and Earl K.), Hill Memorial Library, Louisiana State University, Baton Rouge, Louisiana.

John McClellan Papers, Riley-Hickingbotham Memorial Library, Ouachita Baptist University, Arkadelphia, Arkansas.

Wilbur Mills Collection, Hendrix College, Conway, Arkansas.

Hays Mizzell Papers, Modern Political Collections, South Caroliniana Library, University of South Carolina, Columbia.

DeLessepps Morrison Papers, Howard Tilton Memorial Library, Tulane University, New Orleans, Louisiana.

E. Frederic Morrow Papers, Dwight D. Eisenhower Library, Abilene, Kansas.

Wright Patman Papers, Johnson Presidential Library, University of Texas at Austin.

A. Willis Robertson Papers, Earl Gregg Swem Library, College of William and Mary, Williamsburg, Virginia.

J. N. Rushing, D. D. S. "Scrapbook," Albert Sidney Farms, Jerome, Arkansas.

Richard B. Russell: Georgia Giant. Television transcripts. Used with permission of the Russell Memorial Library, UGA Libraries, Athens, GA 30602.

Richard Brevard Russell, Jr., Papers, Richard B. Russell Memorial Library, University of Georgia, Athens.

Senate Historical Office (SHO), (miscellaneous files, including U.S. Senate and oral history collection), Hart Senate Office Building, Washington, D.C.

Allan Shivers Papers, Texas State Library, Austin, Texas.

Southern States Industrial Council Collection, Tennessee State Library, Nashville.

George Smathers Papers, Special and Regional Studies Collections, University of Florida Smathers Libraries, Gainesville.

The Hon. Howard W. Smith Papers, Albert and Shirley Small Special Collections Library, University of Virginia, Charlottesville.

John Sparkman Papers, The W. S. Hoole Special Collections Library, University of Alabama, Tuscaloosa.

John Stennis Papers, Stennis Congressional Research Center, Mitchell Memorial Library, Mississippi State University, Starkville.

Stuart Symington Papers, WHMC, University of Missouri–Columbia.

Hermann Talmadge Papers, Russell Memorial Library, University of Georgia at Athens.

J. Strom Thurmond Collection, Thurmond Institute, Clemson University, South Carolina.

Harry S. Truman Papers (postpresidential), Harry S. Truman Presidential Library, Independence, Missouri.

John Bell Williams Collection, Mississippi Department of Archives and History, Jackson.

William D. Workman Papers, MPC, South Caroliniana Library, University of South Carolina, Columbia.

SELECTED PERIODICALS

Arkansas Gazette, Arkansas Democrat, Arkansas Faith, Arkansas State Press, Atlanta Journal, Atlanta Constitution, Atlanta Daily World, Atlantic Monthly, Augusta Courier, Austin Statesman, Bainbridge Post-Searchlight, Baltimore Sun, Baxter Bulletin, Catholic Action of the South, Charleston News & Courier, Charlotte Times, Chattanooga Free Press, Chicago Defender, Christian Century, Christian Science Monitor, Cleveland Plain Dealer, Commentary, Crisis, Daily Oklahoman, Dallas Morning News, Ebony, Greenville News, Harper's, Houston Informer, Jackson Daily News, Jet, Las Vegas Review-Journal, Life, Los Angeles Times, Memphis Commercial Appeal, Memphis Press-Scimitar, Memphis Tri-State De-

fender, Montgomery Advertiser, Nashville Banner, Nashville Tennessean, Nation, New Orleans States, New Orleans Times-Picayune, New Republic, Newsweek, New York Amsterdam News, New York Herald-Tribune, New York Post, New York Times, Norfolk Virginian Pilot, Northwest Arkansas Times, Philadelphia Inquirer, Philadelphia Record, Pine Bluff Commercial, Pittsburgh Courier, Progressive, Richmond Afro-American, Roanoke Times, St. Petersburg Independent, St. Petersburg Times, St. Louis Argus, St. Louis Globe-Democrat, St. Louis Post-Dispatch, San Antonio News, Saturday Evening Post, Shreveport Journal, The South, Southern School News, Spartanburg Herald, Springfield Union, The State, Tampa Tribune, Telegram, Texarkana Gazette, Time, Wall Street Journal, Washington News, Washington Post, Washington Star, U.S. News & World Report.

PUBLISHED WORKS

Adams, Julianne Lewis, and Tom DeBlack. *Civil Obedience: An Oral History of School Desegregation in Fayetteville, Arkansas, 1954–1965.* With an introduction by Willard Gatewood. Fayetteville: University of Arkansas Press, 1994.

Ambrose, Stephen E. *Eisenhower: Soldier and President.* New York: Simon and Schuster, 1990.

——. *Nixon.* New York: Simon and Schuster, 1987–91.

Anderson, Carol. *Eyes Off the Prize: The United Nations and the African American Struggle for Human Rights, 1944–1955.* Cambridge: Cambridge University Press, 2003.

Appleby, David. *Hoxie: The First Stand* DVD. Memphis: University of Memphis, 2002.

Aptheker, Herbert. *The Correspondence of W. E. B. Du Bois.* Vol. 3, *Selections, 1944–1963.* Amherst: University of Massachusetts Press, 1978.

Ashmore, Harry. *An Epitaph for Dixie.* New York: W. W. Norton, 1958.

Aucoin, Brent J. "The Southern Manifesto and Southern Opposition to Desegregation." *Arkansas Historical Quarterly* 55, No. 2 (1996): 173–93.

Badger, Anthony J. "'The Forerunner of Our Opposition': Arkansas and the Southern Manifesto of 1956." *Arkansas Historical Quarterly* 56, No. 3 (1997): 353–360.

——. "Southerners Who Refused to Sign the Southern Manifesto." *Historical Journal* 42, No. 2 (1999): 517–534.

——. "The South Confronts the Court: The Southern Manifesto of 1956." *Journal of Policy History* 20, No. 1 (2008): 126–142.

——. "The Southern Manifesto: White Southerners and Civil Rights, 1956." Rob Kros and Eduard van de Bilt, eds. *The US Constitution After 200 Years.* Amsterdam: Free University Press, 1988.

——, and Brian Ward, eds. *The Making of Martin Luther King and the Civil Rights Movement.* New York: New York University Press, 1996.

Baker, James T. *Brooks Hays.* Macon: Mercer University Press, 1989.

Bartley, Numan V. *The New South, 1945–1980.* Louisiana State University Press, 1995.

——. *The Rise of Massive Resistance: Race and Politics in the South During the 1950's.* Baton Rouge: Louisiana State University Press, 1969.

——, and Hugh D. Graham. *Southern Elections: County and Precinct Data, 1950–1972.* Baton Rouge: Louisiana State University Press, 1978.

——. *Southern Politics and the Second Reconstruction.* Baltimore: The Johns Hopkins University Press, 1975.

Bass, Jack, and Walter DeVries. *The Transformation of Southern Politics: Social Change and Political Consequence Since 1945.* New York: Basic Books, 1976.

Becker, Carl. *The Declaration of Independence: A Study in the History of Political Ideas.* New York: Alfred A. Knopf, 1964.

Becnel, Thomas A. *Senator Allen Ellender of Louisiana: A Biography.* Baton Rouge: Louisiana State University Press, 1995.

Bickel, Alexander M. *The Least Dangerous Branch: The Supreme Court at the Bar of Politics.* 2nd ed. New Haven: Yale University Press, 1962.

Binder, Sarah A. "The Partisan Basis of Procedural Choice: Allocating Parliamentary Rights in the House, 1789–1990." *American Political Science Review* 90, No. 1 (March 1996): 8–20.

Bone, Hugh A. "An Introduction to the Senate Policy Committees." *The American Political Science Review* (June 1956).

Brady, Tom. *Black Monday.* Jackson: Citizens' Councils of America, 1955.

Brinkley, Alan. *The End of Reform: New Deal Liberalism in Recession and War.* New York: Alfred A. Knopf, 1995.

Brown, Stuart Gerry. *Adlai E. Stevenson: A Short Biography, the Conscience of a Country.* Woodbury: Barron's, 1965.

Brownell, Herbert. "Eisenhower's Civil Rights Program: A Personal Assessment." *Presidential Studies Quarterly* 21, No. 2 (1991): 235–42.

Bullion, John L. *In the Boat with L. B. J.* Plano: The Republic of Texas Press, 2001.

——. *Lyndon B. Johnson and the Transformation of American Politics.* Pearson, 2007.

Bureau of the Census. *Statistical Abstract of the United States.* U.S. Department of Commerce, 1965.

Byrd, Robert C. *The Senate, 1789–1989.* Washington, D.C.: Government Printing Office, 1988–93.

Campbell, Karl E. *Senator Sam Ervin, Last of the Founding Fathers.* Chapel Hill: University of North Carolina Press, 2007.

Caro, Robert. *Master of the Senate: The Years of Lyndon Johnson.* Vol. 3. New York: Alfred Knopf, 2002.

Carpenter, Elizabeth. *Getting Better All the Time.* College Station: Texas A&M Press, 1987.

————. *Ruffles and Flourishes.* College Station: Texas A&M Press, 1969.

Carson, Clayborne. *The Papers of Martin Luther King, Jr.* 8 vols. Berkeley: University of California Press, 1992.

Carter, Robert L. *A Matter of Law: A Memoir of Struggle in the Cause of Equal Rights.* New York: Free Press, 2005.

Champagne, Anthony. *Congressman Sam Rayburn.* New Brunswick: Rutgers University Press, 1984.

Chappell, David. *Inside Agitators: White Southerners and Civil Rights.* Baltimore: The Johns Hopkins University Press, 1994.

————. *A Stone of Hope: Prophetic Religion and the Death of Jim Crow.* Chapel Hill: University of North Carolina Press, 2004.

Cobb, James C. *The Selling of the South: The Southern Crusade for Economic Development.* Baton Rouge: Louisiana State University Press, 1982.

Cohodas, Nadine. *Strom Thurmond and the Politics of Southern Change.* New York: Simon & Schuster, 1993.

Collins, Robert M. *More: The Politics of Economic Growth in Postwar America.* Oxford: Oxford University Press, 2000.

Congressional Record. Washington, D.C.: Government Printing Office.

Conkin, Paul. *Big Daddy from the Pedernales: Lyndon Baines Johnson.* Boston: Twayne, 1986.

————. *The New Deal.* Wheeling: Harlan Davidson, 1992.

Cope, Graeme. "'Honest White People of the Middle and Lower Classes'? A Profile of the Capital Citizens' Council During the Little Rock Crisis of 1957." *Arkansas Historical Quarterly* 61, No. 1 (Spring 2002): 37–58.

Crespino, Joseph. *In Search of Another Country: Mississippi and the Conservative Counterrevolution.* Princeton: Princeton University Press, 2009.

————. *Strom Thurmond's America.* New York: Hill and Wang, 2012.

Cushman, Clare, and Melvin I. Urofsky, eds. *Black, White, and Brown: The Landmark School Desegregation Case in Retrospect.* Washington, D.C.: CQ Press, 2004.

Dabney, Dick. *A Good Man: The Life of Sam J. Ervin.* Boston: Houghton-Mifflin, 1976.

Dailey, Jane. "Sex, Segregation, and the Sacred after *Brown.*" *The Journal of American History* 91, No. 1 (June 2004): 119–144.

Dallek, Robert. *Lone Star Rising: Lyndon Johnson and His Times, 1908–1960.* New York: Oxford University Press, 1991.

Daniel, Pete. *Lost Revolutions: The South in the 1950s.* Chapel Hill: University of North Carolina Press, 2000.

Daugherity, Brian J., and Charles C. Bolton, eds. *With All Deliberate Speed: Implementing Brown v. Board of Education.* Fayetteville: University of Arkansas Press, 2008.

David, Paul T. *Party Strength in the United States, 1872–1970.* Charlottesville: University Press of Virginia, 1972.

Davis, Kenneth Sydney. *The Politics of Honor: A Biography of Adlai Stevenson.* New York: Putnam, 1967.

Day, John Kyle. "Filibuster." In James Ciment, ed., *Postwar America: An Encyclopedia of History and Politics.* San Juan Capistrano: M. E. Sharpe, 2006.

———. "The Fall of a Southern Moderate: Congressman Brooks Hays and the Election of 1958." *Arkansas Historical Quarterly* LIX, No. 3 (Autumn 2000): 241–264.

———. "The Fall of Southern Moderation: The Defeat of Brooks Hays in the 1958 Congressional Election for the Fifth District of Arkansas." M.A. thesis, University of Arkansas, 1999.

———. "The Southern Manifesto: Making Opposition to the Civil Rights Movement." Dissertation, University of Missouri–Columbia, 2006.

The Declaration of Independence and the Constitution of the United States. Williamsburg: The Colonial Williamsburg Foundation.

Degler, Carl N. *Neither Black Nor White: A History of Race Relations in Brazil and the United States.* New York: Macmillan, 1971.

Dierfield, Bruce J. *Keeper of the Rules: Congressman Howard W. Smith of Virginia.* Charlottesville: University of Virginia Press, 1987.

Dudziak, Mary. *Cold War Civil Rights: Race and the Image of American Democracy.* Princeton: Princeton University Press, 2000.

Dyer, Stanford Phillips. "Lyndon B. Johnson and the Politics of Civil Rights, 1935–1960: The Art of 'Moderate Leadership.'" Dissertation, Texas A&M University, 1978.

Ely, James W., Jr. *The Crisis of Conservative Virginia: The Byrd Organization and the Politics of Massive Resistance.* Knoxville: University of Tennessee Press, 1976.

Evans, Rowland, and Robert Novak. *Lyndon B. Johnson: The Exercise of Power.* New York: The New American Library, 1966.

Fairclough, Adam. "The Costs of Brown: Black Teachers and School Integration." *Journal of American History*, Vol. 91, No. 1 (June 2004): 43–55.

Farber, David. *The Age of Great Dreams: America in the 1960s.* New York: Hill & Wang, 1994.

Faubus, Orval. *Down from the Hills.* 2 vols. Little Rock: Democrat Printing & Lithographing Co., 1980.

Faulkner, William. *Essays, Speeches and Public Letters*, ed. James Meriwether. New York: Random House, 1965.

Fielder, Betty Bean. "Price Daniel, Texas and Segregation." M.A. thesis, Lamar University, Texas. Sam Houston Regional Library, Liberty, Texas.

Finley, Keith M. *Delaying the Dream: Southern Senators and the Fight against Civil Rights, 1938–1965.* Baton Rouge: Louisiana State University Press, 2008.

Fite, Gilbert C. *Cotton Fields No More: Southern Agriculture, 1865–1980.* Lexington: University Press of Kentucky, 1984.

———. *Richard B. Russell, Jr., Senator from Georgia.* Chapel Hill: University of North Carolina Press, 1991.

Fontenay, Charles L. *Estes Kefauver: A Biography.* Knoxville: University of Tennessee Press, 1980.

Franklin, John Hope. *The Emancipation Proclamation.* Garden City: Doubleday, 1963.

Frederickson, George. *Racism: A Brief History.* Princeton: Princeton University Press, 2002.

Fredrickson, Kari. "Confronting the Garrison State: South Carolina and the Early Cold War Era." *The Journal of Southern History* 72, No. 2 (May 2006): 349–378.

———. *The Dixiecrat Revolt and the End of the Solid South.* Chapel Hill: University of North Carolina Press, 2001.

Friedel, Frank. *FDR and the South.* Baton Rouge: Louisiana State Press, 1965.

———. *Franklin D. Roosevelt: A Rendezvous with Destiny.* Boston: Little, Brown and Company, 1990.

Galambos, Louis. "The Emerging Organizational Synthesis in Modern American History." *Business History Review* 44, No. 3 (Autumn 1970): 280–290.

———. "Technology, Political Economy, and Professionalization: Central Themes of the Organizational Synthesis." *Business History Review* 57 (Winter 1983): 471–493.

Garrow, David. *Bearing the Cross: Martin Luther King, Jr., and the Southern Christian Leadership Conference.* New York: William Morrow and Company, 1986.

Gates, Robbins S. *The Making of Massive Resistance: Virginia's Politics of Public School Desegregation, 1954–56.* Chapel Hill: University of North Carolina Press, 1962.

Genovese, Eugene. *A Consuming Fire: The Fall of the Confederacy in the Mind of the White Christian South.* Athens: University of Georgia Press, 1998.

———. *The Southern Front: History and Politics in the Culture War.* Columbia: University of Missouri Press, 1994.

Goldsmith, John A. *Colleagues: Richard B. Russell and His Apprentice, Lyndon B. Johnson.* Washington, D.C.: Seven Locks Press, 1993.

Goodwin, Doris Kearns. *Lyndon Johnson and the American Dream.* New York: Harper & Row, 1976.

Gore, Albert A., Sr. *The Eye of the Storm: A People's Politics for the Seventies.* New York: Herder and Herder, 1970.

———. *Let the Glory Out: My South and Its Politics.* New York: Viking, 1972.

Gorman, Joseph Bruce. *Kefauver: A Political Biography.* New York: Oxford University Press, 1971.

Gould, Lewis L. *The Most Exclusive Club: A History of the Modern United States Senate.* New York: Basic Books, 2005.

Grant, Philip A., Jr. "Senator Estes Kefauver and the 1956 Minnesota Presidential Primary." *Tennessee Historical Quarterly* 42, No. 4 (1983): 383–392.

Grantham, Dewey W. *The Life and Death of the Solid South: A Political History*. Lexington: University Press of Kentucky, 1988.

Halberstam, David. "The White Citizens Councils: Respectable Means for Unrespectable Ends." *Commentary* 22, No. 4 (October 1956): 293–302.

Hall, Jacquelyn Dowd. "The Long Civil Rights Movement and the Political Uses of the Past." *Journal of American History* 91, No. 4 (March 2005): 1233–1263.

Hall, Richard L. "Empiricism and Progress in Positive Theories of Legislative Institutions." In Kenneth A. Shepsle and Barry R. Weingast, eds., *Positive Theories of Congressional Institutions*. Ann Arbor: University of Michigan Press, 1995.

Hamby, Alonzo. *Liberalism and Its Challengers: From F. D. R. to Bush*. New York: Oxford University Press, 1991.

Hamilton, Alexander, James Madison, and John Jay. *The Federalist Papers*. New York: The New American Library of World Literature, 1961.

Hamilton, Charles V. *Adam Clayton Powell, Jr.: The Political Biography of an American Dilemma*. New York: Athenaeum, 1991.

Hamilton, Virginia Van der Veer. *Lister Hill: Statesman from the South*. Chapel Hill: The University of North Carolina Press, 1987.

Harbaugh, William H. *Lawyer's Lawyer: The Life of John W. Davis*. New York: Oxford University Press, 1973.

Hardeman, D. B., and Donald C. Bacon. *Rayburn: A Biography*. Austin: Texas Monthly Press, 1987.

Harris, Carl. "Right Fork or Left Fork?: The Section-Party Alignments of Southern Democrats in Congress, 1873–1897" and "Redeemers versus Agrarians?" In John B. Boles and Bethany L. Johnson, eds., *Origins of the New South Fifty Years Later: The Continuing Influence of a Historical Classic*. Baton Rouge: Louisiana State University Press, 2003.

Haygood, Wil. *King of the Cats: The Life and Times of Adam Clayton Powell, Jr.* Boston: Houghton-Mifflin, 1993.

Hays, Brooks. *A Southern Moderate Speaks*. Chapel Hill: University of North Carolina Press, 1959.

Heinemann, Ronald L. *Harry Byrd of Virginia*. Charlottesville: University Press of Virginia, 1996.

Hine, Darlene Clark. *Black Victory: The Rise and Fall of the White Primary in Texas*. Columbia: University of Missouri Press, 2003.

Hine, Darlene Clark, William C. Hine, and Stanley Harrold. *The African American Odyssey*. Upper Saddle River, NJ: Prentice Hall, 2000.

Hodgson, Godfrey. *America in Our Time: From World War II to Nixon, What Happened and Why*. New York: Random House, 1976.

Holley, Donald. *The Second Great Emancipation: The Mechanical Cotton Picker, Black Migration, and How They Shaped the Modern South*. Fayetteville: University of Arkansas Press, 2000.

Howard-Pitney, David, ed. *Martin Luther King, Jr., Malcolm X, and the Civil Rights Struggle of the 1950s and 1960s: A Brief History with Documents*. Boston: Bedford/St. Martin's, 2004.

Huebner, Timothy S. "Looking Backward: The Southern Manifesto of 1956." *Historically Speaking* VII, No. 5 (May/June 2006): 36–39.

Huntington, Samuel P. *American Politics: The Promise of Disharmony*. Cambridge: Harvard University Press, 1981.

Jacobs, Meg, William J. Novak, and Julian E. Zelizer, eds. *The Democratic Experiment: New Directions in American Political History*. Princeton: Princeton University Press, 2003.

Jacoway, Elizabeth. "*Brown* and the Road to Reunion." *The Journal of Southern History* 70, No. 2 (May 2004): 304–305.

———. *Turn Away Thy Son: Little Rock, the Crisis That Shocked the Nation*. New York: Free Press, 2007.

———, and David R. Colburn. *Southern Businessmen and Desegregation*. Baton Rouge: Louisiana State University Press, 1982.

James, Anthony W. "The College Social Fraternity Antidiscrimination Debate, 1945–1949." *The Historian* 62, No. 2 (Winter 2000): 303–324.

Jeansonne, Glen. "Leander Perez: Demagogue and Reformer" and William C. Havard, Jr., "Louisiana and the Two-Party System." In Mark T. Carleton, Perry H. Howard, and Joseph B. Parker, eds., *Readings in Louisiana Politics*. Baton Rouge: Claitor's, 1975.

Johnson, Haynes Bonner, and Bernard Gwertzman. *Fulbright: The Dissenter*. Garden City: Doubleday, 1968.

Johnson, Walter, ed. *The Papers of Adlai E. Stevenson*. Boston: Little, Brown, & Co., 1976.

Kantrowitz, Stephen. *Ben Tillman and the Reconstruction of White Supremacy*. Chapel Hill: University of North Carolina Press, 2000.

Key, V. O. *Southern Politics in State and Nation*. New York: A. A. Knopf, 1949.

Kilpatrick, James Jackson. *The Sovereign States: Notes of a Citizen of Virginia*. Chicago: H. Regnery Co., 1957.

King, Martin Luther, Jr. *Stride Towards Freedom: The Montgomery Story*. New York: Harper, 1958.

Klarman, Michael J. "How the *Brown* Decision Changed Race Relations: The Backlash Thesis." *The Journal of American History* (June 1994): 81–89.

Klinetobe, Charles. "Jury Trials and Gerrymanders: The Legal Effort to Maintain Segregation in July of 1957." *The Historian* 68, No. 2 (Summer 2006): 221–240.

Kosek, Joseph Kip. "Richard Gregg, Mohandas Gandhi and the Strategy of Nonviolence." *The Journal of American History* 91, No. 4 (March 2005): 1344.

Krehbiel, Keith. *Information and Legislative Organization.* Ann Arbor: University of Michigan Press, 1991.

———. *Pivotal Politics: A Theory of U.S. Lawmaking.* Chicago: University of Chicago Press, 1998.

Lassiter, Matthew, and Andrew B. Lewis, eds. *The Moderates' Dilemma: Massive Resistance to School Desegregation in Virginia.* Charlottesville: University Press of Virginia, 1998.

———. *The Silent Majority: Suburban Politics in the Sunbelt South.* Princeton: Princeton University Press, 2006.

Lawson, Stephen F. *Black Ballots: Voting Rights in the South, 1944–69.* New York: Columbia University Press, 1976.

———. *Running for Freedom: Civil Rights and Black Politics in America since 1941.* 2nd ed. New York: McGraw-Hill, 1997.

Leflar, Robert A. "One Life in the Law: Black Law Students." In *Arkansas, Arkansas: Writers and Writings from the Delta to the Ozarks, 1541–1969,* ed. John Caldwell Guilds. Vol. 1. Fayetteville: University of Arkansas Press, 1999, 569–572.

Leuchtenberg, William E. *Franklin D. Roosevelt and the New Deal, 1933–1940.* New York: Harper-Torch, 1963.

———. *The White House Looks South: Franklin Roosevelt, Harry Truman, Lyndon Johnson.* Baton Rouge: Louisiana State University Press, 2005.

Lewis, George. *Massive Resistance: The White Response to the Civil Rights Movement.* London: Hodder, 2006.

———. *The White South and the Red Menace: Segregationists, Anticommunism, and Massive Resistance, 1945–1965.* Gainesville: University Press of Florida, 2004.

Lipsitz, George. *A Life in the Struggle: Ivory Perry and the Culture of Opposition.* Philadelphia: Temple University Press, 1988.

Longley, Kyle. *Senator Albert Gore, Sr.: Tennessee Maverick.* With an introduction by Al Gore, Jr. Baton Rouge: Louisiana State Press, 2004.

———. "White Knight For Civil Rights?: The Civil Rights Record of Senator Albert A. Gore Sr." *Tennessee Historical Quarterly* 1998 57, Nos. 2,3 (1998): 114–131.

McCubbins, Matthew D., and Thomas Schwartz. "Congressional Oversight Overlooked: Police Patrols versus Fire Alarms." *American Journal of Political Science* 28 (1984): 165–179.

McKeever, Porter. *Adlai Stevenson: His Life and Legacy.* New York: William Morrow, 1989.

McLoughlin, William G. *Cherokees and Missionaries, 1789–1839.* Norman: University of Oklahoma Press, 1995.

McMath, Sidney S. *Promises Kept: A Memoir.* Fayetteville: University of Arkansas Press, 2003.

McMillen, Neil R. *The Citizens' Council: Organized Resistance to the Second Reconstruction, 1954–64.* Urbana: University of Illinois Press, 1971.

Mann, Robert. *Legacy to Power: Senator Russell Long of Louisiana.* New York: Paragon House, 1992.

———. *The Walls of Jericho: Lyndon Johnson, Hubert Humphrey, Richard Russell, and the Struggle for Civil Rights.* New York: Harcourt Brace, 1996.

Martin, James Clyde, Jr., "The First Administration of Governor Price Daniel." M.A. thesis, University of Texas at Austin, 1967, Sam Houston Regional Library, Liberty, Texas.

Martin, John Frederick. *Civil Rights and the Crisis of Liberalism: The Democratic Party, 1945–1976.* Boulder: Westview Press, 1979.

Martin, Waldo E., Jr., ed. *Brown v. Board of Education: A Brief History with Documents.* Boston: Bedford/St. Martin's, 1998.

Mathews, Donald R. *U.S. Senators and Their World.* Chapel Hill: University of North Carolina Press, 1960.

May, Elaine Tyler. *Homeward Bound: American Families in the Cold War.* New York: Basic Books, 1982.

Mayhew, David R. *Congress: The Electoral Connection.* New Haven: Yale University Press, 1974.

Meriwether, James B., and Michael Millgate, eds. *Lion in the Garden: Interviews with William Faulkner, 1926–1962.* New York: Random House, 1968.

Mielnik, Tara Mitchell. "Resisting Massive Resistance: Tennessee's Senators and the Southern Manifesto." March 27, 1997, Albert Gore Sr. Congressional Research Center, Middle Tennessee State University, Murfreesboro.

Miller, Jim. *Democracy Is in the Streets: From Port Huron to the Siege of Chicago.* New York: Simon & Schuster, 1987.

Miller, Merle. *Lyndon: An Oral Biography.* New York: G. P. Putnam's Sons, 1980.

Moe, Terry M. "An Assessment of the Positive Theory of 'Congressional Dominance.'" *Legislative Studies Quarterly* 12, No. 4 (November 1987): 475–520.

———. "The New Economics of Organization." *American Journal of Political Science* (1984): 739–777.

Morgan, Iwan. *Nixon.* New York: Arnold, 2000.

Morrow, E. Frederic. *Black Man in the White House: A Diary of the Eisenhower Years by the Administrative Officer for Special Projects, the White House, 1955–1961.* New York: Coward-McCann, Inc., 1963.

Muller, Herbert J. *Adlai Stevenson: A Study In Values.* New York: Harper & Row, 1967.

Murph, Dan. *The Life of Price Daniel: Texas Giant.* Austin: Eakin Press, 2002.

Muse, Benjamin. *Virginia's Massive Resistance*. Bloomington: Indiana University Press, 1961.

Nichols, David A. *A Matter of Justice: Eisenhower and the Beginning of the Civil Rights Revolution*. New York: Simon & Schuster, 2007.

North, Douglass C. "Institutions and a Transaction–Cost Theory of Exchange." In Alt and Shepsle, eds., *Perspectives on Positive Political Economy* (1990): 182–194.

Old, William. *The Segregation Issue: Suggestions Regarding the Maintenance of State Autonomy*. Chesterfield, VA: 1955.

Olson, Mancur. *The Logic of Collective Action: Public Goods and the Theory of Groups*. Cambridge: Harvard University Press, 1960.

O'Neil, William. *American High: The Years of Confidence, 1945–60*. New York: Macmillan, 1986.

Oshinsky, David. *A Conspiracy So Immense: The World of Joe McCarthy*. New York: Macmillan, 1983.

Ownby, Ted. *The Role of Ideas in the Civil Rights South*. Jackson: University Press of Mississippi, 2002.

Patterson, James T. *America in the Twentieth Century: A History*. Fort Worth: Harcourt College Publishers, 2000.

———. *Brown v. Board of Education: A Civil Rights Milestone and Its Troubled Legacy*. New York: Oxford University Press, 2001.

———. *Congressional Conservatism and the New Deal: The Growth of the Conservative Coalition in Congress, 1933–1939*. Lexington: University of Kentucky Press, 1967.

Pettit, Lawrence K., and Edward Keynes, eds. *The Legislative Process in the U.S. Senate*. Chicago: Rand McNally, 1969.

Polsby, Nelson W. "The Institutionalization of the U.S. House of Representatives." *American Political Science Review* 62, No. 2: 144–168.

Potenziani, David Daniel. "Look to the Past: Richard B. Russell and the Defense of White Supremacy." Dissertation, University of Georgia, Athens, 1981.

Powell, Adam Clayton, Jr. *Adam by Adam: The Autobiography of Adam Clayton Powell, Jr.* New York: The Dial Press, 1971.

Powell, Lee Riley. *J. William Fulbright and His Time: A Political Biography*. Memphis: Guild Bindery Press, 1996.

Rae, Nicol C. *Southern Democrats*. New York: Oxford University Press, 1994.

Reed, Roy. *Faubus: The Life and Times of an American Prodigal*. Fayetteville: University of Arkansas Press, 1997.

Reedy, George. *Lyndon B. Johnson: A Memoir*. New York: Andrews & McMeel, 1982.

———. *The U.S. Senate: Paralysis or a Search for Consensus?* New York: Crown, 1986.

Rhode, David W. "Parties and Committees in the House: Member Motivations, Issues, and Institutional Arrangements." *Legislative Studies Quarterly* 19, No. 3 (August 1994): 341–359.

Ritchie, Donald A., ed. *Minutes of the Senate Democratic Conference: Fifty-eighth Congress through Eighty-eighth Congress, 1903–1964.* Washington: U.S. Government Printing Office, 1998.

Roberts, George C. *Paul Butler: Hoosier Politician and National Political Leader.* Lanham: University Press of America, 1987.

Robertson, David. *Sly and Able: A Political Biography of James F. Byrnes.* New York: Norton, 1994.

Salmond, John. *A Southern Rebel: The Life and Times of Aubrey Williams.* Chapel Hill: University of North Carolina Press, 1983.

Scher, Richard K. *Politics in the New South: Republicanism, Race and Leadership in the Twentieth Century.* Armonk: M. E. Sharpe, 1997.

Schickler, Eric. "Institutional Change in the House of Representatives, 1867–1998: A Test of Partisan and Ideological Power Balance Models." *American Political Science Review* 94, No. 2 (June 2000): 269–288.

Schlesinger, Arthur, Jr. *The Age of Roosevelt.* 3 vols. Boston: Houghton-Mifflin, 1959.

Schlesinger, Joseph A. *Political Parties and the Winning of Office.* Ann Arbor: University of Michigan Press, 1991.

Schulman, Bruce J. *From Cotton Belt to Sunbelt: Federal Policy, Economic Development, and the Transformation of the South, 1938–1980.* New York: Oxford University Press, 1991.

———. *Lyndon B. Johnson and American Liberalism: A Brief Biography with Documents.* Boston: Bedford/St. Martins, 1995.

Scott, Dorothy G. *When the Senate Halls Were Hallowed.* Los Angeles: Corillon Press, 2000.

Silver, James W. "The Twenty-First Annual Meeting." *The Journal of Southern History* 22 (February–November 1956): 60–61.

Simon, Bryant. *A Fabric of Defeat: The Politics of South Carolina Millhands, 1910–1948.* Chapel Hill: University of North Carolina Press, 1998.

Sinclair, Barbara. *The Transformation of the U.S. Senate.* Baltimore: The Johns Hopkins University Press, 1989.

Steinberg, Alfred. *Sam Rayburn: A Biography.* New York: Hawthorn Books, 1975.

Sullivan, Patricia. *Lift Every Voice: The NAACP and the Making of the Civil Rights Movement.* New York: Free Press, 2009.

Tananbaum, Duane. *The Bricker Amendment Controversy: A Test of Eisenhower's Political Leadership.* Ithaca: Cornell University Press, 1988.

Talmadge, Herman E., with Mark Royden Winchell. *Talmadge: A Political Legacy, A Politician's Life, a Memoir.* Atlanta: Peachtree Publishers, 1987.

———. *You and Segregation.* Birmingham: Vulcan Press, 1955.

U.S. Government. *Platforms of the Democratic Party and the Republican Party, 1956.* Washington: GPO, 1956.

———. *Official Report of the Proceedings of the Democratic National Conventions & Committee, 1832–1968.* Washington: National Document Publishers.

United States Senate, Democratic Conference. *Minutes of the U.S. Senate Democratic Conference, 1903–64,* ed. Donald A. Ritchie. Washington, D.C.: Government Printing Office, 1998.

Walker, Anders. *The Ghost of Jim Crow: How Southern Moderates Used Brown v. Board of Education to Stall Civil Rights.* New York: Oxford University Press, 2009.

Walker, Clarence. "The Effects of *Brown:* Personal and Historical Reflections on American Racial Atavism." *The Journal of Southern History,* 70, No. 2 (May 2004): 295–302.

Ward, Jason Morgan. *Defending White Democracy: The Making of a Segregationist Movement and the Remaking of Racial Politics, 1936–1965.* Chapel Hill: University of North Carolina Press, 2011.

Warren, Robert Penn. *Segregation: The Inner Conflict in the South.* New York: Random House, 1956.

Washington, James M., ed., Martin Luther King, Jr., with a foreword by Coretta Scott King. *I Have a Dream: Writings and Speeches that Changed the World.* San Francisco: Harper, 1992.

Wawro, Gregory J., and Eric Schickler. *Filibuster: Obstruction and Lawmaking in the U.S. Senate.* Princeton: Princeton University Press, 2006.

Webb, Clive. "A Continuity of Conservatism: The Limitations of *Brown v. Board of Education.*" *The Journal of Southern History* 70, No. 2 (May 2004): 327–336.

———, ed. *Massive Resistance: Southern Opposition to the Second Reconstruction.* New York: Oxford University Press, 2005.

Weems, Clenora Hudson. *Emmett Till: The Sacrificial Lamb of the Civil Rights Movement.* With an introduction by Robert E. Weems, Jr. Troy: Bedford, 1994.

Weems, Robert E., Jr. *Desegregating the Dollar: African American Consumerism in the Twentieth Century.* New York: New York University Press, 1998.

White, William S. *The Citadel: The Story of the U.S. Senate.* New York: Harper & Brothers, 1956.

———. *The Professional: Lyndon B. Johnson.* Boston: Houghton Mifflin, 1964.

Whitfield, Stephen J. *A Death in the Delta: The Story of Emmett Till.* Baltimore: The Johns Hopkins University Press, 1988.

Whitman, Mark, ed. *Removing a Badge of Slavery: The Record of Brown v. Board of Education.* Princeton: Mark Wiener Publishing, 1993.

Wilhoit, Francis M. *The Politics of Massive Resistance.* New York: George Braziller, 1973.

Wilkinson, J. Harvie III. *Harry Byrd and the Changing Face of Virginia Politics, 1945–1966.* Charlottesville: University Press of Virginia, 1969.

Wolters, Raymond. "From *Brown* to *Green* and Back: The Changing Meaning of Desegregation." *The Journal of Southern History* 70, No. 2 (May 2004): 317–326.

Woods, Jeff. *Black Struggle, Red Scare: Segregation and Anti-Communism in the South, 1948–1968*. Baton Rouge: Louisiana State University Press, 2004.

———. *Richard B. Russell: Southern Nationalism and American Foreign Policy*. Lanham: Rowman and Littlefield Publishers, Inc., 2007.

Woods, Randall Bennett. *Fulbright: A Biography*. New York: Cambridge University Press, 1995.

———. *LBJ: Architect of American Ambition*. New York: Free Press, 2006.

Woodward, C. Vann. *Origins of the New South, 1877–1913*. Baton Rouge: Louisiana State University Press, 1951.

———. "The 'New Reconstruction' in the South: Desegregation in Historical Perspective." *Commentary* 21, No. 6 (June 1956): 501–509.

Workman, William D. *The Case for the South*. New York: Devin-Adair Company, 1960.

Index

CPSIA information can be obtained
at www.ICGtesting.com
Printed in the USA
BVHW03*0149090418
512832BV00005B/17/P

9 781628 460315